CHILD OF THE IRISH BORDER

A Memoir and Family History

NICHOLAS FITZSIMON

SOMERVILLE PRESS

Somerville Press
Dromore, Bantry,
Co. Cork, Ireland

Typesetting and design: Jane Stark
seamistgraphics@gmail.com

ISBN: 978-0-9562231-0-4

Printed in England

CHILD OF THE
IRISH BORDER

A Memoir and Family History

CONTENTS

FAMILY TREES

PREFACE

This book is a little bit of Irish history. It was written in Queensland, Australia in 2006. The author left Ireland almost a half century before, though there were many return visits, sometimes for extended periods. It explores the histories of four families, the family histories of each one of the author's grandparents. These families came of quite disparate traditions, albeit in the small world of recent Irish society. These different traditions are some of the ones which contribute to Ireland's uniqueness, and from time to time have been the cause of its troubles.

In order to relate these four families together, the author has written his personal memoir, growing up in Ireland in the mid-twentieth century, aware of the various traditions, and must apologize for writing with a mindset of that time.

ACKNOWLEDGEMENTS

The author made use of documents, mainly correspondence, now kept in the National Library of Ireland, which relate to the FitzSimon, MacFarlane and O'Connell families. Mr Gerry Lyne is thanked for his assistance in making them available. Thanks are also due to Margaret Brittain for preserving Elliot papers at her home in Co. Meath and to Christopher FitzSimon who guarded much and various archival material. Ted Marr of Hong Kong must be acknowledged for his voluminous work on the Killens.

The author would also like to thank his daughters, Nicola, Catherine and Irena, and son Thomas, for their assistance with research, typing and managing recalcitrant computers, and his wife Joy, who might have preferred him to be doing something more useful, but supported him all the same.

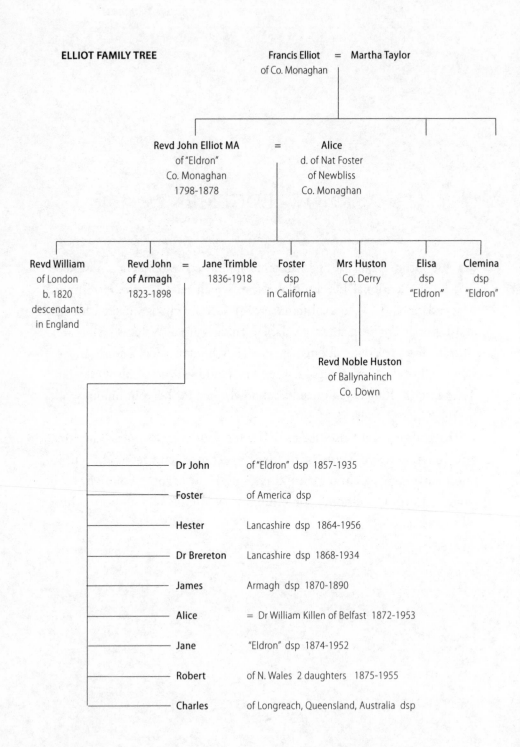

ELLIOT FAMILY TREE

Francis Elliot = Martha Taylor
of Co. Monaghan

Revd John Elliot MA = Alice
of "Eldron"   d. of Nat Foster
Co. Monaghan   of Newbliss
1798-1878   Co. Monaghan

Revd William   Revd John = Jane Trimble   Foster   Mrs Huston   Elisa   Clemina
of London   of Armagh   1836-1918   dsp   Co. Derry   dsp   dsp
b. 1820   1823-1898   in California   "Eldron"   "Eldron"
descendants
in England

Revd Noble Huston
of Ballynahinch
Co. Down

Dr John   of "Eldron" dsp 1857-1935

Foster   of America dsp

Hester   Lancashire dsp 1864-1956

Dr Brereton   Lancashire dsp 1868-1934

James   Armagh dsp 1870-1890

Alice   = Dr William Killen of Belfast 1872-1953

Jane   "Eldron" dsp 1874-1952

Robert   of N. Wales 2 daughters 1875-1955

Charles   of Longreach, Queensland, Australia dsp

CHAPTER ONE

Belfast to Co. Monaghan and the Elliot family

When Julius Caesar conquered Gaul, he wrote a book which famously starts with the observation that "All Gaul is divided into three parts". If he had come to Ireland within the last four centuries or so, he might have written the same about us. He might have seen three predominant tribes, one Gaelic and Catholic, one Anglo-Irish and one Ulster Scottish Presbyterian.

If these three tribes had melded into one, we might have ended up like the English or the Japanese, as one happy homogeneous family. Alas however, we were too prone to squabble among ourselves; we ignored our eighteenth-century patriot Theobald Wolfe Tone, who wished for the day when "Catholic, Protestant and Dissenter would rejoice in the common name of Irishman".

Though some of us Irish continue to squabble over the fruits of our tribal inheritance, some do not; indeed through most of history, the individuals within the tribes have coexisted happily. Not only have they mixed, but they have intermarried, but not on sufficient a scale to prevent the tribes from maintaining their separate identities.

My family is one which crossed the tribal boundaries. Though we seem to have complied with the wishes of Wolfe Tone and call ourselves Irish, we might confuse or mislead those of the majorities who think in terms of a stereotype of their own tribe. I am descended from Catholic, Protestant and Dissenter, and do not need to make apology for any of them.

The tensions arising from the sectarianism which has its roots in our different tribal inheritances, are manifest between Belfast and Dublin, between the North and South of partitioned Ireland and indeed, especially, in Belfast itself, were not new when I was born in Belfast in 1936. We are not done with them yet. With family on both sides of the border between North and South and on both sides of the religious divide, I was brought up on both sides of the divide, and for most of my early days I lived within a few miles of the geographical border itself.

I did not come from the ultra-Protestant Shankill Road, or the lanes off Orange Sandy Row; nor from the Falls or Smithfield, the domain of the "Fenians", as the other lot called them. Eglantine Avenue where I was born is not far from those places, only a couple of miles away, and though its inhabitants were not as likely to march, beat drums, or throw stones at the police, under their outward civility they would no doubt, in the main, have given strong support to one side or the other. It was a territory of the genteel professionals around the Queen's University and the City Hospital, an area which merges towards the territory of the mansions built by the rich linen barons further down the Malone Road.

I was kept at Eglantine Avenue for only a very short time. The address on my birth certificate is Racquet Court Lane, Trichinopoly, South India. That is where my father was, the family home, at the time I was born.

My father was from Dublin, my mother from Belfast. South India was probably different enough from both to be as good a compromise between the two cities as one could get, but I had no opportunity to share in that particular compromise, for I never went there at all. Instead I went, or rather I was taken, to Co. Monaghan, to a place called Ballyleck, a few miles over the border, into what was then called the Irish Free State.

My father had been for some years the officer supervising the South Indian Railway Territorial Army battalion. My mother took the month long voyage home to give birth under appropriate medical care, just as she had done two-and-a-half years before for my brother Christopher. She took a house in Eglantine Avenue, not far from what had been her parents' home in College Gardens. She had Christopher with her this time and her parents as well. Her parents had gone out to stay with her in India and had arranged to have their house in College Gardens sold in their absence. My grandfather had retired at that point. He was a surgeon, an eye specialist and a visiting professor of the university. He lived until 1945, my grandmother until 1953. They were continuously looking for somewhere else to buy after College Gardens had been sold, but never actually got around to acquiring another home.

Coming from a medical background, my mother was probably more conscious than most of the dangers of childbirth in India and would have had great faith especially in the Belfast medical establishment. My cousin John Killen had been born six days before me, also in Belfast, as the medical situation in Monaghan 60 miles away, was presumably considered by his parents to be not much more satisfactory than India. My Uncle Marcus was a doctor there, so I suppose he knew. Marcus came up prior to the births, and was said to be embarrassed to be seen escorting his wife and sister, two nine-month pregnant ladies, about the streets, a common sight in Arabia, not so much so in Belfast. It is just as well my mother had faith in Belfast, as I was born with a fairly rare intestinal condition, pyloric stenosis, and within a week was fading away to nothing, but my grandfather knew a surgeon who could perform Ramsted's operation, recently developed in Sweden for the condition, so I was the first person in Ireland treated successfully for it.

Prior to my operation my mother was visited by my grandmother's cousin the Revd Noble Houston, minister of First Ballynahinch Presbyterian Church, who kindly offered to baptize me on the spot. So I went to the operation fortified against the assaults of the Devil, and with a firm denominational stamp to show it. Christopher had been baptized by the Roman Catholic parish priest of Sandyford in Dublin, so we were off to a good ecumenical start. One can fix the date of my operation as 11 December in the wider course of history for during it my mother listened to the abdication speech of King Edward VIII.

It had been the plan that my mother would return to India with me and Christopher, but as my recovery was slow (I was initially fed with a fountain pen filler), we went to stay with my grandparents at Ballyleck, outside the town of Monaghan; they were renting a part of this curious early eighteenth-century country house. My uncle Marcus had lived in it for a while before he was married, before moving to Aviemore, an imposing building right in the town of Monaghan, from where he carried on his medical practice.

Monaghan was my grandmother's family ancestral county. Her brother, Great-Uncle John Elliot, had practised medicine there since the 1880s from a house some three miles from Ballyleck, called Eldron, which had once been the manse for Smithboro Presbyterian Church. Their grandfather had been minister there for fifty years and had bought the house when he retired. Uncle Marcus took over Great-Uncle John's practice a couple of years before John died in 1935. Eldron was occupied then by Great-Aunt Jane.

Some time in 1937 my mother decided to go back to India alone. Christopher, then 3, went to live at Eldron with Aunt Jane Elliot and I, an infant, but recovered and growing, was left at Ballyleck with my grandparents. My parents came back from India late in 1938 and rented a house called Mount Louise about a mile from Eldron. This house had become vacant on the death of Humphrey, the last of the Evats, local landlords for more than two centuries. Humphrey had only one eye, having lost the other one from a spear thrust in the Zulu War. He was still ferocious enough in his old age to drive a young IRA raider into the freezing lake, the raider being lucky to be let live. Christopher and I were collected and then followed a brief period as living in a traditional nuclear family.

I didn't take at all kindly to my removal to live with these strange people, my parents. I protested loudly for several days. They tried singing to me, but as neither of them had hardly even a rudimentary skill in music, it could have been that it was the singing which delayed my acceptance of the new arrangement. I have no memory of these events; I had just turned 2. Perhaps they were too painful to remember. I do remember being at Ballyleck; at least I still have in my mind the sight of my grandfather and somebody else's legs standing in front of the fire viewed by me from under a table. At Mount Louise I can remember the windows of the house, the back avenue with pools of dark coloured water, and being wheeled in a pusher by a nanny along an icy road, with Christopher running along beside. We could see the moon above some leafless winter trees, but no matter how we urged the nanny to push faster, we couldn't get past the moon; this was very disappointing.

At some point in the spring of 1939 we went to Dublin to stay with my paternal grandparents in Sandyford, South County Dublin. They lived in a modern white flat-roofed house called Whinsfield, which my grandmother was said to have designed herself. Its style was typical of the German Bauhaus school of the late 1920s. It was built on land which had been part of Moreen, an estate in my grandmother's family for 150 years. The main house with a 160 acre farm had been bought by my grandfather from my grandmother's aunt, but by the 1930s, the mortgagee, which was a convent of nuns, had foreclosed and since repossessed it.

My grandparents had a black and white dog called Roy, who attacked me; I had provoked it, persistently trying to gain its attention while it tried to sleep. I got what I deserved before my father separated us.

Not long after, in about May 1939, my father was called on to help separate Jews from Arabs, as their conflict escalated. That conflict, a bit like our one around the Irish border, though in principle much more severe, has not been resolved today. From Palestine he went to Egypt to take part in the Second World War campaign against the Italians in North Africa; he was away for two years.

My mother took a bungalow in Greystones, Co. Wicklow for the summer and then for a short time another one in Sandyford, Co. Dublin, near my paternal grandparents.

I can't have been too happy in Greystones, or perhaps it was a more positive pull to Delgany 2 miles up the road, but it was my expressed intention to run away to Delgany over the period; once I got some distance along the road. On a later occasion in my bid for freedom, I became entangled in the garden fence, scratching my arm. The enforced washing of the scratched arm with disinfectant was very painful. I didn't try to escape again.

Before the end of 1939 I was back in Co. Monaghan. I was left with Aunt Jane at Eldron; Christopher stayed at Whinsfield with the FitzSimon grandparents so he could go to school in Dundrum. During 1940, my mother was invited by Peggy Butler, a relative of hers, to go to live at Annaghmakerrig, a very large house, also in Co. Monaghan, the home of Peggy's mother. So my mother and Christopher took up residence. There would be a lot of other children there. I was considered too young to mix with the bigger children. I remained under the care of Aunt Jane at Eldron. This was the right decision. I had a very happy year, free, yet well looked after. There was never any suggestion that I was spoiled, but before reaching the mature age of 4, I was to be taken and thrown in with the big children in the cold and regimented environment of Annaghmakerrig. I later discovered a claim by pig breeders that if the runt of a litter is taken away and reared independently or with other runts, it will in time flourish; if it is not taken away, it will not survive.

Eldron was a two-storey thatched cottage with two flat-roofed rooms extended from each end, one of which had served as Uncle John's surgery. There was a large and ancient chestnut tree just beside the house, beech, copper beech and elm on the front lawn. Behind the house was a small farmyard. The barn usually contained two cows, and in another shed there was usually a calf; there was a hayloft above and in an adjacent building stood a large black Ford car with beige corduroy seats. From the little hill behind the yard where there were two fields (one of potatoes and one of oats), one could see the spire of Monaghan Cathedral. Inside the house a little hallway gave onto a sitting room, a dining room and a stone-flagged kitchen with its black range. A narrow stair led up to two bedrooms above. There was a bedroom beyond the sitting room, and the former surgery beyond the dining room served different purposes at different times. In the hall there was a grandfather clock and a chaise longue which was covered with a polar bear skin with a stuffed head and glass eyes. The bear had been given to Uncle John in payment for some service. He was called Mr Bear and was my friend; I used to talk to him a lot. I still have him; he is feeling his age having recently had to survive a period on the floor of my son Thomas's flat.

Upstairs was Aunt Jane's bedroom; she later became known as Zane. I had a low bed on one side of the room, while Jane's bed towered up high at the other side. I lay looking up as I practised counting. I could get to 12 quite easily, but beyond that was difficult. Later when I learned other languages, the numbers to 12 seemed to come naturally but beyond, one had to make much mental effort; a dozen is a very significant figure.

Also there was Lizzie's bedroom. I was told I was not to go in there and I think I never did. Lizzie might have been called the maid, but that terminology would create a false impression. She would have been in her fifties; she had orangey-red hair, a big nose and large wide staring eyes. Her time was spent in the kitchen, or in the yard looking after the hens; in the evening she would sit with Jane in the sitting room. At times she would disappear to the house in the village of Smithboro where her three brothers and her sister lived. They had been brought up in a tiny gate lodge adjoining the Eldron land, though belonging to the next door property. Their name was MacMahon, which was that of the dominant tribe of the area and its chieftain in medieval times. Monaghan was not like most of Ulster and much of the rest of Ireland "planted" with English and Scots. The MacMahon chieftains sold their lands around 1620. Some would argue they were tricked out of it by British entrepreneurs (a Welshman, Lord Blayney, got the biggest bit), who brought in numbers of British as their tenants, but large numbers did not arrive until after Cromwell's time and into the early eighteenth century. The Elliots, who originated in the Scottish border country, were said to have come to Monaghan after a period settled in Fermanagh. Our MacMahons were of humble origin; apart from a sister in Belfast, all of Lizzie's generation remained unmarried. There seems to have been a symbiotic relationship between the Elliots and MacMahons, since back in the nineteenth century. One or two of the MacMahon family had been in the employ of Jane's grandfather. Lizzie, who was very important in my early life, had among her brothers, Davy, who was also important.

Jane's grandfather was the Revd John Elliot, the son of a small farmer in the hilly country between Monaghan and Ballybay. John went to Glasgow University where, in 1813, he was awarded the degree of Master of Arts. He became minister of Smithboro Presbyterian Church, which he served for fifty years. He kept a classical school in the days before state education. We find records of him sitting on relief committees, along with the Roman Catholic parish priest and the Church of Ireland rector, dealing out pittances for payment for relief work for the starving people during the famine years after 1846. Co. Monaghan was one of the worst hit areas of Ireland. It had become very densely populated, having been an important flax growing and linen weaving area. By 1846 this industry had become mechanized, and moved to the towns elsewhere in the province, so it was a county of very small farms with landless labourers, who had nothing to fall back on when the potato crop failed. Over the five years after 1846, the county lost one third of its population, perhaps half of this through death from starvation and related diseases. The Revd John would have buried many of his flock, though perhaps not such a large proportion as the clergy of the other denominations, because the Presbyterians were represented more among the stronger farmers than were the others.

The Revd John, let us call him John 1, married Alice Foster from not too distant Newbliss, whose father had been a native of Co. Meath and had children from an earlier marriage. This family was Episcopalian; one of the sons was in holy orders in the Church of Ireland; however there are no stories of sectarian dissension. John and Alice had three sons and three daughters. One of the daughters was married to a neighbouring Presbyterian clergyman and was the mother of the Revd Noble who baptized me; the other two lived unmarried in Eldron until they died. The youngest son emigrated to America, worked as a clerk, and died on the California gold fields. The eldest son William, as a student in Belfast, was so short of cash that because he was starving, so he wrote, he enlisted in a regiment of dragoons. He was said to have been a wild young man; however in time he went to St Bees College in Cumberland to study for ordination in the Church of England. Whether while there or before, he compromised a lady in the household of the Duke of Westminister, who herself was an illegitimate daughter of the Duke or one of his close relations. Following marriage to the lady, the Duke made William his domestic chaplain, and had him preside at the Grosvenor Chapel in Mayfair. The Duke's name was Grosvenor and he owned large areas of Mayfair. Later William was vicar of a large London parish and had descendants who made up a number of my mother's numerous English cousins.

The second son, John 2, became a Presbyterian minister, eventually of the Mall Church in the city of Armagh. He married Jane Trimble, the daughter of Dr Trimble, a native of Clogher in Co. Tyrone, but practising medicine in Castlebellingham, Co. Louth, where he had married Hester Crawley, a local lady with roots among the wealthy linen bleachers of Louth. Louth was, like Monaghan, linen country, before the industry was mechanized and concentrated around Belfast.

In his photographs John 2 appears to be an imposing man with a large nose. He looks too much like the Revd Ian Paisley for comfort; however having read a printed sermon he had once delivered – it would have taken as least as hour to deliver – I would attest that his scholarship would have left Paisley very much in the shade. Indeed his obituary attests that when it would become known that he would preach at a particular church, people would come from miles to hear him. It was from his wife rather than by way of his profession, that the money came to educate the large family.

John 2 and Jane had nine children. The eldest son John 3 and the third one Bertie qualified in medicine at the College of Surgeons in Dublin after studying at the Queen's College in Galway. John 3 became the dispensary doctor in Smithboro. The system of government-salaried dispensary doctors started at the beginning of the nineteenth century, which was an early sign of the socialized medicine to come. Each county was divided into districts, each with a small building, the dispensary, from where the visiting doctor would dispense medicine to the poor, of whom there would be many thousands in each district. The poor could not have had much attention by modern standards, for as well as having very many poor people to look after, the doctor would normally have a private practice as well. A dispensary doctor's salary was small. From the 1880s on, John 3 lived at Eldron with his Aunts Clemina and Eliza. His predecessor at the dispensary, when a young doctor, would perform an amputation by first filling the patient with whiskey, then getting two strong men to hold him down, saw off the stump and then dip the stump in tar. By John's time medical practice was moving towards something more akin to that of the present day.

John, with his cousin Noble Houston, bred rare gun dogs, was a pillar of society, and held high office in the Masonic order. His private practice was large and prosperous. He was remembered by those close to him as a connoisseur and amusing teller of scandalous and *risqué* stories. He died in 1935.

Bertie, who died the year before, had always wanted to be a soldier, but the family was not well off enough for him to become an officer, and to be a ranker would not have been acceptable. He worked as a doctor in Liverpool, but when the First World War came, he immediately joined up in a line regiment. He was sent off as a Senior Captain in the King's Liverpool Regiment to Egypt on garrison duties; training the men and instilling discipline was his role. Judging from the letters he wrote to his mother, he was not only conscientious, but keen on the task. However, not long after arriving in Egypt he was one of the first to land at Gallipoli.

Most of the fighting was in the trenches. Bertie wrote home that he wished that he wasn't so tall, because his head stuck up above the parapet; as he survived he must have been adept nevertheless at bending down. He did not see out the Gallipoli campaign. He took ill with a "strained heart" and was hospitalized back in Egypt. There he remained for a year, not long as a patient, but in charge of the hospital, having transferred from the infantry to the Royal Army Medical Corps. After all he was 46 years old, and with twenty years medical practice behind him, it would have been a much more logical role for him to have. He was made a Major in that corps and came away with a row of seven medals after further service back in England and in France. His military appetite was not totally assuaged however, for when Christopher was born, he sent my mother £10 for her to buy him a sword. I don't know if my mother told Bertie that she spent the £10 instead on buying a pram.

John 2 and Jane's second son died young (of pneumonia) in America, where he had joined the US Coastguard, and another son also died in his twenties just after qualifying as a solicitor in Dublin. The youngest two, Bob and Charlie went to Trinity College, Dublin but dropped out. Bob, along with a friend who had just left, got jobs on a transatlantic line; his friend played the drums in the band, and Bob got a job as a steward. This was bad enough, but when Bob married a stewardess, and one who was a Roman Catholic, that was the end, and he was disowned by his parents, or so it has been said. But I don't think that that is the real story, for there are many letters he wrote to his mother and sisters during the war, letters obviously answered. Like Bertie, he was in the Royal Army Medical Corps, but as a corporal, a hospital orderly, in France. His wife was living in Lancashire with their two daughters, but she was to die not long after. Whatever else he did he wasn't universally approved of in the family. My father was at Eldron with the sisters Alice and Jane some time about 1950 waiting for a visit from Bob who hadn't been seen for decades, listening to the ladies complaining about Bob's lifelong misbehaviour, but when the prodigal arrived at the door "they fell on his neck with much tears and rejoicing".

Charlie was a big and affable man and was a great success in college, socially and at sport, but not at exams. Sadly finance dictated, and perhaps the puritan ethic as well, that he could not continue a sybaritic existence indefinitely, so he was sent out to Australia where following sister Alice's marriage to Willie Killen, there was a vast field of family connections. He was directed onto a succession of sheep and cattle stations by W.W. Killen, then at the head of the Killen empire. Charlie found the rounding up of cattle much to his liking, like playing rugby. When he met W.W., the great man himself, he was greatly dismayed to find that W.W. was a Home Ruler. When he discovered that these Killens were cousins of Viscount Bryce, who was Chief Secretary for Ireland and who also was a Home Ruler, he wrote back saying how the Viscount "needed shooting". Later on Charlie was to write disparaging remarks about De Valera. Throughout his life he kept close touch with his mother and when she died, with his sister Jane.

He served with the ANZACS at Gallipoli, attaining the rank of captain, and was to see quite a bit of Bertie when he was in Egypt. He stayed on in the Australian army after the war and spent a couple of years in England on administrative duties. Back in Australia, he had a business as a wool broker in the town of Longreach in central Queensland. He had an office in the main hotel there, where he also lived. As a pillar of the Presbyterian Church, he was instrumental in raising money for a new building. He liked the Bush Brothers, young travelling priests of the Church of England, but considered that they didn't have enough evangelical zeal. It was his intention that he would retire to Ireland, to Eldron, when he had saved a certain sum of money, but he hadn't reached his goal when the Second World War started. He was taken on by the army with the rank of major, even though he had turned 56. He died of cancer in Brisbane in 1943. His life's savings were largely represented by a collection of opals which as far as one can make out would have been very valuable. The collection was sent to Jane after his death, but it never arrived.

The eldest of the daughters was Hester. Hester was an organizer, a bossy person with clear and strong views. She got her chance to flower after she married her cousin John Foster Stewart, another Uncle John, and another Trinity College dropout. He had been a medical student but went off to join the Mounties, the Royal North West Mounted Police, prior to 1880, when the North West of Canada was a real frontier. He had a medal for helping to put down the Louis Riel rebellion, a frontier war with rebels led by a renegade half-caste Indian. John was known as "Doc," being the next best thing to a doctor in a few thousand square miles. After a full career in the police he was ordained a priest in the Church of England, married Hester and had a parish on the Canadian prairies. In 1916, they came to England where they had a parish in the Lake District. Hester kept the parishioners on their toes and the parish up to scratch. She lived well into her nineties.

The second daughter Alice married William Killen in 1902. These were my grandparents. Jane the third daughter never married. She stayed with her widowed mother in Armagh and was a music teacher. When her mother died in 1918 and the maiden aunts in Eldron both having died not long before, Jane moved to Eldron to live with her brother Dr John.

By the time I arrived to live at Eldron in late 1939, the war had dried up the supply of petrol. So the large black Ford car stood silent in the dark shed. It was a more modern car than the one Davy lost to the IRA. Uncle John bought a car before the First World War, but never learned to drive; Davy was the driver. During the Troubles of 1920/21 Davy, while in the car, was held up by the IRA who wanted it for themselves. A young lad with a rifle got him out of the car. Davy said he was frightened to death because the young IRA lad was so nervous the rifle was shaking in his hands. Davy knew about rifles and how they could go off; he had been a regular soldier with active service in the Boer War. On learning of the loss of his car, John spoke to his neighbour Thomas Toal, a politician of the Nationalist camp, and sometime chairman of the Monaghan County Council. Mr Toal, while not himself an active soldier of the Republic himself, would certainly have known who they all were; he later became a Senator of the Free State. "Don't worry Doctor, I'll have this sorted out," said Mr Toal. A day or two later a different car was delivered up to Eldron. The problem was that John couldn't accept it for it belonged to his colleague Dr Whilta of Monaghan town. The IRA driver, not being as skilled as Davy at steering around the narrow lanes of the county, had piled John's car into the stone wall just below Corinshigo Cross.

Davy had plenty to do besides driving the car. The 25 acres of Eldron constituted what was a tidy sized farm at that time. Other people would come to help for the like of lifting potatoes, ploughing or hay making, but there was always digging in the vegetable garden, milking cows, fixing fences, feeding calves, cutting wood and bringing in turf for the fires. I would be out with Davy as he did his work. It was when I got him into trouble with Lizzie that I remember the events most vividly.

One time Davy was fixing a fence across a ditch or "sheugh" as they say in Ulster. I walked into the sheugh only for it to come up to my armpits, cold winter water, a shock and very frightening. I expect I screamed loud and long. It doesn't take a great depth of water to get up to a 3 year old's armpits. Davy took me back to the house where Lizzie put me into dry clothes and castigated Davy for allowing me to nearly drown.

On another occasion Davy, with me on board, was driving the horse and cart through the gate into the yard. Davy gave me the reins to hold, the horse started to turn and the wheel of the cart knocked a rainwater barrel off its support. Lizzie saw all this from the kitchen window and ran out telling Davy how foolish it was to let a child so young drive a horse and cart.

It was Davy and not me who got the blame there; Lizzie knew well where justice was due. One time I saw the black and white yard cat, which was not at all friendly, and which I didn't like, sitting on the kitchen window sill. I threw a stone which missed the cat, though it made it jump. The stone broke a window pane. Lizzie was furious. I have never thrown stones at a window or a cat since.

If Jane taught me manners and discipline, I do not remember. I do remember her having to pull me back from the tormenting in church of Jimmy Welsh. I think it was more than once she had to. The Welsh pew was in front of the Elliot pew and I would climb over and get Jimmy by the ear. He was several years older than me, and I sensed that he was too well behaved, no doubt embarrassed, to respond in kind. Lizzie was not there to intervene; one could see her, but at a distance on the far side of the church where the MacMahons sat.

I do not remember Lizzie as a disciplinarian but as the person who fed me food I liked. She made porridge, and mashed potatoes with an egg in it, dishes I would choose today, should perchance they be on the menu.

It was a charmed and happy time at Eldron, far removed from the recipients of Adolph Hitler's attentions. This was the time of Dunkirk and the bombing of cities in England, the unspeakable cruelties of the German occupation of Poland, the expansion of the concentration camps and the start of slave labour across Europe. There were even worse goings on with the Japanese in China. But my charmed existence was to end. At the end of 1940, being then 4 years old, I was deemed fit to progress to the to the hurly-burly of the communal life with the big children at Annaghmakerrig. The runt of the litter was ready to fend for itself.

CHAPTER TWO

Annaghmakerrig

I had been to Annaghmakerrig; it was only 8 miles from Eldron, but just for day visits. Once I remember being there for a party where the crowds were so daunting I retired under the dining room table, only coming out on all fours. It is reputed that a grand and patronizing lady bent down and said, "Is little Nicky being a little doggie or a pussycat?" to which I replied consequent on my being in the fields with Davy, "No ma'am, I'm a bullock". With occasional expeditions elsewhere, Annaghmakerrig would alternate with Eldron as home for the next four years and again was the principal family residence between 1948 and 1953.

The Annaghmakerrig estate had never been a large one, at the most about 800 acres, half of which was sold out to the tenants before the First World War. There were a lot of trees, new plantations of softwood, and stands of oak and beech from earlier times. Pride of the place was the lake, half a mile long and a quarter mile wide. The house looked down onto the lake. In the mid-nineteenth century there was a modest two-storey house on the site, the home of the local doctor, Dr Moorehead, who had married a Foster from the nearby village of Newbliss, of the same household as the wife of Revd John Elliot of Smithboro; hence our family connection. During famine times a young lieutenant by the name of Power came to the district to supervise relief work. He came back after distinguished service in the wars in New Zealand, Hong Kong and Canada and married the doctor's daughter. He went on to become General Sir William Power, Quartermaster-General of the British Army. When he retired from the army he was Agent-General in London for

New Zealand. The present house was built by him in 1876 with Victorian bay windows, three storeys, and wings that extended down to the stable and farmyards; it is among the biggest dozen or so houses ever to have been built in the county, and the half dozen or so amongst them still standing. Sir William spent most of his time in England after he left the army, but was frequently at Annaghmakerrig, where he died in 1911. There were attempts to draft him to sit in Parliament for the county as he was acceptable to both Catholics and Protestants, some feat in the turbulent years after Parnell, with dictatorial Roman Catholic bishops and militant Orangemen. He declined politics however. In my day there were locals who still referred to Annaghmakerrig as "Sir William's".

Sir William's daughter Norah was married to a Scottish doctor, Clement Guthrie, who had a practice in Kent. There, her son Tony and her daughter Peggy were brought up, with Annaghmakerrig the place for summer holidays. After the First World War, and when Dr Guthrie died, Norah came to live in Annaghmakerrig permanently. She was turning blind, and although she did not suffer from total blindness, she was never cured. We called her Mrs G. From Sir William's time and into the 1920s, the place had as agent cum caretaker, one James Dane, a relative common to both Elliots and the Power-Guthrie household, and it was largely through him that the connection between the families was kept alive.

I can't say if Annaghmakerrig made any impact on me at the age of 4; my memory of the place is coloured through my experience of living there through many later years. A few aspects do stand out the main stairs, the playroom, the turf shed, and the lake. But they stand out from this early time by association, the place where certain events took place.

I do not look back on my early days at Annaghmakerrig with much pleasure; on balance the bad outweighs the good. The bad comes from the contrast with Eldron. The house, like most big houses in Ireland with their high-ceilinged rooms and a reluctance to burn more turf or wood than could be avoided, could be brutally cold. One had to wear uncomfortable quantities of clothes, and one still caught colds, coughs and sore throats. The compact, small roomed, thatched-roofed Eldron did not present such a problem. I did not like the food. Gone were Lizzie's porridge, potato dishes and eggs. We had foul stews with vegetables like leeks and onions and white cabbage, puddings with currants in them, and worse still I was made to eat them. It is probably a consequence at the attempts at force feeding that I cannot to this day eat several of the dishes that were put before us children in the big breakfast room where we were fed. Then there were the problems of socialization which was now enforced upon me.

I have said I was not spoiled at Eldron, but I mean deliberately given my way without resistance. But the environment at Eldron did not require rebellion or antisocial behavior. I was therefore in a fuller sense, thoroughly spoiled, and I now had to bear the consequence. I wonder how I would have coped if I had been incarcerated in Germany in Dachau or Bergen Belsen, which at that time were fully functioning.

Very soon after arriving it was Christmas, a magical event to be lived with ever after. There was a big party for all the children on the estate. Besides the six children in the main home there were four families with several children in each. The Dalys lived in a wing of the main house which stretched down the stable yard; there were five girls. Then there were the McGoldricks, Maguires and Burns, who occupied the three gate lodges; it is possible that the Maguires didn't come till the next year, and that the Watsons whose father worked on the place, at one stage were there; at any rate there would have been upwards of twenty children. We were ushered into a room called the study, and what a sight. In the middle of the room was the tree, covered with lighted candles and coloured shiny things. It went right up to the ceiling, and when one is only 3 feet tall a 12 feet tree is pretty high, especially when one is not expecting it. We stood and marvelled and then Peggy called out everyone's name from a pile of presents around the base of the tree. We were then sat around the big table in the dining room, under the pictures of the Power ancestors, Sir William with his feathered hat, moustache and sword, and given cakes and other sweet things, sharp contrast to the daily fare in the breakfast room. There were games in the drawing room, "The Farmer Wants a Wife", "Nuts in May", "Blind Man's Buff". I was not sufficiently socialized to enjoy such activities which under the direction of Peggy were to be an ongoing feature at Annaghmakerrig. Nevertheless the sight of the Christmas tree and the cakes in the dining room had been sufficient to overcome any dissatisfaction the drawing-room games may have caused me.

The winter of 1941 was an exceptionally hard one. The lake froze over completely and the adults flew about on it on skates. I think they had only one pair so it was one at a time. My mother had learnt to skate in Switzerland in the 1920s, but as she was there for only one season, she can't have been very good. Nevertheless it looked quite remarkable to me. Hubert, Peggy's husband, about whom I will have more to say later, pushed us about in wooden chairs. This was exciting fun; the only pity was that I didn't get enough pushes.

Mrs G. was the head of the household. Someone must have told me to give her a present for her birthday so I brought along an artistic creation, a picture of something I had drawn. She couldn't see it of course, and probably couldn't see much of me either, so Bunty explained to her what was happening. She said that she was 74 but could remember when she was 4, my age. I sensed her pleasure; from then she was no longer remote, never to be approached with any trepidation. Not so Bunty. I learnt to treat Bunty with circumspection. She was then twice my size; it was years later when I was twice her size before I could approach her without trepidation. As her name implied, she was very short, maybe less than 5 feet; she was one who would brook no nonsense. She had been a hospital matron and was Mrs G.'s companion, assistant, and ruled the household with meticulous efficiency.

There were several women in the kitchen and its surrounds. There was a cook called Kate who was enormously fat; whenever I hear the word "obesity" I picture Kate and I am never comfortable when I hear my daughter Catherine, a thin person, referred to as Kate by her husband and friends, it is so wrong. I learnt when 4 years old irrevocably, that "Kate" is the name of a fat person. The others are now shadowy; I don't remember them all. They had their roles; Chrissy was a housemaid and had a black and white uniform, she brought the afternoon tea to Mrs G. and Bunty in the drawing room; she was nice. Her sister Florrie was a nanny; she was dangerous I thought, and best avoided. When Chrissy married we all went to the wedding in Clones Church. Although these people were classed as servants and they may have kowtowed to the adults, there was nothing servile when it came to dealing with the likes of me. There was also a lady who was not a servant, but a governess.

There were classes held for the older children: Christopher who turned 7 that year, Julia Butler, Peggy's daughter who turned 6 and a girl called Jennifer. Peggy and my mother participated as formal educators. I can only remember my mother teaching me, and that is only a glimpse of a story about the Crusades. I managed to acquire a piece of wood for a sword, though what I really wanted was a shield with a red cross on it. I also asked that my name to be changed to Richard, after the Lionheart. Neither of my requests met with success.

There was also "playing school". This was led by the Daly girls. The Daly's large extended family lived in a wing of the house and the five girls went to the local national school at Crappagh, a mile or so away and could give instructions in Irish. The youngest girl Joan was not much older then me, and was not a problem, but the older ones, especially Laura and Susie, liked to boss one and make one sit in a row and put up one's hand to answer a question. Playing at "church" was a similar exercise. I didn't mind these activities but know I wasn't very enthusiastic. The saving grace of living at Annaghmakerrig and my support in escape from the regiment of women to whom we were subjected was the presence of Joe.

Joe Hone was, though a couple of months younger than me, much bigger. He was as big as Christopher. They both weighed 4 stone; I was only 3 stone. Joe had been taken on by Peggy and Hubert as a foster child and fulfilled the role of surrogate brother to Julia. He had arrived at Annaghmakerrig just before me, as his parents, who having need of finding support for six children, had them distributed amongst friends and relations. The father had been somewhat eccentric, involved in the Spanish Civil War and something of a black sheep, before being incapacitated with tuberculosis.

Joe and I would go about in the horse and cart with Seamus McGorman, a strong young man who worked on the farm, and for whom I had great respect. We also did things which were apparently naughty, like climbing on the roofs of the yard buildings and dissecting a frog with a pen knife, and did things which we recognized were really naughty. Joe put sand in the petrol tank of the car, immobilizing it, so that a planned expedition to a dancing class in Clones had to be he abandoned. The girls and the ladies were disappointed, but Bob was devastated. Bob Burns was the chauffeur; he even had a chauffeur's cap. He did a lot of other things like mowing the lawns, tending the fires and lighting the lamps, but the car was his pride. There must have been petrol longer at Annaghmakerig than had been available at Eldron, but I don't think the car came out again until 1945. Bob kept it polished and shining in its garage throughout the war. We got about by pony and trap most of the time.

There was a big party in Clones at my Aunt Mat Killen's family house. I don't remember how we got there. It must have been Easter, as there were coloured eggs hidden all over the place for one to look for. Joe was not the only naughty boy in the county. It was there I first met Walter Greacen who having just got hold of John Killen's toy carpenter's set (which I very much envied), was reputed to have sawn through the leg of a Chippendale settee.

Naughtiness nearly put paid to Joe's life at this early stage. We were strictly forbidden to go to the lake, let alone get in the boat. One day we went there, and were having a wonderful game with Joe in the boat and with me holding the rope, pushing the boat and pulling it back. But the boat got away and started to drift. Joe panicked and jumped out. I saw him with the water up to his neck, panicked myself, turned tail and ran back to the house. I found my mother and told her I had drowned Joe. I think I believed I had drowned him, this was not just colloquial Irish hyperbole, "There wasn't a drop of breath in him. I killed him. I killed him stone dead, so I did". My mother ran down to the lake throwing off her clothes as she went, to dive in to save him, but as she rounded the bend at the boathouse she met a very wet and sorry Joe. If he had jumped a couple of seconds later he would have been in the deep water and that would have been the end of him. When my mother got back to the house she found I had put myself to bed – being put to bed was the punishment for the most heinous of offences. When he arrived back at the house Joe also put himself to bed, without having to be told to do so.

My mother was unquestionably my refuge during the early days at Annaghmakerrig. She was the successor to the people at Eldron as my guardian in the face of the society in to which I was not yet integrated and which controlled the practices and routines of daily life. I did not associate her with the lawmakers, Peggy, Bunty, the servants (so called) and the big Daly girls, who I felt were oppressors if not actually malicious. It was a question of being on terms with authority. One needs self-confidence to deal with authority and I had little of that then. Joe had all the airs of self-confidence. As an old and hardbitten veteran, I have dealt successfully with the military, religious and political police of a number of unsavoury dictatorships, but that was fifty years later. Such dealing would be very easy compared to the struggles of life at Annaghmakerrig in 1941.

It is only in hindsight that I know my mother was having an anxious time. My father had been at the wars for two years and having survived so far, was now on his way home on the high seas on a long and roundabout route, with German surface raiders and U-boats at the height of their activity. My father had been in the campaign under Wavell, which had forestalled the Italian invasion of Egypt, and went on to rout the Italians in Libya. In February 1941 he had been given temporary command of his battalion and after the victory, when a new permanent commander had arrived, he was given the job of escorting 12,000 prisoners of war into captivity. I do not know where they all went, but he eventually proceeded from Durban in South Africa, from where he sent me a postcard with a picture of a wild black man with a spear, via New York, eventually to Dun Laoghaire. He said he saw New York but didn't go ashore. I did something similar twenty years later when driving form Montreal to Philadelphia. I thought I would stop in New York for a look around, but after circling Manhattan a couple of times and finding nowhere to park, I drove out the other side without stopping.

I mark my mother's anxiety by the fact that it was at this time she taught Christopher and me, or at least went through the words of the hymn "Eternal Father strong to save, whose arm doth bind the restless wave". Whenever I hear this hymn, or its catchy tune, which also does for a rather naughty song which starts, "It almost broke the family's heart when Lady Jane became a tart", I think of the corner of my mother's bedroom by the fireplace when I was introduced to it. The hymn had a puzzling reference in it to "waters dark and rude". I could not understand this because the term "rude" was related to the activities of the lavatory and to certain organs of the body exercised there. I myself had not at this stage had any religious education; indeed I didn't have any formal such instruction until I was about 12 at school. I never in my life went to Sunday School , though I think the older children did; the Daly girls were full of it. Churchgoing on Sunday in rural Ireland was a normal routine for all but a few eccentrics. For me it was simply a chore like being sent with the mob to the Doohat post office nearby, or the even worse imposition of having to go picking blackberries. Some morsels of theology did filter through. The second of the Ten Commandments has a reference to "the water which is under the earth". On looking at a hole dug in a potato field which had water in it, Christopher explained to me that the water was the water under the earth. I wondered how the idols one was not to bow down to could be in it.

We went to Dublin to meet my father. He came into Dun Laoghaire, (my grandfather called it Kingstown) on the mailboat. We were very excited. I had told Joe one time when he was being difficult, that my father, being a soldier, had a gun and would shoot Joe when he came back, so I well knew the reason for the long absence. There was a wooden barricade over which we looked and we saw him with a suitcase open on a bench for the customs man. We shouted "Daddy" but he took no notice; my mother said there were a lot of men called Daddy. She called "Simon", which is the name she used for him; he looked up then. When he came through the gate there was an inordinately long time as he stood with my mother in what might be called a clinch. Then he came and spoke to me and Christopher. I don't remember anything else until we were back at Annaghmakerrig . He came too, but can't have stayed for long because he was only on wartime leave and had to take up a post in Scotland. I do believe I enjoyed his stay, he was to teach us "gym" which was to involve climbing ropes and swinging on bars, but I was not really old enough for that and so there was too much boring stuff like swinging one's arms and touching one's toes.

It wasn't necessary for Joe to be shot, for by the time my father arrived, or not long after, Joe departed, along with the Butlers, Hubert, Peggy and Julia. Hubert's father had died, so Hubert inherited the family house, Maiden Hall in Co. Kilkenny, so there they went. Hubert had been a distant figure, and though never an intimate, he was important in my life. At Annaghmakerrig he was marking time after coming back from Austria where he had been helping people escape from the Nazis. Quite a lot has been written about Hubert; he was a light under a bushel which was not widely seen until his old age forty and more years later.

Jennifer and her little sister, along with her nurse, also left, and the servants were thinned down by one or two. The organized yet frenetic life of 1941 became more manageable. There was just Mrs G., Bunty, my mother, Christopher and I, though there would be visitors often for lunch or to stay. There were of course the ubiquitous Daly girls however. Christopher and I at some point were considered big enough or civilized enough to have luncheon, which was the main meal of the day, with the adults in the dining room. Christopher and I, having been instructed by Bunty, were privileged to lay the table. There was always soup, a main course and some sort of pudding. Water biscuits and cheese were always available. This was a big improvement from the force-feeding of the mob of children in the breakfast room. The ambience of the dining room was quite a contrast from taking lunch with Davy McMahon at his house in the village of Smithboro, where a big basket of boiled potatoes was put in the middle of the table with a piece of butter on a plate and one helped oneself. These were always good potatoes. How different again that would have been then to lunch in Poland or Russia where Hitler's armies were now pounding Moscow and Leningrad, but I had no knowledge of wars and politics. My earliest understanding of politics was when Christopher told me of a man called De Valera who would put Mrs G. out of the house and make her live in the boathouse. I thought that this would be a frightful thing to do. I had, despite the limits of her involvement and her distance with me, become very respectful of Mrs G. So burnt into me was this idea, that years later when my rational mind at one point told me that the Fianna Fáil party was the one to be supported, because Dev was the most superior statesman in the country, I remained suspicious that I had it wrong. Dev might have been a dangerous ogre underneath.

In the late summer we had a seaside holiday with Uncle Marcus Killen, Mat and their two children, John who was my age and Margaret, a year younger. We went to Bundoran, the first of two Bundoran summer holidays. As Christopher and I were not going to school, I wonder if holiday is the right word; at any rate it was another scene. We stayed in a boarding house from where one could see the flashing at night to the St John's Point Lighthouse. Marcus was a great fisherman. He caught mackerel off the rocks below the house and once we walked all the way over Finner Strand, past sandhills which were fun to slide down, to the estuary of the River Erne where we saw Marcus land a great fat salmon. It was not the famous Salmon of Assaroe, the oldest and wisest living being in Ireland, which dwells in those waters, but Mat cooked it and it was delicious. My memory of Bundoran is rather negative, being of cold winds and rain. One was supposed to enjoy bathing in the sea; I can only remember the cold of it. We went back on the Bundoran Express, which stopped at Newbliss some 3 miles from Annaghmakerrig. This train was called the Bundoran Express, not because it went particularly fast or because it was non-stop: it stopped everywhere, but one could go all the way from Dublin to Bundoran without having to change at Dundalk, Clones or Bundoran Junction.

I find it hard to keep track chronologically of events and places over the next couple of years. Some of the time we were at Annaghmakerrig and some of the time at Eldron; indeed some of the references I have just made could well be about later events. These places were the bases, but there were excursions, short ones to Dublin, and then two long periods away in 1942 to Newcastle, Co. Down and in 1943 to Strabane in Co. Tyrone. These later two were related to my father's movements. He was variously posted to Edinburgh and Bristol. His penultimate posting was to Newcastle, Co. Down and in January 1943 he was in hospital in Derry for a sinus operation, after which he was invalided out of the army. After leaving the army, he spent quite some time at Annaghmakerrig, but never at Eldron. The pattern was that my mother would make extended visits to him in Britain, and we would be put in Eldron while she was away. He was certainly at Annaghmakerrig one summer for that was when he gave me my first swimming lessons. With a walking stick hooked into a raincoat belt under the arms, one was towed behind the boat. It can't have been successful, for it was another couple of years before I could swim properly. He said it was much better to be safe and humane than to do as Humphrey Evatt of Mount Louise did, which was to throw his children out of the boat and let them learn on their own.

The men I had most to do with at this time were Brian McGoldrick and Eddie Daly. Brian was then quite old, and retired not long after. He lived in the back gate lodge with his wife Mary. Mary was "Big Mary" as opposed to her daughter "Wee Mary". She was a jovial woman who came up to the house to help with the laundry; there were no washing machines then. In the family were also Bridget, Patsy and Micky Joe. Micky Joe had a racing dog, a greyhound. Patsy kept a ferret in a wooden box (you could see its red eye through a hole). There was a rope for carrying the box on the way to the rabbit warrens. Brian worked on the estate. I learned much later that he and Mary had come from the wild mountain country near the source of the River Shannon and had come to Annaghmakerrig a long time before in answer to an advertisement put in the paper. Brian was a great man to sing. He taught me my first song which was "Brian O'Lynn". "Brian O'Lynn had no breeches to wear, so he got an old sheepskin to make him a pair, with the skinny side out and wooly side in, they'll be warm in winter said Brian O'Lynn". In my mental picture of Brian he is wearing leggings and smoking a pipe, though I might be mixing him up with a picture of Brian O'Lynn from some songbook. They were a bright and friendly family, Catholic and much closer to the old Gaelic culture than the rest of the people in and around Annaghmakerrig who were mainly Protestant, and despite many having Irish names, they were largely anglicized and somewhat dour in comparison to the McGoldricks. Mrs Annie Daly, Eddie's wife, also sang.

Once a week she would spend a morning in the dairy making the butter. She would push a wooden churn backwards and forwards for a very long time until the butter suddenly appeared. There was a strange rhythmic sound emanating from the dairy as this was going on; it was Annie Daly singing in time to the churn. She was in fact, though it was hard to detect, singing hymns. This was a sign of the Protestant culture. Actually she didn't go to church; Eddie and the five girls all went to the Church of Ireland; Annie was a Presbyterian, but whether the fact that she didn't go had anything to do with antipathy to Episcopalianism, the given reason was that she had to stay home to cook the Sunday dinner. At any rate she made up for her absence with her own liturgy in the dairy.

Perhaps it is from later on that I got to know Eddie, a big grave man with a white moustache, for I think of helping him harness the horse into a cart and I can hardly have done that when only 5 or 6. My memory of him ploughing up the West Park with two big black horses was a wartime activity, compulsory tillage. After the war there was never again the exciting activity of threshing when the huge threshing machine and the steam traction engine came and all the men would be there to pitch in the sheaves of oats from the rick, and when they got to the bottom of the rick, the rats would start to dash out, to beat the gauntlet of dogs and urchins like me. In peacetime there was only enough tillage to provide oats for the horses and potatoes for the household and a couple of pigs. There was hay made every year for the four or five cows which Eddy milked, and for other cattle. The land was poor; marl underlay the topsoil, making for water-logging. The extensive stone outbuildings had little use. Only about 50 acres were farmed after the 1930s, when most of the property had been planted with trees by the Forestry Department.

CHAPTER THREE

FitzSimon Grandparents, the MacFarlane Family

We went to stay with the Butlers in Kilkenny for a month or so before the Christmas of 1942. On the way we stayed with my paternal grandparents in Dublin. I liked to stay with my FitzSimon grandmother, who was still, though turned 70, a very lively person. She was very skilled at cooking chicken with parsley sauce, a treat we had when we stayed. It was a practice in later years, when we stayed with her around Christmas for a few days that she would take us to the pantomime to see Jimmy O'Dea or Cecil Sheridan, and to the pictures, with tea in Roberts café or the restaurant of the Green Cinema.

My grandfather Dan kept to himself, or at any rate did not become involved with children, though when Christopher was staying at Whinsfield, Dan would take him to Mass at Sandyford. I seem to remember that Dan wore tweed plus fours, and sat in the dining room where he kept whiskey and soda and bottled stout in the sideboard. He may have drunk quite a bit, but I never heard any suggestion that he was an alcoholic; he was unlike his brother, to whom we will come shortly.

During the war years travelling even in the city was not easy; one had to wait in a queue for what seemed hours for the number 44 bus to Sandyford. When it was time to go to Kilkenny we had to get up in the dark at six o'clock to be collected by Mellon's taxi from Dundrum to take us to Kingsbridge Station.

Both of my grandparents had been born into the landed gentry with what would appear to be silver spoons in their mouths. But close

MACFARLANE AND MCKAY FAMILY TREES

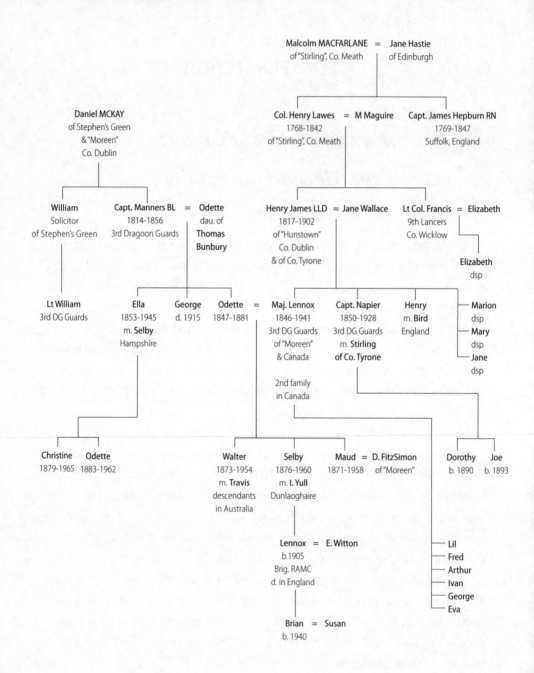

Malcolm MACFARLANE = Jane Hastie
of "Stirling", Co. Meath | of Edinburgh

Daniel MCKAY
of Stephen's Green
& "Moreen"
Co. Dublin

Col. Henry Lawes = M Maguire
1768-1842
of "Stirling", Co. Meath

Capt. James Hepburn RN
1769-1847
Suffolk, England

William
Solicitor
of Stephen's Green

Capt. Manners BL = Odette
1814-1856   dau. of
3rd Dragoon Guards Thomas
                Bunbury

Henry James LLD = Jane Wallace
1817-1902
of "Hunstown"
Co. Dublin
& of Co. Tyrone

Lt Col. Francis = Elizabeth
9th Lancers
Co. Wicklow

Elizabeth
dsp

Lt William
3rd DG Guards

Ella
1853-1945
m. Selby
Hampshire

George
d. 1915

Odette =
1847-1881

Maj. Lennox
1846-1941
3rd DG Guards
of "Moreen"
& Canada

2nd family
in Canada

Capt. Napier
1850-1928
3rd DG Guards
m. Stirling
of Co. Tyrone

Henry
m. Bird
England

Marion
dsp

Mary
dsp

Jane
dsp

Christine   Odette
1879-1965   1883-1962

Walter
1873-1954
m. Travis
descendants
in Australia

Selby
1876-1960
m. I. Yull
Dunlaoghaire

Maud = D. FitzSimon
1871-1958   of "Moreen"

Dorothy   Joe
b. 1890   b. 1893

Lennox = E. Witton
b.1905
Brig. RAMC
d. in England

Lil
Fred
Arthur
Ivan
George
Eva

Brian = Susan
b. 1940

examination shows that the silver was already tarnished when they were still in their infancy. My grandparents at this point in 1942 were probably at the nadir of their financial fortunes.

My great-grandfather Christopher FitzSimon was forced to sell about half his property to pay off mortgages, the year my grandfather was born. He had inherited an estate of some 3,500 acres which was valued at £2,200 per annum in 1862 when he took out a mortgage of £17,000. His father, also Christopher, known as Poor Dear Fitz had made over the property, lands in Wicklow and Dublin, just before he died in 1856. Poor Dear Fitz had inherited the estate which had been in the family nearly 200 years by then. He was married to Ellen, daughter of the "Liberator", the great Daniel O'Connell, and while MP for Dublin at Westminster, supported his father-in-law. Later he had a lucrative sinecure "Clerk of the Crown and Hanaper" worth £1,400 a year, which the government of the day had bribed him with to get him to resign his seat in Parliament. He said that he needed to spend more time with his family. This was not seen as treachery by O'Connell, who liked to see his relatives well looked after.

Poor Dear Fitz was responsible for building at Glencullen the old church, the school, and the police barracks, and pushing through the road to Rathfarnham through the Pine Forest. He and his son Christopher were both educated at Trinity College and both called to the Bar. Christopher never practised law; he inherited the estate when aged 26 and thereafter farmed the Glencullen land rather then let it out to tenants as it had been previously, and as were the Wicklow lands. He employed up to thirty men on the farm. They earned 1s. 6d. a day. He was the High Sheriff of Co. Wicklow in 1862, and was said to have kept great state, but I suspect that the need to raise a mortgage in 1862, and the fact that when he died in 1883 he was bankrupt, was also due to his overindulgence at playing at cards. There are stories of his near great wins and real great losses. Working against him from the 1870s was the opening up of land in North America and the Antipodes with newly invented agricultural machines, and refrigeration ships to bring meat and butter, with which Irish and European farmers had difficulty competing. Also the late 1870s was a period of bad weather and bad harvests. Poor Dear Fitz and Ellen had another son Henry and three daughters, who grew up and married, and when some provision was made for them, the estate was further diminished. The early history of the FitzSimons and Glencullen is dealt with in Chapter 14 below.

After Christopher died bankrupt, his children were made Wards in Chancery, and what was left of the estates was administered by solicitors. These solicitors must have done their job well, because when my grandfather's elder brother "Uncle Christie" reached his majority and took over, the debts had all been paid off. Unfortunately, Uncle Christie did not take long to run up some debts himself. Whereas his father's vice had been cards, Christie's was drink, and he was to die at the age of 43 of cirrhosis of the liver. He had wanted to marry my grandmother but I guess she was too smart. She settled for the bank clerk younger brother Dan.

My grandmother's father did not inherit anything. It was his father known as "Old Mac", who dissipated an estate, and was to die bankrupt in 1902. These people were MacFarlanes, whose forbears had come from Scotland in the eighteenth century.

These Irish MacFarlanes were, to use Brendan Behan's term, archetypical Horse Protestants. They were a proud and passionate lot. There was a belief that they were heirs to the Scottish clan chieftaincy, the Macfarlane of Arrochar, descendants of the Earls of Lennox. Great efforts were made in the twentieth century, especially by my father's cousin Lennox MacFarlane, to establish the claim. He also had it in his head that there was money to go along with the title. His cousin Rhoderick MacFarlane in Australia, who by primogeniture was the theoretical heir, wrote to Lennox to say that Lennox could have the title if he, Rhoderick, could have the money. Lennox wrote back to say that that was a very generous gesture, but alas there has been no recognition of the chieftaincy, or sign of any money either. We have established that our branch did come from the house of the chief at Arrochar but my cousin John MacFarlane in Canada, who has researched the family history in detail, has put forward the theory that the problem is that our branch is illegitimate.

Our branch stems from Malcolm MacFarlane who left Scotland in the mid-eighteenth century on government business, first to Portugal and then to Ireland where he eventually settled having bought land in Co. Meath.

In earlier times the clan had a reputation, even by highland standards, for feuding with neighbouring clans and stealing their cattle and sheep. The moon was called "MacFarlane's Lantern" owing to their propensity for night-time activity. Their Highland traditions may well have been ingrained in the bones of their successors among the Irish gentry, amongst whom they would continue a somewhat muted form of piratical marauding, curbing their passions and eccentricities as they wrestled with the restrictions of Victorian respectability; perhaps they were not too different from many of their class.

Of Malcolm's sons, the elder, Henry Lawes, as an army colonel, was Captain General of the Irish Wagon Train; that is he was in charge of military supplies, a post which would have given him much opportunity to feather his own nest, a practice which today would be seen as outright corruption. Then, though if one was not nimble on one's feet and one stuck in one's hand too deep, one could still get into trouble;however such practice was not seen as all that much of a misdemeanour; it was of course a sought after position. He bought considerable property in North County Dublin; Hunstown House was his residence. The second son, James, had a career in the Royal Navy, fighting the French on "The Glorious First of June" and retiring eventually in England as a captain. In between, he won a large amount of prize money, having captured a French merchantman, towing it out with sailors at the oars of rowing boats from under the guns of Fort St Louis on Mauritius. A third son Edward, according to his father's will dated 1808, was left the house, Stirling, at Clonee, Co.Meath, the property bought on the original migration from Scotland, along with rents of £430 a year. He later removed to England. Another son disappears from the records after being cut out of the will;we don't know why.

It was Henry Lawes's eldest son Henry James, Old Mac, born in 1819, who inherited Hunstown. The second son, "Uncle Francis", was left the rents of several townlands adjacent to Hunstown, but spent most of his career with the army in India where he distinguished himself at the Battle of Goojerat in 1849 against the Sikhs. He led the charge of the cavalry. Ultimately as lieutenant colonel, he rose to command his regiment, the 9th Lancers. After he retired, he lived in Delgany, Co. Wicklow along with his daughter and his wife who was his first cousin, the daughter of the naval captain uncle.

Henry James, my grandmother's grandfather, married a Miss Wallace from Co. Tyrone who brought with her into the family about 1,600 acres of not very good land at Ballygawley in Co. Tyrone, along with ground rents in the nearby town of Aughnacloy. The family then would spend part of their time there, as well as at Hunstown House near Dublin. Henry Lawes sat on the bench of magistrates of both counties. To rise in the world he stood for Parliament for the University of Dublin seat, but wasn't elected. The university did however give him the degree of Doctor of Law. Perhaps his downfall ultimately was due to him trying too hard to rise in the world. He was a busy man, but he had lost all his property before he died in 1902. As a country gentleman and landowner he was very much involved in local government. As a guardian under the Poor Laws, a role undertaken by many of the gentry, the thrust of the work was the administration of the workhouses. These were dreadful places where the starving poor at least had a roof over their heads. They were set up just before the great famine of 1846, but with the famine they were crammed to overflowing, and the inmates were lucky to survive the rampant infectious diseases. It took some time for the system to be improved; part of the process of improvement was the ongoing nineteenth-century professionalization of the public administration, and in this Henry James was to share, being appointed in 1879 to the position of Local Government Inspector on a salary of £800 a year. He had for the previous twenty-one years been Chairman of the North Dublin Union. With his salary and his estates he would have been very well off, but he was probably living beyond his means.

He appears in photographs as a strong and severe character. There is no evidence of him treating his family badly but there is evidence that he dominated them all. His photograph albums show what must have been an abnormally high propensity for sycophancy and social climbing, more than would have been likely for the normal bureaucrat toadying for advancement. He had pictures of such as "My esteemed friend the Bishop of Bath and Wells", "My dear friend the Marquis of Normanby", " My long and most highly respected colleague Viscount Lifford", and many more with such titles. It is said that when his wife was seriously ill and near to death, a servant dispatched to bring him home could not extract him from a card game at a party with the Duke of Marlborough. He became bitter as he became older and was passed over for promotion. His sycophancy doesn't seem to have helped; perhaps it was a hindrance. He had expected to become the head of the department, a position which carried a knighthood as well as a bigger salary. He carried on a correspondence with a succession of Lords Lieutenant and Prime Ministers, first explaining why he should be promoted, and then after he had resigned in protest, why he should be compensated. The letters become more and more shrill and make one think it had deteriorated into an irrational obsession. In time, as an old man, after the mortgagees had foreclosed on Hunstown, he had to be dragged away from haranguing and abusing the people attending the auction who he considered had no right to be there.

Henry James, Old Mac, as he was more commonly known, had three sons and three daughters. The eldest daughter, Marion, was one of the first ladies to attend Alexandra College, Dublin. Fragments of her school reports remain; these date from the early 1870s and are only remarkable in that they appear little different than if they had been written a hundred years later regarding curricula and the comments on the performance of the pupil. Perhaps Alexandra was ahead of its time. We also have fragments of her diaries. She seems to have travelled around the country visiting friends quite a bit, and corresponded a lot with a former school friend who had a teaching job in Germany. There is frequent movement between Hunstown and Tyrone. When living at Hunstown House she was busy about the place and driving into the city on her own or with her mother several times a week. She was also active in the local church where she played the organ for Sunday services; this would have been Clonsilla Church of Ireland Parish Church where many MacFarlanes are buried in the surrounding churchyard. One gets the impression that she was the de facto mistress of the household even before her mother died, and most certainly was afterwards. After Old Mac went broke, and Hunstown house was taken over by the mortgagees, it was Marion who picked up the pieces and organized the exodus, taking Old Mac and her sisters, Jane and Mary to find sanctuary with Uncle Francis's daughter in Delgany, Uncle Francis MacFarlane by then being dead. None of these ladies married.

On the other hand, all Old Mac's three sons married. The first to do so was my grandmother's father Lennox. Lennox, along with the second son, Napier, both graduated from Trinity College and were then commissioned in The 3rd (Prince of Wales) Dragoon Guards. This was an expensive regiment, both to get into by way of the purchase of the commission, (Uncle Francis had sold his commission at about the same time his nephews joined up, getting £3,500 for it) and to keep up the expected lifestyle which apart from the need for the brilliant uniforms, swords and mess bills, being in the cavalry one had to own a particularly good horse. Army pay and allowances went nowhere near to meeting such expenses. Old Mac was still well off then, so only the best in style would do for the family. Lennox, who was born in 1846, married in 1870 Odette McKay, an orphaned heiress of modest fortune, so he was thus established. Napier did not marry until much later. Indeed Old Mac, being dissatisfied with the rate of progress of Napier's courtship, and complaining that Napier was too shy, intervened himself, making Napier's case to the lady in question, successfully.

Napier had a degree in Engineering, and after leaving the Dragoon Guards continued his army career in the artillery. We find him at one point, as a captain in the militia, The Royal Cork Artillery, on manoeuvres in Donegal and attending courses in England. He was my only forbear of athletic distinction, being middleweight boxing champion of the British Army. He lived on the Tyrone property which had belonged to his mother and in which with his sisters he had a share after she died.

About 1905 the Tyrone property was sold and he went with his family to live at Newbury House, Raheny, Co. Dublin. There is a lot of evidence of Napier and his family attending the Lord Lieutenant's social functions at the Castle. Whatever were his politics (he was not an activist), he was an Orangeman; his daughter Dorothy had his sash in the house until the house fell in.

Dorothy was, for a lady, an early graduate of the university; she had a gold medal for Philosophy. She had a long career racing greyhounds; she drove around in a Ford van to the race tracks (and everywhere else) with the greyhounds in the back. It is said that despite her dedication to the sport she was not often a winner. Napier died in 1928 and his unmarried son Joe, not long after. Dorothy lived on until 1986, well before the time the once fine Georgian house Newbury had progressively collapsed. I last visited her when on a trip to Ireland in 1974, by which time the roof over the hall and stairs was completely gone and to get from the drawing room to the kitchen one had to walk on duckboards to keep one's feet out of the mud. In the kitchen there was a goat which normally belonged to a group of tinkers, who camped on the lawn, and with whom Dorothy had from time to time some sort of symbiotic relationship.

Old Mac's youngest son Henry was something of a black sheep. He enlisted in the Dragoon Guards as a trooper and took part in the Egyptian campaign of 1883, but was eventually commissioned as an officer, by which time it was no longer necessary to purchase a commission. He was to cause his mother distress when he raided the family home one night and stole his father's favourite black stallion. This sort of thing however was not unique. Some relations, being aggrieved that they did not have certain family silver, and having failed to get it by legal means, raided the house when they knew that the family were away. When the housekeeper saw the carriage drive up, she guessed what they were after, and quickly hid the silver away, thus thwarting the plot. Henry settled in England and his descendants cut themselves off from the family in Ireland. Perhaps his father-in-law, who was a Doctor of Divinity in Yorkshire, took him in hand, and reoriented him and his successors to a more English type of respectability.

Going back to the eldest son Lennox, my grandmother's father; he was to bring up his family in Moreen, his wife Odette's property at Sandyford in South County Dublin. There were three children of the marriage: Maud, my grandmother (who was actually born in Stirling, Co. Meath, the original MacFarlane house, which had been bought about 1770), Walter and Selby. In the gate lodge there was Lil, later known as Aunt Lil, who was the result of circumstances which caused, so it is believed, Lennox's departure from the Dragoon Guards. Lennox had had an affair with the wife of a brother officer, and what made the offence worse was that it was while the brother officer was away on active service. This was not Lennox's only such dalliance. There was more than one of the local retainers held to be one of the "Major's gets". Lennox, after leaving the Dragoon Guards, became a major, like Napier, in the Royal Cork Artillery. He most likely had met Odette through her cousin William McKay who was also (as had been Odette's father Manners McKay) in the Prince of Wales Dragoon Guards. This William disappears under a cloud having virtually bankrupted his father, who was left to pay off his gambling debts. The father, William McKay senior, who had been a wealthy Dublin solicitor, went to live out his days in a London hotel; he kept a mistress in Paddington, so he can't have been entirely broke. Odette's parents both died when she and her two younger sisters were very young so the children were brought up by their mother's Bunbury family in Tipperary.

Odette too was to die very young, in 1883. In the language of the day, she was said to have "died of a broken heart", on account of her husband's infidelities. There were several instances when she fled to Hunstown; she seems to have had sympathy from her sisters-in-law. She had no nearby family to flee to, with her parents long dead and her sisters living in England. Her husband Lennox was exceptional among MacFarlanes, in that he was the only one with whom she had a problem. We find Lennox, when he wanted her to return, writing to Francis in Delgany, " for God's sake, Uncle, could you talk to Odette; you are the only one she respects".

It appears that it was during Odette's absences that Lennox was most prone to rage. We read of the maids also fleeing when he came in drunk, roaring at them and swearing. On one occasion he was brought before the Dundrum magistrates for horsewhipping a manservant.

My grandmother, Maud, remembered the occasion not long after Odette's death, when Lennox arrived up the avenue with a woman carrying an infant. The woman was an illiterate dancer from Liverpool, a mistress, and the infant was Fred, the first of five children they were to have together. In 1895, when his eldest son Walter reached the age of 21 and inherited Moreen, Lennox, along with his second family moved to Co. Meath, taking Aunt Lil from the gate lodge as well. In 1898 he took this family to Canada, first to the prairies where they lived in a pioneering sod hut and then to Vancouver Island. My cousin George MacFarlane had a description of him sitting in the middle of the hut on his rocking chair, in the one spot where the rain was not coming in, reading his Bible. When Queen Victoria died, he held a special service with the family for her repose. He was, like most of the family, a religious man in the manner of the Irish gentry of the time. There is evidence of great remorse after his temper and passions had led him into rages and conflicts. Life must have improved after the move to the island. On the prairie, the boys, (there were four of them, scarcely into their teens), would catch rabbits for the family and sell them so that they could give the money to their mother, and not to their father for him to buy his whiskey. On the island they were closer to civilization, and Lennox was able to go to the social functions of the Provincial Governor; indeed he was eventually to be married to a society lady in the cathedral in Victoria. His long time partner and mother of most of his children, lived thereafter in the boathouse.

Lennox was a remarkably talented horseman. Not only did he ride in races at official tracks, but he had a track on Moreen where he ran less formal races. He was reputed to "fix" these races; horse culture had a lot more to it than simply riding. There are two newspaper articles put together after interviews with him reminiscing in 1936, when he was 90 years old. Both stories are long and convoluted. One is about a race he rode on a horse which belonged to a boastful and unpopular officer. The aim was to put down the officer, who could not handle the horse, whereas Lennox, as the most skilled rider in the regiment would show him up. The other was about a retainer on the Hunstown estate known as Peter the Fish (his uncle sold fish), scheming to sell a horse to an English dealer. The horse had had its ears cut off, punishment to the owner for paying rent to a blacklisted landlord, a common practice during the land wars of the time. Peter had gone to great lengths to get two horse's ears from an abbatoir and to fix them in place on the cropped horse so well that the dealer was totally taken in. Flurry Knox in the novels of Somerville and Ross could not have done better. One wonders if Somerville and Ross knew the MacFarlanes.

Despite his behaviour, and some long estrangements, Lennox always seems to have made amends, enough that his descendants by and large, and at a distance, remember him with some respect. His sins such as philandering, knobbling horses at race meetings and attacking his servants while drunk, were not seen as mortal ones whatever disturbances they created at the time. He lived until he was 96.

Shortly after my grandparents were married, Walter put Moreen on the market and left for Australia. My grandparents approached my grandmother's Aunt Ella, who was Odette's sister, and had inherited that part of the Moreen estate which had not passed to Odette and then to Walter, to buy Moreen at the auction. This aunt had married a wealthy businessman (he had made a fortune in scrap metal and met the aunt at Malta on a cruise in the Mediterranean). The arrangement was that she would then lease the property to Dan. That was in 1898, the year my father was born.

Dan was now able to live the life of a gentleman, at least some of the time. He hunted with the Bray Harriers, played golf and sat on the magistrates' bench as a JP. But he had to work too. He ran the Moreen farm as a dairy; it was what one would today call a vertically integrated business. Every morning after the cows were milked, carts would head off for the suburbs of Rathmines, Rathgar and Ranelagh, and the maids of the bourgeoisie would come out to fill their jugs from the churns in the cart. Invoices were sent out to the customers headed "Tigh Lorcan Dairy, Telephone, Dundrum 51". This dairy business went on till the First World War; it ceased rather than develop into the modern style of dairy with glass bottles and pasteurization and refrigerated storage. Dan had a hand as well in managing the Glencullen estate of his brother Christie. He had in fact gone to live in Glencullen before he was married, an escape from life as bank clerk in Rathmines and then in Bunclody, Co. Wexford, a life which he hated. Life was fun at Glencullen with his brothers and sister. They were the nucleus of the Glencullen cricket team, which played on the front lawn. After the match, the Glencullen band would play, and a barrel or two of porter would be broached. They put on theatricals in the big barn as their parent's generation had done before. There was excellent grouse shooting on the mountain. Only 50 acres of Glencullen was farmed after the lawyers took charge in 1883; the rest of the agricultural land was let to tenants, about 700 or so acres, as much of it as had been let in earlier times. There was another 1,000 acres of mountain on which sheep would graze from time to time, but the grouse took precedence.

I was always given to understand that Grandfather Dan helped Christie on the estate because Christie, a clever chap who had been at Trinity College, was busy with other things. This I found to be a cover up to preserve the family good name. The only evidence I could find of Christie being busy was with the bottle. Dan helped because of Christie's incompetence. There was one harrowing period when Christie was being pursued for breach of promise of marriage and for getting the lady pregnant, a Miss Daly from Liverpool. She sued him for £1,000 but settled on the steps of the high court for £100; one wonders if she really was pregnant, and if there was a child, what happened to it. There are letters Christie wrote to solicitors saying he was being blackmailed, though it arose from "my own stupidity". He had the case handled by different solicitors from the normal family ones. He was probably very embarrassed by it all.

Of the other brothers, Dick died just after being commissioned an officer in the Royal Irish Constabulary; Ned had a spell at the university, then went to South Africa where he was a policeman during the Boer

War, later farmed and died there unmarried in 1939. Christie died in 1910 and Dan, my grandfather took over. He ran the estate thereafter but continued to live at Moreen. Sister May resided in Glencullen House until 1914 when she went off to England to do war work and after that the house was let from time to time. Christie didn't leave any debts but there were death duties to pay. He had sold the last of the Wicklow estate, a farm called Ballinamona in 1907 for £3,700, enough to pay off his debts, which included £1,000 he had borrowed from his sister May. The Glencullen rental was presumably enough to keep his wine merchant at bay for the rest of his life. A Glencullen saying, "For every pound the FitzSimons got in rent they spent two", seemingly ceased to apply for this period.

Dan then raised a mortgage of £11,000, which was used to pay the death duties, buy out Moreen from the aunt in England, and leave a bit to invest in a cattle dealing business. The cattle dealing replaced the dairying; Dan and his partner, a farmer from Kilternan, had a stand at the cattle market where he would have to be at four o'clock in the morning.

Around the same time my grandmother's two MacFarlane aunts died. They had taken refuge in Delgany with their maiden lady MacFarlane cousin after old Mac went broke. They left my grandmother the very fine house in Delgany which she promptly sold, and the proceeds went to buy some flats in London, which thereafter became Maud's principal interest. Checking up on the flats provided a need for frequent visits to London, the cost of which would be just about covered by the rents.

The Delgany aunts had had some considerable resources to pass on to various relations and to charities, having owned most of the town of Aughnacloy in Co. Tyrone, inherited from their mother and kept out of the clutches of their father. They left a lot of money to the Church of Ireland of which all the MacFarlanes were pillars. The ladies played the organ in the church and also left behind shelves of bibles, prayer books and religious tracts.

Maud had quite a social life. Her great friend Constance Gore-Booth introduced her to Dublin Castle and the social whirl of the Lords Lieutenant. She also had some tenuous links with the artistic and intellectual set of the day. Her friend became the Countess Markievicz and took up the cause of Ireland; she was one of the leaders of the 1916 Easter Rising and in the War of Independence. Before the rising, the Countess rented one of the cottages on Moreen and would bring out young lads from the city to give them military training. Maud never became involved in politics, nor Dan either. He was a man who liked to sit on the fence. When my teenage father saw the Countess's lads hopping about among the whins on their military manoevres, Dan told him to say nothing to anyone, and this despite my father being down to go to Sandhurst. Some years later Michael Collins came to Dan to "get permission" to use the Glencullen barn as an arsenal. Dan's reply was "How would I even know you were using it?"

Maud was involved in community affairs, being secretary to the local Jubilee Nursing Association for fifty years. Though she did not follow the intense evangelical life of some of her forbears, she remained a pillar of Kilternan Church of Ireland Church, singing in the choir even after she became stone deaf in her eighties, nobody having the gall to suggest that it might be time for her to retire.

She had married my Roman Catholic grandfather in the Roman Catholic Church in Westland Row. I never heard of any dissension between them on this score or between the two families, though perhaps there had been some. This was a time when rivalry between denominations was intense and sectarianism could lend to a great deal of grief. The Church of Ireland had lost its political dominance. Before the Church of Ireland was disestablished in 1870, the Church of Ireland archbishop took precedence over the Roman Catholic one in any official function. After 1870, the government protocol people, on wondering what to do, decided that as the Roman Catholic one, Cullen, was a cardinal, he would take precedence. This was too much for the Protestant one who never attended the castle again. The Roman Catholic establishment was now exercising its influence. For instance, any political election meeting for the Nationalists would typically have ten to twelve priests on the platform. The Protestants preferred the Unionist party, but tended to keep their heads down while their church leaders tried after a while to concentrate on non-political issues.

The fact that my grandparents were able to exist amicably on religious grounds was no doubt helped by my grandfather being free of any vestige of fanaticism. He was not even what was called a "good Catholic". It is possible he would have been called a "bad Catholic". He said that the only reason he ate fish on Friday was that he liked fish and would eat it three days a week if he could get it. He had a dispute with the parish priest in Sandyford to do with the boundary of Moreen and the church grounds, possibly to do with the church grounds being a donation a 100 years before by my grandmother's ancestor from part of the Moreen estate. The result was that he stopped going to Mass for years.

My father started off life nominally as a Catholic but soon went to a non-Catholic school, Earlsfort House in Dublin. With his mother, who he adored, an active Protestant, and his father, who was rather distant, a non-active Catholic, as well as the school, he must have been a bit confused. This would become apparent later. He had a little sister, but she survived only a few months. She was, according to Maud, caught in the pram in the rain when her nurse went into Flavins bar in Sandyford for sustenance, leaving the pram outside. My Uncle Henry known as Tib, who was much younger, was sent to school with the Jesuits at Clongowes and wanted to be a priest. My grandfather to whom such an idea was anathema, managed to torpedo such a career. Tib instead was sent to Trinity College, but dropped out in his third year after a couple of failed attempts at "Little Go", the final Freshman exam. In due course he was to be found a position as a helper, in effect he was a lay brother, with the nursing order, the Alexian Brothers, in their hospital at Warrenpoint in Co. Down where he was to remain until his death in 1985.

My grandparents' life continued in the early 1920s comfortably enough, but with the new government of independent Ireland, the twenty-six counties, the writing was on the wall. The late nineteenth-century Land Acts culminating in Wyndham's Act in 1905 made provision for tenant farmers to be bought out from landlords. The Irish land holding system had been a vexatious issue for a very long time. In many countries, such as Russia and Mexico, the peasants rose in bloody revolution to relieve themselves of their oppressive landlords. Some countries such as

England had reasonably fair land holding laws and landlords with an ability and incentive to invest money in the farms, rather than bleed their tenants dry. Ireland was closer to the former countries than the latter. The attempts by the British Government to resolve the issue were rather half-hearted, but under Prime Minister Balfour, the government devised a plan which was a successful compromise. If the tenants on an estate put up a proposal to buy out the landlord which the landlord accepted, the government provided the money with terms of repayment over a long period. Unfortunately as hindsight was to show, Christie would not accept the proposal put forward by his tenants. The sticking point was that the tenants asked for arrears of rent to be written off; there were some tenants who hadn't paid rent for two years or more. Christie scrawled across the proposal in pencil "Not enough".

After 1922, the new Free State government made the transfer of tenanted farms from the landlord to the Land Commission compulsory; there would be no more landlordism in the twenty-six counties. So ended a system which had been in place since the invading Normans in the twelfth century had started to replace the old Gaelic system with their continental practice. In Russia at this time the Bolsheviks were busy shooting the landlords, but the Free Staters were relatively benign. True, many landlords had been induced to leave, mainly in the West where their houses were burnt down. But this was done by irregulars; the new government was one for law and order. The new government paid compensation to the landlords for the land taken over, but at only sixteen times the annual rental valuations as against twenty-four times under the British. As well, by 1927 when the Glencullen tenanted land was transferred, the rents were down from pre-war levels. So the compensation package wasn't enough to cover the big loan Dan had taken out, which initially would have been equal to about half the value of the property but now was more than the value of all of it. Dan struggled on for a bit negotiating with banks, but by 1930 with the worldwide depression setting in and not much sign of belt tightening – Dan liked his horse and his whiskey and Maud her trips to London – the mortgagees foreclosed on Moreen. My grandparents moved into Whinsfield, a house which they built on the last acre of the Moreen property. Moreen had been in Maud's family since 1770, and its loss was keenly felt by my father who had grown up there.

They kept going for the next twelve years by selling off bits of property which had not gone to the mortgagees or the Land Commission. There was the freehold of Foxe's pub in Glencullen, there was 30 acres of the Glencullen farm and a cottage there which had been built as a dispensary, in 1940 the actual Glencullen house, and in 1942 about 300 acres of the mountain to the Forestry Department. When we stayed with them on the way to Maiden Hall in 1942, Whinsfield had also gone, and they were renting a cottage called Sea View from a dentist called Yates. When I later came across him as my school dentist, he was known as "Butcher Yates", albeit unfairly.

Dan was just about to sell some important family silver, a set presented to Christopher, Poor Dear Fitz, on his election to Parliament in 1834, when my mother salvaged it by buying it herself. She had a low opinion of her father-in-law with his, as she saw it, profligate and idle ways. He may have been a profligate but not as bad as some, and circumstances had been against him. He was certainly a contrast to my mother's worthy puritan Ulster relatives. The following year things were to turn a bit better. There was with the war, a shortage of imported coal, and hence money to be made selling large quantities of turf from Glencullen Mountain. This bonanza went on until 1947. In 1943 my grandparents bought Kilgobbin House, helped initially with a loan from my mother. It was a small but distinguished early Georgian house which cost very little to buy but needed modernization, adding the like of a kitchen, lavatory and a septic tank. In all these moves they were never more than a mile or so from Moreen or 4 miles from Glencullen. Dan died there in 1948. Maud stayed on till 1953. One can say he might have ended up richer if he had been smarter, greedier, or more energetic, but one can say that about most people. My father maintained that Dan worked very hard when he was younger. My mother on the other hand maintained that though he had the opportunity to make good money in the 1930s and 40s as an arbitrator in the Land Commission courts, if the weather wasn't right or something else interfered, he wouldn't bother to attend.

CHAPTER FOUR

Newcastle, Strabane, Eldron

Our stay at Maiden Hall was the last contact I can remember with the Butler family for several years. It was a good visit. I was not force-fed food I did not like. Maybe I was treated more as a guest, though I doubt that. Peggy's predilection for organizing children had changed; perhaps a factor was that I was, at 6, more attuned to intellectual activities which had been meat for the older children at Annaghmakerrig. It was not necessary to escape with Joe to mischief, with the usual consequence of getting into trouble. Peggy was good at organizing our activities. Making things with plasticine, weaving with raffia, drawing and painting, but above all reading aloud was her forte. We had the *Babar the Elephant* books and *Mary Poppins*. Pamela Travers, who wrote *Mary Poppins*, was a friend of the Butlers; she was Julia's godmother and had adopted one of Joe's brothers. Books to me were no longer emotionally disturbing. At Annaghmakerrig I had once attended a reading session. The book had in it a fat brown creature called "Bugaboo". He was an apple pip with teeth who lived at the bottom of a hole and ate people who fell into the hole. This was so terrifying that I ran out of the reading session and never attended another one. Beatrix Potter's Tom Kitten who was tied up by Mrs Rat and rolled up in pastry as a pudding was deeply disturbing, even though he was rescued before the end of the story. I was also very sorry for a salmon who looked very friendly in the picture book, but was caught and made into a jar of salmon mayonnaise. At 6, however, I could handle such trauma.

It was a house where the intellect, art and discussion of issues were fostered. I had to wait until I was an undergraduate before I could consciously appreciate this; even then the intellect of Hubert was too distant. I am jumping the gun. I must by then have had some understanding of the ability to write, for Joe convinced me that it was necessary to write a letter to Santa Claus if he was to bring me anything at Christmas, which was getting close. The letter would go up the chimney. A letter was written, but it would not go up the chimney; it just lay on a ledge. It did disappear eventually, but I was never confident that Santa got it and that in time was borne out, for my request was not granted.

The move after the visit to Maiden Hall was to Eldron. My mother went to join my father in Britain, so Christopher and I were left with Aunt Jane at Eldron. By now Davy had retired and, I think, died fairly soon after. The big car had gone from its shed, but ironically, it was then that I had an opportunity to go in it; it had been sold to Joe McGovern in Smithboro who drove it as the one and only local taxi. Davy's place working the farm had been taken by alternative visits from the Howe brothers, Harold, Reuben and Andy. Andy taught me how to throw a stone. He was remarkably skilled; if he had had the opportunity I am sure he could have played cricket with the best, for Australia or the West Indies. He didn't make a habit of stoning the crows, but I had seen him when he needed some dead ones to hang up among the oats to deter their relatives, knocking them nonchalantly from the trees, such was his accuracy. Later, after the war, he emigrated to Canada where he had a job putting the heads on dolls in a factory. There wouldn't have been scope to exercising his throwing talent, but I am sure he made a better living than wrestling with the stony grey soil of Monaghan.

Christopher and I became very adept at climbing the trees. He liked to sit in the branches; I was more inclined to go up and down. We both would run down to the "Line", the railway line which ran through the property; the "Flyer" would thunder and roar past twice a day each way. This was the passenger train from Belfast to Cavan. A big black hissing engine and so much more exciting than the occasional goods train which trundled by slowly.

The "Flyer" would bring the Belfast newspapers. Dublin was a remote place from Smithboro; it needed two changes, Clones and Dundalk, and all day to get there. The people of the west of Co. Monaghan took a long time to get used to the idea of Partition, the imposition of which I have always thought to be the greatest travesty the island has had to bear in the twentieth century. Monaghan is an Ulster county and its contact with the outside world, at least the west part of the county, has always been up the valleys of the Blackwater, the Bann and the Lagan to the North. I date the consummation of Partition as 1957, when the railways were shut down, and buses and cars made Dublin less remote. It was then that my Uncle Marcus in Monaghan town switched his allegiance from the *Belfast Newsletter* to *The Irish Times*.

I had a role, to walk into the village to collect the *Belfast Newsletter* from Mr Kerr's shop when it had arrived in a bundle from the railway station. Whether I could read the words from the paper I do not know, but I certainly understood the concept of the map. Every day I would open the paper to see the arrows which indicated the advance of Montgomery's Eighth Army across North Africa. By the time it got to Tunis, we were back in Annaghmakerrig for the summer. That was the summer of 1942, which was spent in Newcastle, Co. Down.

To get to Newcastle was a tortuous journey with several changes. Crossing the border was also a fairly tortuous exercise in itself even in the train. During the war, shortages of many things on one side of the border would be different from the shortage on the other. Smuggling was the boom industry. It continued to be so for many years after the war. Otherwise respectable people would smuggle goods for their use. My mother once went over the border on her bicycle to get candles which were virtually unobtainable in the South – remember we had as yet no electricity. She wrapped the candles around herself under her coat, but peddling the bicycle was warm work and the day was warm anyway. When she got home she was encased in a solid corset of melted candle wax.

Crossing the border thus meant interminable waits on each side as the customs men went searching through the whole train, checking everyone's luggage. On the northern side, the military police were equally slow as they checked out every man's papers in case he was a deserter from the British Army going south or a Nazi spy going north.

My father had a posting to Newcastle, so we rented what was a mews house in a big garden behind a boarding house owned and run by a Mrs Griffin. We did not stay very long in Newcastle, but long enough for Christopher and I to go to school for the Summer Term. I got into trouble for anti-social behaviour. I knocked a girl's lunch into a flowerbed; I think I was being boisterous rather then being malicious, but the teacher castigated me (unfairly I thought), whereupon I attacked the teacher with my belt which had a buckle shaped like a snake. My mother was brought in and had to take me home in disgrace.

There were some big boys at school who were Boy Scouts, or rather the junior version, Wolf Cubs. Christopher, who was 9, got to be one. I must have still been too young. One of the boys brought in a bit of a plane which had crashed on Slieve Donard, the big mountain which dominates Newcastle. Another plane crashed on the beach. This was about as close to the war I ever got, though I had a child's gas mask. Newcastle has a long wide sand beach. One could have donkey rides on it. I was given a ride which was supposed to be a treat and anticipated with excitement, but it turned out to be a great disappointment. I had expected to go galloping all over the strand on my own, but all that happened was that I was led by the donkey man, the donkey only walking.

The Americans arrived in Newcastle while we were there. Mrs Griffin's gardener, a bad-tempered old man could not abide the Americans whom he considered to be as bad as the Germans. The Americans were not as respected as well as they might. There was a popular rumour, which manifested anti-Americanism, that a sentry challenged approaching footsteps in the dark, and when he did not get the password, opened fire, only to find in daylight the he had shot a donkey. We children going to school appreciated the Americans when we walked past their lines of trucks. They would hand us out sweets. They put on a show for the civilians; I had expected to see their tanks rushing about, and though a couple of them did drive a short distance, the main entertainment was a game of baseball, which to me was incredibly boring. My father was attached to a battalion of the South Staffordshire Regiment. I do not know what they were doing or why they were in Newcastle but my father, a major, who had been a temporary lieutenant colonel in North Africa, had a servant, a batman he was called, who babysat us; he was a nice chap and had a funny English accent. My father was soon posted to take command of a battalion of the East Surrey Regiment in Scotland, and after some time, we went back to Eldron.

My role of going to the village to collect the newspaper recommenced; I now daily followed the arrows on the map as the allied armies advanced across North Africa. Sometimes I would go to the post office on an errand. The post office was at the far end of the village in Toal's shop. We did our shopping in Kerr's shop at the near end, which was more convenient. Mr Kerr had a bald head and wore a brown dustcoat. He was assisted by his son Wilson, who had horn-rimmed glasses and also had a brown dustcoat. Wilson went off to train for ordination in the Church of Ireland. Location was not the only reason for patronizing Kerr's. I suspect that most of the Protestants did so, and the Catholics would have gone to Toal's. Mr Toal was a senator and had a big new pebble-dashed two-storey house near Magherarney Chapel. Having the post office was probably a perk, and a consequence of holding high office. Unlike Annaghmakerrig and its surrounds where sectarianism was virtually non-existent, something I noticed in later years when I knew all about sectarianism, that some families went to the chapel in Killeevan, some to the meeting house in Newbliss and some to the church at Aghabog; that was the end of it. In and around Smithboro, religious differences were more pronounced; there was a definite suspicion of the "other lot" and a noticeable tendency for social mixing to be with one's own lot.

Going through the village to Toal's could be something of a gauntlet. Whenever he saw me, a little chap who lived in a house on the left of the street would run out to attack me. I don't remember how the feud started let alone why. He was a spirited chap, as he was smaller than me, and I would respond to his attack in kind, driving him off. I quite enjoyed the thrill of the battle, knowing that I would always win. There were occasions when his mother would come out and drag him away; it was to rescue him rather than discipline him for attacking a passer-by. I never drove him off to his door, rather just fought clear and proceeded on my way though he might come at me again; he would never learn that he could not get my measure. I can still remember the look of hatred on his mother's face, looking at me as she pulled him back to the door. I can't remember any words. It was a row of mean cottages he came from; his clothes were ragged and he was decidedly not clean. I have often wondered in later years whether his attack was a response to hearing his elders saying "Look at that stuck up, la de da wee brat in his fancy clothes – he needs a beating" or even "Look at that stuck up la de da wee Protestant brat etc.". At 7 I had not learnt the antipathies of class and religious divisions, but these were so ingrained in society that it would not be long before they were washed right through me.

This feud, my battles with that lad, became sufficiently notorious for disturbing the Smithboro street that the police became involved. A Garda was sent to have respective mothers, or in my case Jane, to restrain us. I think that stopped the attacks. The authorities were always conscious of a sectarian incident escalating. It is said in some philosophy that a butterfly's wings flapping in Tokyo could set off an earthquake in South Africa. Around the border country a fight between a couple of urchins might end with a Catholic or Protestant being burnt out of his house. In 1921, the rough handling of a Catholic youth by a Protestant special constable in the village of Roslea some 3 miles from Smithboro on the Fermanagh side of the border, set off a chain of events which resulted in several deaths and a dozen houses being burned down. It was reported in the Monaghan newspaper that the Protestants around Smithboro were sitting up at night in fear lest their houses be attacked. There had been twenty years of peace, but memories are long; some amongst us thought that the sectarian tiger was dead by the 1960s when he was only sleeping. He woke up then with a vengeance.

There was another danger spot on the way to the village; this was the blacksmith's shop of Mr McGeoch. Mr McGeoch had a large family of small boys. They would show severe antagonism as I would pass by. I was very wary of them, but they would never come out of their yard, limiting possible warfare to the hurling of epithets with naughty words in them. I don't think I responded in kind. With my sheltered upbringing to date at the hands of ladies and old men, I hadn't yet learned how to shout insults. Perhaps any lack of response on my part may have implied a weakness, or a show of supercilious superiority, which would heighten the rage of the McGeochs.

We got to know the son of one of the Gardai. He was a big boy who went on the train to Monaghan to the secondary school. I think that Uncle Marcus recognized the need for some such role model. When my mother was staying she had taught us to ride the bicycle, running along holding it steady. Now we had bicycles or at least the use of one from some quarter. The Garda's son would take us fishing, teaching us, that is. One would have one's rod, a long pole cut from a tree, with a line, hook and cork which stretched along the bar of the bicycle and off we would go. One kept in mind the cautions of Lizzie which would make one quite apprehensive concerning the dwellers in the waters where one would fish. Just about every lake or bog hole had some sort of unpleasant being in it. Drumsnat Lake had a hand which would come up and get you. Magherarney had an evil eye in it; one lake had a "Dragoon" in it, which my uncle Marcus thought might have been a dragon. There was a lake near Annaghmakerrig, Drumate Lake, where there was a monster which would come out at night and graze with the cattle. There was a small bog hole just down the road from the Eldron gate which Lizzie said had no bottom in it and in which there was something of such unspeakable horror that it didn't bear thinking about. Lizzie's MacMahon ancestors were living there before St Patrick passed through so she should have known what was in the bogs and the lakes. The Presbyterian religion to which she belonged, might have tried to eradicate the old knowledge, but it hadn't succeeded.

We would nevertheless go to the lakes and not least to the Ulster Canal, less than a mile away. It hadn't been there long enough to harbour the supernatural but it teemed with sticklebacks or "stridlies" as we called them. The canal, (today one can hardly see where it was), then had plenty of water in it though it hadn't actually been used by boats since the 1920s. Its life had been short. It was opened in the 1830s to connect Lough Neagh to Lough Erne and brought prosperity along its route, but the competing railway which was laid almost on the same route some twenty years later, eventually killed the use of the canal, and a generation after this, road transport killed off the railway.

In the lakes we caught perch and roach, but these were inedible. Pike, which were edible, were beyond us; they are best caught with a spinner, a much more professional activity then a worm on a hook. The trout and its cousin the royal salmon were in the rivers for the game fishermen with their science of tying flies and their art of playing the fish.

There was a more concerted effort to attend to my and Christopher's academic education. A friend and former teaching colleague of Jane, Miss Hogan, came to stay and gave us lessons – my mother did so too when she was there. I was on to long division, the most painful of all exercises. Miss Hogan was a lady dressed in grey with a grey bun and seemed to be a bit severe but wasn't really. Sundays she would walk to the Church of Ireland at Drumsnat, and I sensed that she thought this was superior to going to Smithboro with the Presbyterians Jane and Lizzie.

As autumn passed to winter we moved to Strabane in Co. Tyrone. Strabane is very close to Derry and my father had been put into a hospital there for an operation on his sinuses. I was told that the problem was due to him getting sand up his nose in the North African desert. I myself was put of out of action for six months when I had sinusitis in the Arabian desert at a much later date. I don't think that it had much to do with the sand, but it is a condition which is hereditary. He was operated upon by my mother's cousin, Jim Killen, a nose and throat surgeon who lived in Derry.

My mother, Christopher and I had rooms (I think we were classed as paying guests), in a big brick Victorian house called Milltown House, which belonged to a hardware merchant called Mr Harper, near the River Mourne at the edge of town. Miss Hogan showed up on the scene. I think Strabane may have been chosen not only because of its proximity to Derry, but also because of the presence of Miss Hogan who had moved to live in Strabane. At any rate Miss Hogan would come up to the house to give us lessons. It was at this stage that I had a breakthrough in reading. All of a sudden I found that I could understand the whole story just by following down the page, rather then puzzling out individual words.

CHAPTER FIVE

Father and Mother

My father came to stay at Milltown House while he was convalescing. He was now invalided out of the army. I heard later from one of his military colleagues that he was bitterly disappointed at having to leave his profession so young (he was 44), and had had full command of his battalion for only six months. The records show that he relinquished command because of ill health, just a month before the battalion left for the Algerian landings, of Operation Torch under Eisenhower, so no doubt super fitness was required. The battalion were involved in the Italian campaign for the next two and a half years. There was stiff fighting there; being invalided out meant at least that my father survived.

Manners, as my father was known to his parents, was born the same month that his father acquired Moreen; that is where he was brought up, and it remained the family home for upwards of thirty years. Nearly all his schooling was in Dublin. From an early age he went to a school called Earlsfort House, which took its name from the terrace where it was situated. It was generally known as "Lep's", after the name of its headmaster, Monsieur Lepeton; in time the school evolved into what is now Sandford Park. At the age of 15 he was sent to an English public school called St Edmonds in Ware, Hertfordshire, which had been patronized by his Redmond cousins. Perhaps things did not work out to expectations there; at any rate, by the time he was 16, he was back at Lep's. Lep's was a small school, judging by a photograph of the rugby team which shows a motley collection of youths, ranging from small, perhaps 12 year olds, to almost adults. The classes were of only about seven or eight boys. Manners, whose reports indicate that he performed reasonably well at most things, usually came about third or fourth in the class.

Lep's was followed by attendance at an army crammer, which specialized in pushing pupils through the entrance exam to Sandhurst. The course at Sandhurst had at that time been shortened. The exigencies of war were such that large numbers of young officers had to be replaced as they were being shot down like flies in the trenches. Manners was practically colour-blind; he maintained that if it had been peacetime he would have failed the medical, but the examining doctor fudged the result of an eye test which required the separation of different coloured threads which he, Manners, was unable to do. However, the shortage of potential candidates for the trenches prevailed. Having passed through Sandhurst, he was commissioned second lieutenant into the Third Battalion of the Prince of Wales Leinster Regiment in December 1917. The Third Battalion, formerly the King's County Militia, was the training battalion for the regiment.

In May 1918 he arrived in France with the Second Battalion of the Leinsters, and was to take part in the Fourth Battle of Ypres. In September 1918 the allied forces were starting the final push which was to end the war. On 30 September, whilst leading his platoon along the side of the Ypres to Menin road attacking German machine gunners in the village of Gheluwe, he was shot in the stomach, and so was out of the war, which ended with the Armistice six weeks later. He was awarded the Military Cross for his part in the action.

The Leinster's headquarters was at Birr in Co. Offaly and this is where he spent 1919 and part of 1920. As the Troubles (The War of Independence) escalated, the Irish regiments were posted out of the country. Of course they spent most of their time abroad anyway garrisoning the Empire anyway, but in 1920 they couldn't be left in Ireland at all. It was one thing to keep the Burmese or the Zulus in order, but not one's own friends and relations. The government could not trust which side in the Troubles would have their sympathy. In the early part of the nineteenth century a third of the British Army was made up of Irishmen. This proportion was to decrease by the twentieth century, not least because of Ireland's falling and Britain's rising populations, but there were still sizeable numbers joining up. In the First World War, the casualties among Irish troops as a proportion of total population was of the same order as that of the English, despite Ireland not having conscription. The attempt to introduce conscription in 1918 contributed significantly to putting public opinion behind the hard men of the IRA, who were to come into their own in 1920/21 and gain political independence for twenty-six of the thirty-two counties in 1922.

The Leinster Regiment was sent to Colchester in the east of England and then to Germany. When I became aware of the events of 1920/21 and of Irish history and politics as a schoolboy and undergraduate, I would ask my father about them, but he had precious little to say. I felt that he should have been more articulate. I put it down that he was wrong not to have been more interested in the shift taking place in Irish society and political life. I now think, from some conversations much later, and finding occasional letters, that he was, as I believed, indifferent to the goings-on. But also I sensed another element which was later, a degree of resentment at what happened, and hence an unwillingness to speak or even think about it, about the collapse of the comfortable life of the country gentry.

What he did like to talk about was the social and sporting life. Hunting with the Ormond Hunt, tennis parties, croquet on the lawn and balls in country houses was what went on. Michael Collins and De Valera were of no more significance than the wild tribesmen of the Asian deserts.

In her novel *The Last September*, Elizabeth Bowen marks September 1914 as the end of the idyll of the Irish country gentry, but it seems things hadn't changed around Birr by September 1919. It was to be 1920 before the writing on the wall was fully appreciated by the gentry, maybe after a few of their houses had gone up in flames. By then my father had been shipped off to Silesia, where a Franco-British division of troops (the British Army troops mostly belonging to Irish regiments) was holding the line between Germans and Poles. There was to be a plebiscite to decide how Silesia would be partitioned between them; in the meantime they were at each other's throats.

It was in Silesia one day that he heard the regimental band strike up. The band was not due to be playing that day, so he went to investigate. He met with a sergeant and asked him what was going on. The sergeant said, "Haven't you heard sir, we're free!" The news had just come in of the signing of the treaty of December 1921 between the British government and the Irish revolutionaries. Within a few months, however, it would mean that the band, the sergeant and my father would be out of a job. The treaty was ratified by the Dáil, the hitherto illegal Irish Parliament, and all the Southern Irish infantry regiments were disbanded.

After the colours of the Leinster Regiment were laid up and the men sent home, some officers turned to civilian life, others were scattered. A few joined the new national army of the Irish Free State. One cousin, Maurice O'Connell, served in the Irish Army for more then twenty years; a captain in the British Army, he never rose above that rank in the Irish Army. It was common belief in the family that lack of promotion was due to the antipathy of the new masters towards the old ones. After the French Revolution, there were former royalist officers in the armies of Napoleon and the Soviets had former Czarist officers, but not very many perhaps. These officers would be easy to understand if they were flexible enough to overcome their pride and prejudices. It may have been easier to make the transition at least amongst the French, where the army was more professional than the British. Our family forbears in France did not take kindly to the change. General Daniel O'Connell, an Irishman, commanded the Swedish Regiment in the French Army, the men of the regiment being mainly Germans. He was first and foremost a professional at arms, with a sizeable salary. He was offered a high position by the revolutionaries, but actually he did not take it. The British officer class by and large, did not make money in the army; indeed up to the 1870s they usually had to pay to get their commission and promotions. Their role was to uphold the status quo with its social class divisions.

The social class distinction in the British Army is still there, diminishing since the 1870s but had not diminished when my mother's uncle Bertie wanted to be a soldier. His class status was in the way. He was not rich or upper class enough to have been seen as officer material, yet to have signed on in the rank and file would have branded him as black sheep in his straight-laced family. He had to wait for his chance with the outbreak of the First World War in 1914. There was also a pecking order of regiments bound up with the social origins of the officers.

My father sought employment elsewhere in the British Army. His parents had uncles and cousins who had all been in cavalry regiments; the Third Dragoon Guards could almost have been called a MacFarlane family regiment. But by 1922, the cavalry was beyond the family's financial resources. Looking for other family connections, he discovered a Lieutenant Maguire on the MacFarlane side who is the subject of a famous painting leading the "Forlorn Hope" at the siege of San Sebastian against the French in 1814. Maguire's regiment was the Fourth Regiment of Foot, the King's Own Royal Regiment of Lancaster. My father was taken on by it, and straight away sent to Burma. I was told by an officer who had served under him years later, that he had great difficulty adapting to the democratic nature of an English line regiment. If, in 1922, an English regiment could be described as "democratic" in comparison to the Leinsters, the mind boggles at how feudal would have been life in the Leinsters then.

In Burma, such being the climate, it was the practice to get up very early and finish military duties before midday. The officers had champagne for breakfast. From a letter to my grandfather, there is talk of the hockey team, boxing, and we learn of a vast array of game birds and animals abounding in the rice fields and jungle, and some details of the expeditions to shoot them. There is also recognition that the Empire had to be held, even if there mainly for the sport of young gentlemen; there is mention of some priest who stirred up trouble, and on whom one had to keep an eye. At one stage he had a posting to the Andaman Islands. These tropical islands in the Indian Ocean had on them the main penal colony for the Indian Empire. He told me it was the most idyllic posting he ever had, with tropical sea and no strenuous duties; the main responsibility was to keep the troops from getting bored by organizing swimming and cricket on the beaches.

Father may not have been totally happy with his lot and his prospects. He had heard that the newly founded police force of the Irish Free State, the Garda Síochána (the Civic Guard), was to employ some former British army officers and wrote to my grandfather asking him to find out about this. He appeared to be keen on the idea, but I never heard or saw any more about it, or any other suggestion of career changes.

Burma was followed by two years on the North-West Frontier of India, at Rawalpindi and the hill station of Murree. In 1926 he was in England at the regimental headquarters in Lancaster. During Father's stay in Lancaster he first met my mother, Gladys Killen. She had a range of relatives living in the area, all on her mother's side. She had been born in Belfast and spent her early days in Helen's Bay, a few miles away on the shore of Belfast Lough. Later the family moved into the city to College Gardens. She spent a year at school in Switzerland and a couple of years at Alexandra College in Dublin, but otherwise Belfast was her home. For a while she did secretarial work for her father, but her main course of employment was fashion advertising in newspapers. There were many Killen relatives in Belfast who made up a close interlocking, not quite incestuous community. Pairs of brothers married pairs of sisters and second and third cousins. She seems to have had quite a social life. She worked in advertising with a childhood and lifelong friend Consie Wadsworth, who moved with her family to Lancaster in the mid 1920s, and it was to visit her and a number of Elliot relatives which took Gladys to Lancaster, where she stayed for extended periods.

By the time my father had moved on, back to the North-West Frontier of India in 1928, they were engaged. There was disapproval amongst the Killen and Elliot clans at the idea of Gladys marrying a Roman Catholic. Rather than ignoring their relatives, my parents waited until they had all been won over. Nearly all of them dropped their objections quickly when they recognized that Father was not a dangerous or subversive republican, nor a fanatic bent on promoting popery. On Father's side, most close contact was with the Protestant MacFarlanes anyway; Grandfather Dan was unlikely to object and his sister Aunt May wouldn't say boo to a goose. The last one to hold out with her objections was Aunt Hester, the eldest of the Elliot sisters. She was at this time living in the English Lake District where her husband, Uncle John Foster Stewart, was vicar of a parish which was not far from Lancaster. Hester was very much a boss and had the parishioners toe the line. After she came to accept Gladys's marriage, she was the strongest supporter of my father, who in her eyes could do not wrong.

My parents had to wait another two years before they were married, until Father, now a Captain, came back. After the North-West Frontier, he had spent a year in the Sudan on the Red Sea coast, a hell hole if ever there was one with blistering heat and no facilities.

The wait for the wedding lengthened. Gladys's younger sister Pauline was dying. I never heard a word but the greatest praise for Pauline, who died at the age of twenty-one; she had contracted a rare form of tuberculosis of the spine arising from a hockey injury. My grandmother never got over the loss.

Eventually my parents were married in St Mary's Church of England Church in South Kensington, London. This could be seen as neutral ground between Presbyterians of Ulster and the Roman Catholics of Dublin, though the more extreme among both sides might have equally seen the arrangement as unacceptable. However the extremes of tribal theology were not at issue; the grand social occasion ruled the day. It was a full dress military wedding involving officers in scarlet with medals and swords. There was a big turnout of relations, though Grandfather Dan was missing. This would not have been his antipathy to the denomination of the ceremony, as I have heard it said; it would have been his dislike of travel. He lived in Dublin practically all his life and said that he had never been to Howth, 10 miles away, but would visit it before he should die. He never did.

The honeymoon can't have got off to too good a start. They spent the first night in a hotel in Basingstoke where there were fleas in the bed. They lived in Lancaster for the next year. Mother spoke of the gay social life surrounding the regiment. They went for picnics in the Lake District, and to Aintree for the Grand National. The pay of a captain was not very much and Father had no money of his own. Mother's parents had made over to her an investment which might have brought in £50 a year; not much, but this was the time of the Great Depression and it would have bought quite a lot. They also paid the wages of a maid for Mother, which would probably have been less than £50 a year. In 1933 they went to Egypt for a year or so and then on to India, which would be their home for four years. Once when I said to an Egyptian, by way of what I thought was friendly small talk, that my parents had lived in Egypt; I was rather taken aback when he said, "Well we didn't really <u>hate</u> the British", as his friendly reply. It hadn't entered my head that as Egypt hadn't been a colony fighting for its freedom, that the British presence would have been resented. I should have known, for Mother, who was not an intolerant or bad-mannered person, had shocked me (I was a left-leaning teenager), when she said that she learnt only three words of Arabic and they all meant "Go away". Such ingrained but unconscious racial arrogance was naturally bound to cause resentment. The British can still be like that, the French are similar, but now it is the Americans that lead the field in creating resentment in Third World countries when they display their ethnocentric arrogance.

My parents, though starting from a position that "natives" were on a lower plane, held that they should be treated kindly and fairly. There were then, and there are today, bullies who would treat the "lesser breeds" brutally and with contempt. One year Father was president of the Trichinopoly Club. An Indian was proposed for membership and there was an attempt to blackball him. Father said that if the Indian couldn't join he would resign his presidency. This Indian was elected. Mother told me this story as a lesson in proper moral behaviour; but I suspect the Indian was a professional man of good family, a cricketer and maybe with a degree from Oxford or Cambridge and who wouldn't have been an immediate threat to the white gentlemen in the club.

My father's job in India this time was to train the South Indian Railway Territorial Battalion. He was the regular officer who supported the part-time reservists made up of railway employees. With the job went a bungalow with a big garden and a private railway carriage which could be hooked onto a train to go to wherever business dictated. Mother would go too; she particularly liked trips to the west coast where there are wonderful beaches.

It was necessary to have about a dozen servants about the house. To the modern politically correct Westerner this would seem to be the height of arrogance, and the mistreatment by the colonial monsters of the downtrodden natives. But that was the system with roots going back long before the British came to India, when native princes and aristocrats lived in much greater splendour than any of the later Europeans. It had a moral justification in that the rich had an obligation to provide employment, to give support and protection to the poor. Anyway if one was to have any servants at all it had to be a large number. This was due to a demarcation system which would leave the old unionized British shipyards way behind. The man who looked after the horse, the Syce, could do nothing else; nor could the Punkawallah, who worked the ventilation fan. The cook and the laundry man were exclusive specialists. The caste system to some extent dictated the specialties: for instance cleaners would be untouchables. Administration of a household was a complicated business; if an untouchable's shadow was to fall on the butler's dinner, the butler couldn't eat it. My mother was never one to enjoy administering households. In India she had a manager of some sort, a majordomo cum sergeant major to coordinate her household empire.

There was an extraordinary formality of living according to formulas of ritual designed around rank. One needed to know who to call on and who not to call on, who to receive, who to invite to dinner and when, and how to sit them, with whom to leave visiting cards, and what could be discussed and what not. It is often explained that this was the British pre-war society, where social class was significant, but in India enormously exaggerated, like life at the Court of Louis XV1 at Versailles. Behind the rituals was a subconscious apprehension and perception that it was necessary to put on a show for the Indians of the mystique of a dominant race. I am sure however, that the culture of the club and the elaborate etiquette of the memsahibs evolved from a more brutal one which the British took over from the earlier Mughals, the sixteenth-century Moslem conquerors of the subcontinent.

I am even more sure that Mother, as a 30 year old, would not have dreamt of such sociological theory. The customs were somewhat perplexing, but it was exciting and immense fun.

Invalided out of the army, Father stayed with us in Strabane while he recovered; we all went out to see friends of the Harpers, the Herdmans who lived at Sion Mills. In fact they owned Sion Mills, a huge linen mill around which the village of the same name had grown up. We were able to see around the mill which had banks of whirling machines and linen thread going in and out of them. What was far more interesting was a little factory in the grounds which was making ammunition for the war. There was a box full of imperfect anti-tank shells which were being discarded; Father took one as a souvenir and put it in his pocket. They were less then the size of a shoe and weighed a kilogram or two. I helped myself to one, but it was too big and heavy for my pocket, which tore away from my coat, causing some consternation and I had to put it back, my one and only gesture to the war effort.

Then Father was off to seek civilian employment in England. He was to spend the next two years involved in Civil Defence and firefighting in and around Manchester. He elected to go to the more mundane Manchester rather than Madagascar where someone had tried to get him to look for some mineral (it might have been diamonds), but his first employment was equally, at least for him, esoteric. It can't have been for more then a week or two, but he appeared on the stage along with Robert Helpmann in *Hamlet*. Father was the second soldier on the left in the burial scene. This job he owed to Tony, son of Mrs Guthrie of Annaghmakerrig, though the circumstances of the appointment were more due to a fiddle by Tony to get him a UK work permit, rather than my father having thespian ambitions. Tony was then becoming established in a career which was to make him one of the world's leading theatre directors.

When he left Strabane, Mother, Christopher and I went back to Annaghmakerrig, but with another summer holiday at Bundoran and a further stay at Eldron to come.

CHAPTER SIX

Garth House, Bangor

While I stayed at Eldron for a few months with Jane and of course Lizzie (and for most of the time Mother was there as well), Christopher was sent to school in Monaghan. Monaghan was only 6 miles away, but as there was no car and the trains were few and far between, he went to live with Uncle Marcus in the town. Marcus, with Aunt Mat, John, who was my age and Margaret, who was a little younger, lived in a big terrace house called Aviemore which overlooks, indeed dominates, the town. It had been bought by my grandfather for £1,000 when Marcus was taking over Uncle John Elliot's medical practice, and was about to marry Mat. There was a big overgrown garden and there were a lot of outbuildings at the back.

Mother and I were frequent visitors at Aviemore. We would go on the train from Smithboro in the morning, and come back in the afternoon. It was always an exciting visit, not just the trip on the train, exciting though that was, but all the activities which were so different from Eldron. The first difference was that whereas at Eldron, one climbed trees, at Aviemore one climbed walls. When they had visited Eldron, John and Margaret had to be taught how to climb trees; they hadn't the skills I had learnt over the years; now the situation was reversed. They led me up and along the garden walls and over the roofs of outbuildings at the back of the terrace houses. Another aspect of urban living was that there was more scope for warfare with urchins. I don't remember actual physical violence, but one particular nest of urchins just up the street on the other side would respond to provocation with insults and epithets. "What are you looking at? Donkey face!" stayed in mind.

It was going back to Smithboro on the train that I first saw a sign of the demon drink. It was many years later that my sheltered life opened up to further encounters with the joys and ravages of the demon; in fact I didn't really take in that it was the work of the demon that we had to look at in the railway carriage. Mother and I were in a compartment waiting for the train to leave when a man with a florid face, in a cap and raincoat and carrying the sort of stick that one beats the rump of bullocks in the fair with, came in, sat down, and immediately vomited copiously on the floor. He then got out of the carriage again, whether from embarrassment or to get air. Mother pulled me out into a clean carriage. To me, vomiting was a rare and serious medical condition, something I had done only once or twice in my life when I felt very ill, and said something to that effect. I asked whether the man was going to die. Mother said that there was nothing wrong with the man, only drink. In his old age my father reminisced of a similar experience. When he was about 4 years old, he was staying with his nurse on Derrykerrib Island in Lough Erne where she came from, a remote and still then Irish-speaking part of Fermanagh. He saw a young man coughing up what he thought were his whole insides only to be told it was just the Poteen.

From that year, and for the next twenty, the Killens would spend the month of August at Dunfanaghy in north Donegal. We went there from Eldron that year. It was a long and tedious journey; though only about a hundred miles, it took all day, changing trains and crossing the border with its wartime harassment into and out of Northern Ireland. The train went as far as Letterkenny; from where we went on by bus. There were some old women in the back of the bus speaking in Irish. I found this quite frightening, as I had never before heard any language other then English.

Unlike earlier summer holidays at Bundoran, I do not think of Dumfanaghy as cold and uncomfortable. I remember swimming in a rock pool. Despite earlier lessons in Annaghmakerrig Lake, my swimming hadn't progressed greatly, but before we left I could competently swim across the pool. Mother would read to us, as she always had done – we were into Arthur Ransome at this age. The Killens didn't, as far as I recall, go in for reading aloud; I felt that they didn't appreciate Mother reading, but they had, to my delight, the cartoon characters from the *Irish Independent*, Curly Wee (who was a pig, and a Count at that) and Gussie Goose, and that marvellous nineteenth-century psychopathic German work, *Struwwelpeter*.

In September 1944, after the Dunfanaghy holiday, we moved to Bangor in Co. Down. This was to be the start of a more conventional and settled life. It was the first time in many years that my mother was to be the head of the household rather then a guest of some sort, of friends or relations. It was to be the start of a run of continuing formal schooling for Christopher and me until we graduated from university. It was to do with schooling that we moved to Bangor. Mother had found out about a small prep school called Garth House of which she liked the sound; both my parents visited it and interviewed the headmaster and proprietor, Captain W.N.M. Hutton.

We went to live at 144 Seacliffe Road, which belonged to a Mrs Magee, who was well known to the family having originally been from Monaghan. Mrs Magee's daughter Sheila had a husband who was away in the navy, and a small child, Jeffie. They had made the top floor of the house into a flat that could be reached from a bridge made onto the embankment behind, and we took over the lower two floors. The house was at the end of a terrace; it had bay windows. There was only a small front garden before the road which actually formed a sea wall, the water at high tide coming over the rocks right up to it. At low tide one could be down among the rock pools with their crabs and shellfish and seaweed within seconds of leaving the house.

Christopher started at Garth House in the Autumn Term, but there was no place for me. There was a suggestion that I might go to the Grammar

School in January. I quite liked this idea, because the Grammar School cap was blue with yellow stripes and much more handsome then Garth House's wine coloured one. As it happened, a place at Garth House became vacant in January and so there I went, and would go for the next five and half years. In the meantime I went to a little school run by a Miss Featherstonehaugh in the tennis club. There were about ten pupils all around my age. It must have been a happy place. I have no bad memories and perhaps learnt some things there. Two things I learnt were that in *The Pilgrim's Progress* there was a demon called Apollyon – Mrs Featherstonehaugh read *The Pilgrim's Progress* to us – which was very frightening (I am still a bit frightened of it), and I also learned the concept of "being up for" a side. The latter arose after we learnt about the Battle of Bannockburn. Dermot McIlveen, who was to follow me to Garth House, asked me who I was up for, the English or the Scots; he was up for the Scots. Alas I didn't know who I was up for, the concept was quite puzzling, but in time I got to grips with it such that I have remained violently partisan for some side or other for the rest of my life, though I have never been very consistent over the long term who I would support, football teams, political parties or whatever.

Whereas I could accommodate myself within Miss Featherstonehaugh's little school without stress, Garth House was quite a shock. It was so big, so many big boys. It took me a long time to fit in as it was so scary. But actually, even by prep school standards it was small, about sixty pupils in total, half of whom were boarders, but it all seemed very big to me.

I had had a term at school in Newcastle two years before but it made little impression, perhaps I was only there in the morning and went to one classroom, but from the beginning at Garth House one was at immersed in the school community. One learnt from one's peers how to conform to the schools routine and to what one's peers thought was suitable behaviour, indeed to conform to their attitudes.

The day at school was a long one; it started with a bicycle ride across the town of Bangor. Bangor then had a population of 20,000 and was essentially a dormitory for the Belfast middle classes. There was an old town centre with a main street which ran down from the railway station to the harbour, late nineteenth-century and early twentieth-century terraces, running into 1920s and 1930s villas stretched along the Lough shore for a mile or more each side of the harbour. The town was a holiday resort for those not lucky enough to be able to go to the Mediterranean or suchlike. Mother once took us to the Belfast Museum and Art Gallery to see a huge painting called *Getting aboard the Bangor Boat*. She took us because the central figure in the picture was a big man in a hat who was my grandfather. It was not a portrait of my grandfather as such, but he had been a friend of the artist, who had put him in the picture along with the happy Belfast holidaymakers going to Bangor for the day. There was no Bangor boat in my day; one always went by train on the Belfast and Co. Down Railway from the station on Queen's Quay.

The first term, being winter, we had football four days a week, which was fun. On Friday we had PT and boxing, neither of which was fun. At boxing, in order that I might be paired with some one of my age and size, I always had to fight Miller or Fyffe. It was all right fighting Miller as he would swing his arms around wildly and not land a punch, but Fyffe had a very vicious and accurate jab which would get me on the nose. My nose bled very easily but at least this would have the fight stopped. PT meant swinging one's arms and bending and such like but there was an interminable amount of marching. I could never keep in step, and would put the others out of step too. Not long after my first term, boxing was dropped from the curriculum, and PT changed from marching to vaulting over a wooden horse from a springboard, which was great fun. Perhaps this change was made because the headmaster and proprietor, Captain Hutton, was more humane then his predecessor Captain Swanson; Hutton had taken over about a year before I arrived, having been Swanson's assistant before some war service which earned him his title of Captain. Perhaps it was part of a paradigm shift in the wider world as the war ended and militarism was waning. Some of the militarism was to stay. We were all divided into platoons, six in all with a captain and a corporal. Getting ready for lunch was when, and only when, the platoons and their officers were functional. This was in an area where there was a changing room, showers and lavatories, known as the Boy's Hall. Everyone was lined up by platoons to be inspected, the officer would shout "hands" where upon one showed him one's palms. Then, when he would shout "over", one would show him the back of our hands. The more sadistic would make one go and wash one's hands again, the even more sadistic would slap the hands with a gym shoe if he disapproved of the presentation. Then the whole school would march in single file by platoon to the dining room. Members of staff would sit at the ends of the tables. It was a two or three course meal which was usually enjoyable if, like me, one liked tinned corn beef and brown gravy, and if not exactly cordon bleu, it was closer to that than what most of Europe would be having for lunch then. For my first two terms, as I was very young, I, and a few others, would have to lie down in a dormitory after lunch. Fyffe, who bled my nose at boxing, was one of them. He it was who once started to boast how rich his father was, which was such a new concept to me that I had to ask my mother if my father was rich, and was disappointed when she said he wasn't. I don't remember any comment in the dormitory from Ava on the issue, though he was normally very talkative. Fyffe's father owned a chemist's shop in the main street, Ava was the Earl of Ava, whose father was the Marquis of Dufferin and Ava and owned one of the greatest landed estates in the country. Ava didn't appear at school one day; we were told his father had been killed in Burma and he was now the Marquis and too important to come to Garth House any longer.

I was probably reasonably well settled in by the end of the first term, comfortable enough with my age group, but still apprehensive of the big boys who I don't remember as being particularly pleasant. There was one big boy, Rawlinson, who was exceptional. He went out of his way to ask me if I was all right after I had been knocked down and my nose bled (not Fyffe this time). I had been hit full in the face by a kicked football when standing on the touchline watching the school team play a match.

My second term was the Summer Term, when the war in Europe ended, and I was introduced to cricket. My earliest memory of cricket was being very bored fielding, and not taking much notice, and as I played with a half crown my grandfather had given me, it rolled away in the grass and was lost. This was an enormous sum of money for an 8 year old to have, and though I am sure I didn't appreciate its monetary value, I knew the loss was a tragedy about which I didn't dare to tell anybody.

When I earned my first shilling, I felt as rich as Croesus, and was conscious of my financial power. From early June, after morning classes, the whole school marched down to Pickie Pool for swimming. Pickie was built into the sea, so that it had the sea water at its normal temperature. It was 100 feet wide, a lot less then the 50 metre Olympic size of the present day, yet it was one of the main pools in the country for swimming sports. Whenever one could swim across the pool, one was allowed into the deep end and one was awarded one shilling. The same day I had my shilling, I was approached by a boy called Ross, a couple of years older than me, who had ideas of how my shilling should be spent. I went along with him on the way home from school to the harbour where a man hired rowing boats for one shilling. So we went out rowing on the bay. When I arrived home and told of my success and subsequent adventure, to my surprise Mother was furious. It was the danger I had been in – she wasn't cross with me, but she complained to Captain Hutton and to Ross's mother and went to the boatman and lectured him on his irresponsibility. I understood her fuss but didn't agree with the need for it, as I was now a competent swimmer and I was with a quite big boy. Ross was all of 10.

Christopher had his eleventh birthday and there was a picnic on the beach with boys of his age. Ross was at it, but that was before he (in my mother's eyes) disgraced himself. Before the term ended there was the annual school picnic to the Copeland Islands. This was my first of six such expeditions, always looked forward to. This first time there was an air of mystery, as the boys who had been there before talked about what they would do when they got there, mysterious because one didn't have a picture in one's mind of the place. There was something of excitement communicated, but for me, year on year, it was not the place or the trip which I learned to appreciate, but the activity of running about with a group for a whole day, making simulated war on other groups over the rocks and in the bracken. It must have been quite an undertaking organizing the bus trip to Donaghadee – 6 miles from Bangor, as the song goes – and the motor boat to the island. There was all the food and drink to be carried. It was on the Copelands that I learnt that I didn't like fizzy lemonade and sandwiches which invariably became laced with sand when dished out. We always wore light clothes because it was a summer expedition, but more often than not it was cold and wet. The climate of Bangor was no worse then anywhere else in the country, but I have heard it described as bracing.

As our home on Seacliffe Road looked out over the Lough, one could see the ships going up and down. We had a telescope and would look at the ships and at the other side at Carrickfergus Castle where King William landed, as everyone learned at an early age. This last year of the war there were masses of ships going to and fro to the armies in France and the Low Countries. They must have grown careless after the victory, for subsequently, two ships, one at each end of the town, ran onto the rocks. A big one ran aground just by the road to school, but it was soon towed off. The other one rotted way over the years in Ballyholme Bay. It would have been a year or two later when the school managed to visit the warships, the *King George V*, a battleship, as big as one ever there was, and the aircraft carrier *Theseus*. In the latter I was allowed to sit in an aircraft and being then well read in Biggles, able to ask intelligent questions like, "Which is the altimeter?" On the battleship all I can remember was a cook in the galley frying eggs. He was frying hundreds of them and could break them neatly with one hand at one or two a second.

My maternal grandparents, the Killens, stayed with us for some time in the summer. I hadn't seen much of them since they handed me back to my parents when I was 2 years old, though they would show up and stay from time to time at Eldron, so the link was never broken for long. My grandfather, who was called Bogey, was then 80 and I feel I remember him well, though I do not remember anything he said or did, apart from him sitting reading. My grandmother I remember more from later. At this point my only memory of my grandmother was her taking me to church. I do not know why I was the only one in the household who would go with her. She took me to the Trinity or Third Bangor Presbyterian Church in the main street. Once I had a fit of coughing which was so prolonged that I became aware that it stopped the preacher in his tracks, and my grandmother took me out, walking between rows of tall adults. I suspect that I was the only child in the congregation.

Father had visited occasionally from his job in England but sometime about June we heard that he was taking up an appointment in Co. Clare and that was where our home was to be. At the end of July, Mother, Christopher and I went off to Clare by way of Dublin with a stay at Kilgobbin House with my FitzSimon grandparents. My Killen grandparents went to stay with Uncle Marcus in Monaghan. I was not to see Bogey again. We had not been long in Clare when the news came that he had died. Concerned about his dog, he had gone out the back door , slipped, fell and broke his hip. He was taken to Monaghan Hospital where he died soon afterwards. He was buried in Smithboro churchyard among the Elliots but in the same grave as his daughter Pauline.

CHAPTER SEVEN

The Killens

There have been two views of the origins of our branch of Killens. There is no doubt that they are of ancient Gaelic stock, but are they Irish or Scottish? According to the late Dr MacLysaght, the genealogist, the Killens of Co. Antrim are MacKillens or MacCollins who were a family of Galloglass, axe wielding soldiery, in the hereditary employ of the southern MacDonalds whose lands included the islands of Islay and Jura. These MacDonalds, or MacDonnells, through marriage with the Anglo-Norman Bissetts, acquired the coast of Co. Antrim in the fifteenth century and moved their principal seat there. The present MacDonnell, the Earl of Antrim of Glenarm Castle is the clan chief. The Killen forbears would have crossed over with the clan chief in the fifteenth or sixteenth century. That is the theory of Scottish ancestry but it is somewhat academic to distinguish between Scots and Irish in that place at that time. The seaways were then highways rather than barriers. The ancient Kingdom of Dalriada covered both Co. Antrim and south-west Scotland. The word Scot originally referred to the Irish, the Gaelic language and the culture was the same on both sides of the Minch, the sea which separates Scotland from Ireland. From Fair Head in Antrim one can see the houses on the Mull of Kintyre, if it is not raining.

This Scottish view of Killen origins owes its persistence to the reputation of the late Dr MacLysaght. That there are people in Antrim called Killen who are of Scottish origin one need not doubt, however I am now sure that as far as our branch of the Killen family is concerned the issue is irrelevant.

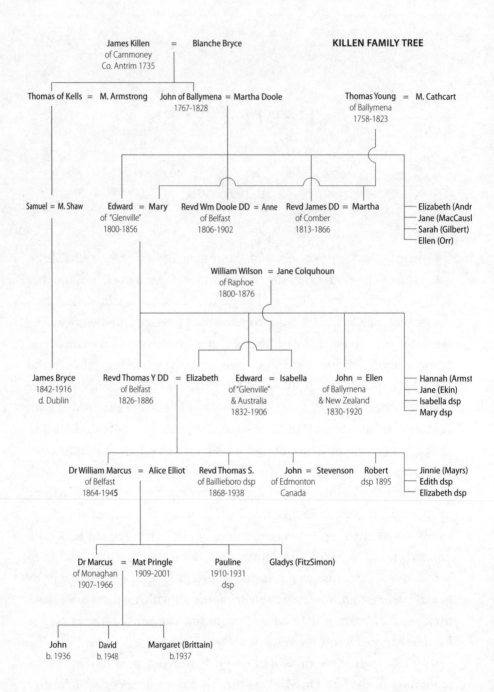

KILLEN FAMILY TREE

James Killen = Blanche Bryce
of Carnmoney
Co. Antrim 1735

Thomas of Kells = M. Armstrong   John of Ballymena = Martha Doole
                                   1767-1828

Thomas Young = M. Cathcart
of Ballymena
1758-1823

Samuel = M. Shaw   Edward = Mary   Revd Wm Doole DD = Anne   Revd James DD = Martha
                     of "Glenville"   of Belfast   of Comber
                     1800-1856   1806-1902   1813-1866

— Elizabeth (Andr
— Jane (MacCausl
— Sarah (Gilbert)
— Ellen (Orr)

William Wilson = Jane Colquhoun
of Raphoe
1800-1876

James Bryce   Revd Thomas Y DD = Elizabeth   Edward = Isabella   John = Ellen
1842-1916   of Belfast   of "Glenville"   of Ballymena
d. Dublin   1826-1886   & Australia   & New Zealand
                                                  1832-1906   1830-1920

— Hannah (Armst
— Jane (Ekin)
— Isabella dsp
— Mary dsp

Dr William Marcus = Alice Elliot   Revd Thomas S.   John = Stevenson   Robert
of Belfast   of Baillieboro dsp   of Edmonton   dsp 1895
1864-1945   1868-1938   Canada

— Jinnie (Mayrs)
— Edith dsp
— Elizabeth dsp

Dr Marcus = Mat Pringle   Pauline   Gladys (FitzSimon)
of Monaghan   1909-2001   1910-1931
1907-1966   dsp

John   David   Margaret (Brittain)
b. 1936   b. 1948   b.1937

Our family historian W.D. Killen, who was born in 1806, says that the Killens were natives of the Lecale district of Co. Down since the time of St Patrick, and indeed even today there are large numbers of people there with the name. But W.D. Killen goes no further back with historical detail than his grandfather James, who had a farm on the slopes of the Cave Hill in Co. Antrim. So what was James doing there if he was not of the clan of Lord Antrim's Galloglasses? There are two good reasons. Firstly, the Cave Hill is within a day's hard walk (or two days of a more leisurely stroll) of the Lecale centre of gravity of Killen settlement. Secondly, and more significantly, we have record of one Thomas O'Killen (Thomas is a recurring name in our branch), a farmer in Carnmoney, the parish at the northern end of the Cave Hill, 100 years before the time of W.D.'s grandfather. Whereas "Mac" in a name can be Irish or Scottish, "O" can never be anything but Irish.

This James Killen married one Blanche Bryce, who was descended from Edward Bryce, the first Presbyterian minister to come to Ireland from Scotland. It was the view of my grandfather (my grandfather was nearing 40 years old when W.D. died, and the close relations maintained among the family, and the fact that Grandfather lived within a mile of W.D., his great-uncle, would indicate that he knew him quite well) that W.D. had thought that James's immediate forbears were Roman Catholic and he didn't want to know about them. This was confirmed to me by an Australian relative who had a quite firm family tradition that Blanche would not marry James until he became a Presbyterian himself. But such anecdotes can always be a bit shaky as historical evidence. It is intriguing that Thomas O'Killen in the mid-seventeenth century was instrumental in providing land for the Carnmoney Presbyterian Meeting House, though there is no record of him having been a member of the congregation. W.D. in his two volume *Ecclesiastical History of Ireland*, lists Killens along with a number of other native Irish famlies who adhered to the Protestant Reformation in the sixteenth and seventeenth centuries, so perhaps he was thinking of the family of Thomas O'Killen. The numerous Killens living today in Lecale appear to be entirely Roman Catholic. Thomas may not have resided in Carnmoney himself. He was the "farmer", that is he held lands on lease, more than a 1,000 acres, from Lord Donegall the head landlord, and then would have rented out sections to the tenants who did the work. It would have been quite usual for such middle men, entrepreneurs like Thomas, to establish their children or descendants on their leases, so it would be a normal situation for one to find a continuity of Killens in the district. It was not uncommon either for intelligent landlords to facilitate their tenants' religious requirements, even if they were not of the same denomination as themselves.

The best evidence, therefore, establishes our Killens as being of native Irish origin, but to establish why they adopted the Presbyterian religion needs further research. Whether Thomas O'Killen was a Presbyterian or not, there is a strong inference that later Killens, forbears of James, were. According to the survey of the parish of Carnmoney of 1838, made when the area was becoming economically influenced by the growth of Belfast, the parish was four-fifths Presbyterian. There was only a handful of Roman Catholics, people who had only recently arrived from Derry and Tyrone, attracted by the opportunity for employment in the new cotton mills around Whiteabbey on the Lough shore. There was even then no Roman Catholic place of worship closer than Belfast, while there were four Presbyterian churches, two quite large, and a Church of Ireland one. The Presbyterians had previously been violently opposed to the Episcopalian Established Church of Ireland, who in times past had let the parish church decay into a ruin, and did not always provide a resident minister, but would collect the tithes nevertheless. By 1838 the Established Church was taking its responsibilities more seriously and so was receiving less Presbyterian ire. Given that there is no mention of attitudes towards the Roman Catholics, usually seen as even worse than the Episcopalian Establishment, might further suggest that there just were no Catholics in the neighbourhood.

The surveyors of 1838 dwell considerably on how the area had improved over the previous twenty or thirty years, especially the habits and morals of the people. The people were less prone to drunkenness, though they were still prone to frequent whiskey drinking – on the Sabbath they would adjourn for whiskey after the sermon to public houses placed adjacent to the churches. The "other immorality" was not seen to be too prevalent or too much of a problem; premarital intercourse, it was claimed, was in the main indulged in by the women to get away from their fathers and by the men to squeeze as large a dowry as possible from prospective in-laws. The basic diet was still potatoes, but there were increasing numbers of two-storey houses with slate roofs, typical for the larger farmers, as against the single-roomed thatched cottages of the peasants. Schooling was considered to be not of high quality and had not changed for generations, yet the people had always learned enough to be able to read their Bibles. They were described even at this late date as being still very Scottish. They were said to have remembered very little by way of tradition, but their accents, proverbs, sayings, music and dancing were all Scottish.

The Scots of Carnmoney were Lowlanders. The more fertile land along the shores of the Lough were taken up early in the seventeenth century by soldiers of the garrison of the great Carrickfergus Castle nearby. By 1657 they had penetrated so far into the hill that by then a Presbyterian congregation was meeting there in the townland of Ballyduff, where later the village of Carnmoney developed. Ballyduff was one of the townlands leased by Thomas O'Killen. This is no argument that Thomas was of the Gallowglass MacKillens who were settled further to the North and were Highlanders every bit as foreign to the Lowlander colonists as Lecale Irish. Indeed the Lecale Irish may have been less foreign. Lecale was long settled by the Normans and is a much less rugged country than the Scottish islands or the Glens of Antrim. One would suspect that Thomas's descendants intermarried with the Scottish colonists before the marriage of James Killen and Blanche Bryce in 1766. All the names recorded in Canrmoney graveyard in 1838 with the exception of Killen are lowland Scottish ones.

W.D. Killen was a man of his time. If he lived today he would eclipse the Revd Ian Paisley with his fundamentalist and anti-papist polemic, but he was a scholar of some consequence and a lucid writer. He held the Chair of Ecclesiastical History in the Assembly College in Belfast and had several books published. His best work was a two volume *Ecclesiastical History of Ireland* published in 1878. He served as Moderator of the General Assembly of the Presbyterian Church in Ireland, as did his brother and nephew. When the Killens became Presbyterian they did so with a vengeance. The brief bit of family history which W.D. left us is in his autobiography which is called *Memoirs of a Long Life* and covers most of the nineteenth century. Curiously, he has little to say about his wife or children. The book concentrates on church history and has a tendency to argue points he made in sermons decades before. James Killen of Cave Hill and Blanche Bryce had a son John who moved to Ballymena before 1800 and opened a shop there. John married a Miss Martha Doole, who inherited an estate in Glenwhirry nearby, previously in her mother's family, the Millars. The old Millars did not approve of Martha marrying John (not quite of their social class), but accepted him when they realized that he was a good churchman and a good man at business. John had left the whiskey swillers of Carnmoney behind, though perhaps it was his mother, Blanche who taught him respectability, even in Carnmoney. W.D. describes Blanche as a "prayerful woman" and tells how she approved of her daughter-in-law Martha spending £5 on the purchase of a silver ewer, saying "I see you want to be respectable". Martha had thought that she would be reprimanded for extravagance.

The property of some 600 acres in Glenwhirry, known as Glenville, was farmed by the Killens until the 1870s. It is high country bordering on the mountains. There is a little river, which runs eventually into Lough Neagh and in which there are various species of trout. The road leading up the hill from the river bridge past Glenville House is to this day known as Killen's Brae.

A forbear of the Millars in the district was a seventeenth-century covenanter called Willie Gilliland whose anti-government exploits inspired a number of ballads. Later Killens were very proud of their descent from Willie, who was celebrated in a somewhat epic poem by another descendant and relative (albeit a remote one), Sir Samuel Ferguson.

W.D. makes no mention of any family involved in the 1798 rising in the north-east. He admits that many Presbyterians were involved, but by the time he was writing a hundred years later, he was reflecting the change in political allegiance of the Presbyterian community at large. Rebellion against the Crown was not at all respectable and the less one was associated with it the better. The enemy was no longer Britain and the Monarch. There was enough to do confuting Rome and popery. The area from Ballymena to Belfast was the epicentre of the rising which ended with the defeat by the military at the Battle of Antrim. In his book *The Year of Liberty*, Thomas Packenham tells how after the Battle of Antrim, an officer who was looking at a cartload of corpses, rhetorically asks "Where are these wretches from?" at which a bloody head emerged from the pile and says "I'm frae Ballyboley". Ballyboley is just over the hill from Glenwhirry.

W.D omits to make any mention of William Orr who was to marry Ellen Killen, W.D.'s sister. William Orr was transported to Botany Bay for alleged involvement in the rising. It was later determined that it was a false charge, trumped up by an aquaintance who bore a personal grudge against William. William, without knowing that he had been exonerated, escaped from Sydney in an open boat, and after an epic journey, landed at Penang, the East India Company centre in Malaya, where he spent several years amassing a fortune. He returned to Ballymena where he opened a prosperous business, bought a big house and married Ellen. (At an earlier time, a FitzSimon, one Michael, was accused of taking part in the Blessington rebellion – actually he had, but it had been may years before – by a jealous neighbour who wanted Michael's land. Michael was not as lucky as William Orr, as he had his head cut off).

W.D. describes his father John as an upright businessman and a devout servant of the church, "he was a model of temperance and a lover of peace". He doesn't appear to be the type to be out rioting with rebels – one day there were 30,000 rebel supporters demonstrating in Ballymena alone, where they occupied the courthouse and killed some guards. Apart from W.D. who spent most of his life in Belfast, John had two other sons, one James, who also became a clergyman and Doctor of Divinity, and Edward who took over the business in Ballymena and the farm in Glenwhirry, and four daughters, all of whom married. One daughter married a Co. Derry man called McCausland, who rose to great wealth in Belfast and became Lord Mayor of the city.

Edward of Ballymena married Mary Young of a Ballymena family. Two of their sons, Edward and John, set off in 1852 for Australia along with a cousin, Charles Young, lured by the prospect of gold. They went to Victoria where John, Edward and Charles had a claim on the diggings at Bendigo, but this was not a success. They sold the mine and went into business with a bullock wagon supplying the diggings. Charles sent for his wife to follow him, and in due course she arrived at the port of Williamstown. She was so dismayed at the sight of the place that she refused to disembark. The story goes that Edward went out to the ship and persuaded her to come ashore in a rowing boat. In time the Youngs had a farm and Charles was to sit as a member in the Parliament of the Colony of Victoria.

When Edward senior died in 1856, John and Edward junior returned from Australia and Edward took over the Glenwhirry property. He lived there for nearly twenty years; he was married to a Miss Wilson from Raphoe in Co. Donegal and his children were born in Glenwhirry. It is said that he was to suffer from the damp and cold in those Antrim hills; we have a description of him near to death with his old uncle W.D. kneeling beside his bed praying for his recovery. Consequently he determined to sell the farm and to emigrate to Australia again, but with a family this time. About the same time John who had been running the Ballymena business, emigrated with his family to New Zealand where he was to have many descendants.

Edward Junior's eldest son, William Wilson Killen, finished his schooling while living in Belfast with the family of his father's older brother, the Revd Thomas Young Killen, who was to continue the Killen practice of two brothers marrying two sisters and was also married to a Miss Wilson from Raphoe. William Wilson's cousin in the Belfast household, with whom he shared a bed, was William Marcus Killen, my grandfather. W.W. would pay the younger W.M. to scratch his back, which has been pointed out to me as an early manifestation of W.W.'s. entrepreneurial and managerial ability. W.W. went on to become a grazier of great wealth, an MP and a cabinet minister in the Australian Federal Government. W.W.'s younger brother, another Edward, who also became a large scale grazier, started off as a clerk in the bank at Jerilderie. He should have been at work the day of the famous raid by Ned Kelly and his gang, but for some reason he was not present. Perhaps the raid was an inside job?

These settlers, along with a son of W.D. known as Captain Killen, a former ship's captain, had many descendants in Australia, in time running into hundreds. There would be other immigrants to Australia at later times from the Killen/Young extended family. Descendants of Youngs are also numerous. The Youngs were also a Ballymena family, said to be of Huguenot origin, and they provided three sisters for the brothers Edward senior, W.D. and James Millar to marry. One of these Ballymena Youngs I have seen described as the first Englishman to climb Mont Blanc; there is something astray in the description.

The Revd Thomas Young Killen, D.D., my great-grandfather, who, I heard it said, got the expensive education which justified his brother Edward getting the farm at Glenwhirry, was Presbyterian minister in Ramelton in Co. Donegal, Ballykelly, Co. Derry, and then at Duncairn on the Antrim Road, Belfast. His wife's uncle, William Wilson was MP for Co. Donegal, and was known as "The Honest Attorney"; attorneys presumably were considered by and large not to be honest. He was a contemporary of Isaac Butt, but died young and unexpectedly, before Parnell took the lead of the Irish parliamentary party. Home Rule was not an important issue for William, or at least he is not recorded as speaking on it. What he did speak about was tenants' rights – he took the side of the small farmers against the landlords. The Wilson family had a large property at Raphoe. They were "gentry", but the fact that they were Presbyterian rather than Church of Ireland, might explain to some extent why William chose the more radical side of politics.

There was one Killen whose politics were very radical. Thomas Young's second cousin was James Bryce Killen, who was born in 1842 at Kells in Co. Antrim, and died in Dublin in 1916. He went so far to the radical side that he appears to have been disowned by his respectable and non-revolutionary relations; that he married a Roman Catholic probably didn't help either. After leaving school in Belfast, he entered the Queen's College there, the forerunner of Queen's University; he also studied at the Queen's College in Cork where he probably met his wife, she being a native of that city. He also studied at the Queen's College in Galway and was given the L.L.B.law degree some time before 1867. He was called to the Irish Bar in 1869. Shortly thereafter he emigrated to America, suspected of Fenianism. He returned to Ireland and in 1872 he was editor of the *Northern Star* in Belfast. Over the next ten years he wrote poems and contributed articles to many publications. He was to be imprisoned in Kilmainham on account of his seditious speeches and writings. He was also charged (along with Michael Davitt the Land Leaguer) with seditious libel after a meeting at Sligo in 1879. As a senior member of the National Labour League, in 1887 he mobilized the unemployed in Dublin and brought thousands onto the streets. He told a crowd of 3,000 at one rally on Harold's Cross Green, that the land and all the instruments of production belonged to the community and that the worker was "justified in using any means whatever in order to get rid of the idle class that fattened upon his misery". He was forbidden to address the students at his old university. He continued with his journalism in Ireland and again for a time in the 1890s in America, but was to die in Dublin in poverty. According to his son, the politics, along with the drink, ruined his marriage and his legal career. One of the Australian Killens had a story of one of the family having lost his ear at a riot in Limerick, an easy thing to happen when the dragoons with their sabres went to break up a crowd of protesters. I wondered if it was James at Limerick, but later learned that James went to his maker with both ears in place, so the owner of the missing ear remains a mystery. I asked Kathleen MacCausland what she knew about James, who was her father's second cousin. Kathleen was then well over 100 years old and James had been dead for eighty years, but she was quick to disassociate herself from the subject muttering she didn't know anything about "any murderer".

There were no other firebrands, political or otherwise. There were occasional eccentrics. Cousin Eddy Killen, who lived in London, was an inventor who made several fortunes with inventions that worked, and lost the fortunes on inventions that didn't work. One of his inventions was the cinema tip-up seat. W.D.'s grandson Jim, who was a surgeon in Derry – the same one who operated on my father's nose – was very much of the city's Protestant Establishment, but unique among such an Orange and Unionist group, he was a life-long Nationalist, who when he retired preferred to live on the Donegal side of the border. Jim's sister Alice lived most of her life in Paris; she had a doctorate from the Sorbonne for her studies on horror novels. More typical of the society in that family were a brother who emigrated to Australia where he grew fruit on irrigation land, and another, Bruce, who was a Belfast stockbroker and every Sunday afternoon would drive with his wife and sister-in-law Kathleen MacCausland to Donaghadee or some such place at a like distance, have afternoon tea, and then drive home.

Thomas Young Killen was not untypical of his generation of Presbyterian clergy. He was strongly evangelical; he was very enthusiastic about the great Ulster religious revival of 1859. This revival, which bordered on hysteria in some places, brought vast numbers into the churches. It was essentially a phenomenon among the Presbyterians, but it spread among other denominations as well. He was minister of Ballykelly in Co. Derry at the time. His thinking would be recognizable today among conservative theologians, as it seems to be free of the polemical anti-Catholicism of his uncle W.D. After moving to Belfast he served a term as Moderator of the General Assembly. He was to die soon after, leaving a young family with not much money. His eldest son was William Marcus Killen, my grandfather, who I knew as "Bogey".

William Marcus (Willie) was a final year medical student at Queen's College, Belfast when his father died. His education had cost nothing as he had scholarships. He had previously been at Inst., the Royal Belfast Academical Institution, which by then had evolved into the big secondary school which it is today, from when W.D. had been there in the 1820s, when it was an embryo university with the training of

Presbyterian clergy a main aim. Willie was able to earn enough money after he qualified to assist in supporting his siblings through their education. His brother Tom was to become the Presbyterian minister of Bailieboro in Co. Cavan, where his sister Edith went to live with him and keep house – Tom never married. The next brother Robert became a solicitor, but died when not much over 30, and the youngest John, started to train as an architect but did not complete the course, going to Canada where he settled as a real estate agent in Edmonton. The older sister Jinny married a Belfast merchant called Mayrs.

Willie had finished his medical education with a course in midwifery at the Rotunda Hospital in Dublin. It was there that one day he saw a crowd of people at O'Connell Bridge looking at the river, and saw that they were watching a child who had fallen in and was apparently drowning. Willie dived in and saved the child only to be told by an onlooker that there was no need for such action as there were too many children in Dublin. He then went on to Vienna to learn the latest in eye surgery, which was to become his speciality. While in Austria he did some mountain climbing, but did not reach the heights of his Young cousin, the first "Englishman" to climb Mont Blanc. His whole working life, some forty-five years, followed at the Benn Hospital right beside where his mother and family lived in Clifton Street, Belfast. The Benn was the hospital for ear, nose, and throat surgery as well as for the eye; he operated on all these organs, however it was in advancing surgery on cataract removal which established his reputation. He was a visiting professor at Queen's, since 1908 a university in its own right. His nephew Bryce Mayrs became a full-time professor at the university. Bryce started off as a student of surgery but lost his arm in France during the war (rather ironically due to an accident when he fell off his bicycle behind the lines, rather than having it hacked off by a Prussian cavalryman) and so gave up surgery for pharmacology. Willie had wide interests in his profession, and at one stage was offered the position of president of the Cancer Research Council, but whatever consideration he gave the offer, it would have meant a move to London which my grandmother did not favour. He was, if not a polymath, a scholar of breadth; he read classical

Greek for his enjoyment, could speak German, and was something of a student of Egyptian hieroglyphics.

He married my grandmother Alice Eliott in 1902, when he was 38 years old and the following year, when my mother was born, they went to live at Helen's Bay on the Lough shore, three stops on the railway on the Belfast side of Bangor. Marcus and Pauline were born some years later. About 1918 they moved into Belfast to 32 College Gardens, near the university. He was a big and imposing man, with a reputation for generosity; he charged people fees which they could pay, and didn't charge if they couldn't pay. Consequently, though the family was comfortably off, there was never any sign of much money. I remember a large red armchair which had been the contribution from a convent of nuns where he had always given his services free.

Like many intelligent and learned people, he was what is called absent-minded, extremely absent-minded. After he got a car about 1920, he had the habit of setting off into town in it, and then forgetting about it, coming home on the tram. Losing his car became so commonplace that the police gave up ringing him when they came across it, but just had it driven back to the house. To my mother's consternation, she discovered three years after his death, that she had lost a fortune. It is a complicated story, the essence was that Willie had had his brother John buy some remote land in Canada early in the century, in order, it was said, to help him. Nothing happened on the land and when my mother was married, Willie said that he would make it over to her. When oil was struck on the land in 1947, it was found that Willie had forgotten about making the land over to Mother, and had later made it over to his nephew, John's son, who had started farming it but was having a hard time during the depression. This issue was to become something of a saga which I will come to later.

Willie retired on the spur of the moment deciding to go to visit my parents in South India, and had Bryce Mayrs sell the house after he and my grandmother had sailed. In India, his demeanour and manner fitted well. He would sit under a tree and numbers of Indians would gather around him, to ask him questions, or just to sit and take in his charisma. He became what they call there a guru.

His politics were conformist, but apart from being one of the hundreds of thousands who signed the Ulster Covenant of 1912 against Home Rule, he was not an activist. He did not approve of Orangeism, as he was a mild-mannered and tolerant man. He told my mother that he preferred the Episcopalian Church of Ireland to his own Presbyterian one, but desisted from any apostasy because of the hurt that this would cause in the extended family. I never heard a bad word said of him. It was always praise, but most of what I know of him came from my mother who was most biased in his favour, despite his having forgotten to pass on to her the oil well in Canada.

Of the descendants of John Killen of Ballymena and Martha Doole there are now none of the name in Ireland, apart from the unmarried daughter of my late first cousin John, though there are still quite a number of descendants through female lines. Killens of this clan branch can however be found in America, Africa and England, and in Australia and New Zealand they are extremely numerous.

My Killen forbears were nothing like as eccentric as my MacFarlane ones, but of all my ancestors with their generally Conservative and Unionist conformity, they alone would now and then throw up a refreshing element of Radicalism and Nationalism. I did indeed find one curious eccentricity which must be embedded in the genes when I found Australians of the clan referring to the "Killen Farewell". It is a noticeable phenomenon that when a group of visitors has taken leave of a household, got into their car and would seem to go off, members of the household would stand around opening up further topics of conversation with them which could go on for up to an hour or more. The odd thing is that I remembered how Killen clan members would do just the same in Ireland.

Mrs MacFarlane (née Wallace)

Odette MacFarlane

Alice Killen (née Elliot) and Gladys Killen (m. FitzSimon)

Dr William Marcus Killen

Reverend John Elliot and Family

Eldron, Co. Monaghan – home of the Elliots

Isobel MacFarlane, May FitzSimon and Maud FitzSimon at Moreen 1903

Henry James MacFarlane "Old Mac"

Lieutenant-Colonel Francis MacFarlane

CHAPTER EIGHT

Mount Callan

Mount Callan is in West Clare. The west of Clare, like Galway and Donegal, is quite distinct from its east. The east of these counties is much like the rest of Ireland. The west is the rugged, boggy, wet, Atlantic coast. The coastlands, from being relatively empty, became very heavily populated in the eighteenth and early nineteenth century, but from the time of the famine of 1847 until now, the population has been in decline. The famine was not by and large so severe on the actual coast as further inland; for when the potatoes failed there was fish and seaweed, and boats could bring in the Indian meal. However, once a pattern of emigration was set, it became a logical course to leave the tiny farms where little livelihood could be scratched from among the rocks and bogs. There was very little in the way of pickings to attract a landlord class; development was limited. There were only three or four major resident landlords of consequence in the whole of West Clare, a branch of the O'Briens, and the Macnamaras of Ennistymon, both descendants from ancient chiefs of the area, being two of them. Even when the West Clare Railway was built in the late nineteenth century, there is little evidence of improvement to the economy. The railway's legacy is Percy French's song "Are you right there Michael, are you right?"

The Mount Callan property had originally been owned by the church, but it fell into the hands of the Synge family. The Synges contributed a great number of bishops, deans and other dignitaries to the Church of Ireland, and someway thereby they acquired the land which most likely was contributing very little to the church coffers. In the mid-nineteenth century a Miss Synge married a Tottenham. There was a sporting lodge on the property which was extended into a two-storey L-shaped dwelling with farmyard and gardens laid out nearby. There, Captain Robert Tottenham brought up his family of four sons in the interwar period, but had moved to Wicklow by 1945 to the main Tottenham house. His son Robert, who was to inherit Mount Callan, was then, (after war service in India), in a plaster cast and unable to look after the place. My father was given the job.

The property covered more than a 1,000 acres on the eastern slope of Slieve Callan, from the top of the mountain at 1,100 feet, down to some river meadows. A good deal more than half the land was mountain heather and bog with two well wooded glens. The farm land was grazed by 200 or 300 cattle. A dozen or so cows were brought into the farmyard and milked each day. There was a black Angus bull called George. There was no attempt to grow crops apart from a few potatoes for domestic use and a few oats for the horses. Hay was made, poor hay it was, but also silage much more suitable for the wet, misty, damp climate. Silage was little known in Ireland in those days. Land was also owned in the north of the county, in the Burren, that rock-covered land where one of Cromwell's generals said "there was not enough water to drown a man, not a tree where you could hang a man and not enough soil to bury a man". Amongst the rocks however, grew the best grass in Ireland, so herds of young cattle were driven up to the Burren from Mount Callan every summer, the ancient practice of booleying.

Apart from old Austin Woods, who was nearly 80 and who worked in the garden – he was the last of the native Irish speakers – there was his son Gus, Jimmy Lernihan, John Henchy, John Scullane and his young cousin Pakky, who worked on the farm. John's sister, Big Nora was the cook in the house and their cousin Margaret was the maid; Nora left soon after and was replaced by Mary Ann, another cousin. All these people lived in cottages on the property. Their wages were small, but at least sure. The agricultural labourers' wages at the time were about £2 a week – when we arrived, my mother was appalled to find Margaret was only getting 6 shillings a week. She doubled this to 12 shillings a week. All the families would get an occasional 10 or 20 dollar bill in a parcel of tea or the like from relatives in America.

When we arrived at the end of July, Father had already acquired a Ford 10 panel van, and access to petrol. He met us from the train at Limerick. An expedition so far was then for him a rare event. To go to Ennis 16 miles away, for shopping, would later become a regular weekly or fortnightly event. The post office was at Inagh, where there were only a couple of houses. That was 5 miles away, and the postman, Paddy the Post, would come on his bicycle; he brought the newspaper whenever he came. Soon after we arrived, the war with Japan ended, but as there was no radio in the house, we didn't know this for several days.

We had no radio at the start, but we did have electricity. There had been no electricity at Annaghmakerig or Eldron. It was all oil lamps and candles there. Mount Callan had its own hydropower generator. This was worked from a little dam on the mountain above the house. The dam also served as a swimming pool. The plant had been put in about 1920, and was still working seventy years later. It was enough to light the house – there was even one of those newfangled contraptions, a refrigerator – or run a circular saw in the yard, but not the two together. There was a wheel valve to turn on the turbine which was too heavy for me to turn when we arrived, but when we left after nearly three years and I had grown enough, I had no such trouble. When I visited many years later I noticed that Robert Tottenham, by then living there, kept the lights on all day; he said it was cheaper on the system than turning them on and off.

An exciting event was the unpacking of my parents' luggage – some wooden packing cases arrived from wherever they had been stored for the last seven years. They had packed the boxes when they left India, but had never been confident enough that they were to remain in one place long enough to warrant unpacking. The boxes had in them all sorts of ordinary household effects like linen and towels, but also ancient Indian silver and wooden ornaments. What was exciting was that our family was establishing a home. The year in Bangor had provided what was almost a home, but one felt that it was Mrs Magee's house, what with her family on the top floor and in evidence about the place. Before that, of course, we were quite clearly staying with other people, and conforming to their practices. Mount Callan was not our house or estate, but it felt that way, although there were a couple of visits from various Tottenhams at different times.

The Tottenhams were an archetype of the Anglo-Irish family. There was a framed glass-fronted chart of the family tree hanging in a passage; there were on it Marquises of Ely, Loftuses of the house of the Elizabethan Archbishop of Dublin, Tottenhams of New Ross, from where one who held the parliamentary seat had ridden all night to Dublin for a crucial debate and whose vote carried the decision. He had not had time to change his clothes and ever thereafter the toast of his party at dinners was "Tottenham in his boots!" Of the four boys of the generation when we were there, two were in the British Army and one in the Navy and the youngest, Dick, was to take up a career in banking in the Far East. They had all been to English public schools, but when at home would speak with the local Co. Clare accent. When Christopher and I heard about their speaking like this, we too learnt how to imitate the accent and would always speak in it with the locals. This would seem to be a variant on colonial practice where one would speak to one's African servants in Swahili; however, though this might have been patronizing, we certainly didn't see it like this. Rather it was an expression of involvement with the people, and I don't think that there was any resentment. One time when Aunt Jane had come to stay from Eldron, she heard us talking with Margaret Scullane, the maid, in our unmistakable Clare tones. She said to Margaret, "They don't talk like that in Monaghan", to which Margaret commented, "Sure, I suppose they must have an accent up there."

West Clare today has the reputation of being a centre for traditional Irish music *par excellence*. It was a place which, in its isolation, never lost all of its culture. It wasn't, like in the east, necessary to revive it. The Gaelic language was gone. Old Austin Woods the gardener, who would have grown up in the 1880s, was the last and only native speaker, but the old stories and customs were still around.

The pilgrimage to Croagh Patrick in August is well known and attended by thousands. But the ascent of a mountain for the feast of Lughnasa was in times past, and going back thousands of years, practised in many places in Ireland. Mullyash in Co. Monaghan was such a site into the early nineteenth century. The annual ascent of Slieve Callan was one of the last pilgrimages to survive. We arrived at Mount Callan when the practice was just about becoming extinct. The people for some time had not gone up the mountain, but simply assembled in a meadow at the bottom. Even that had stopped by the time we left.

In the farmyard there was a kitchen, a room with a big hearth where the calves' and pigs' food was cooked. The turf fire did more than this, for it was often a gathering place in the evening. There would be the smoking of pipes, discussions and stories. There was one story I learnt off by heart, for I heard it more than once. It was all about a king's son who went off on quests, and had adventures such as playing ball with the Devil and beating him at cards. At the end of each episode the King's son would set off again, always "with his hound at his heel, his hawk on his hand and his fine black horse to bear him" travelling "over rivers and valleys and mounts like Mount Callan". The principal storyteller was Mick Tierney. Mick was not of the immediate community, but had a farm not far away and had been to Australia, not as a migrant but as a tourist having won a sizeable sum in the Irish Hospital Sweepstake. He probably went to visit relations. Though recent emigration was mainly to America, there was a time when more people from Clare went to Australia than from anywhere else in Ireland.

Unfortunately I never knew any musicians or singers, but I suspect they were about somewhere; we were not a musical family and would not have sought them out as I myself would later on when I had a smattering of musical education. There was a gramophone in the house – I think it must have been ours rather than the Tottenhams, as it was a novelty to Margaret the maid. She brought some records to play on it. Probably they were the best and most near to traditional one could buy, before the revival and commercialization of traditional Irish music in the 1950s and 1960s. She had "Haste to the Wedding", " Johnny the Daisy", "The Maid of the Sweet Brown Knowe" and the Kilfenora Ceilidhe Band.

At Christmas, or rather on St Stephen's Day, for it was on St Stephen's Day that the "Wren, the Wren, the king of all birds was caught in the furze", and that we were visited by the Wren Boys. A half a dozen young men would go from house to house, give a little performance and collect money. They came into the kitchen where they were given something to eat and drink and then to the tune of a few bars on an accordion a couple of them would do a little bit of a dance. Pakky Scullane who worked in the yard was the best man to dance.

At Mount Callan I started to learn to shoot and to ride. Shooting was limited to an old air gun which was so weak that I am pleased to say in hindsight that I never managed to kill anything. I did manage to frighten some crows; one time I clearly heard the slug hit a crow's wing, but the crow flew off without much of a squawk. The first time I was allowed to take out the gun on my own, I made with great anticipation to where I knew there were rabbits. There were a lot of rabbits about in those days. I stalked carefully, close up to some, and fired at one. The slug fell to the ground half way to the rabbit. The rabbit did not even show me the courtesy of running away.

As well as the two horses which worked on the farm there was an old pony. In the past, the pony's job had been to pull the trap, but now that cars were back on the road, he was living a leisured retirement. He would now be saddled up for my pleasure and could be made rather unwillingly to trot, even to jump over a low ditch. He had never been trained for riding, and resented the imposition. It was hard work for an inexperienced rider to get him to conform. I had only one really good ride, which was when I had to take him to the blacksmith at Crowe's Bridge, 2 or 3 miles away. He was quite well behaved going there but when we started for home there was no holding him; he galloped the whole way. By and large, wrestling with this animal, mentally and physically, was too difficult, and may explain why I never took to horse riding.

Sometimes there was a visit to the sea at Spanish Point. There is a fine beach there. One summer our friends, the Perrys, took a house there and I at least stayed some nights there. As usual when I think of the sea bathing in the Atlantic, I think of the cold. Spanish Point was only about 8 miles from Mount Callan, yet it was always a major expedition to go there. There was a Church of Ireland church there which we attended occasionally. The rector, Canon Elliot was renowned as a catcher of crabs. People would come from all over the country and beyond to go crabbing with him. I saw him in action. He would be fully dressed in long trousers and a black jersey and would disappear completely underwater in a rock pool. After an interminable time, when one was beginning to think that he had drowned and would never be seen again, he would emerge, holding by the claws, a crab so big that its body was the size of his head. The canon would have on his dripping face a meek little smile of achievement.

Protestants were very thin on the ground in West Clare. There would only be a small handful attending the canon's services at Spanish Point or Ennistymon. He also looked after the congregation at Kilfenora where the church is actually a cathedral. The congregation (when present), consisted of two elderly ladies. That was the whole diocese. It hadn't warranted a Protestant bishop of its own since the Reformation. Nor for that matter has it had a Catholic one of its own either. In the absence of such, the position was occupied officially by the Pope himself.

It is possible that expeditions by car to Spanish Point and even the more necessary ones to Ennistymon for shopping, were strictly limited by Father's aversion to spending money on petrol. After a year with the little Ford van, grandmother Killen bought us a car. British cars were hard to come by and European ones non-existent immediately after the war, but not so American ones. We acquired a big brand new American Ford V8. It would have used a lot of petrol. Though it was not brought out often, it did go on more than one occasion to Monaghan and the North. I think that the cost of running it was the reason why within a couple of years it was exchanged for a Ford Prefect, a little British car whose modesty was a contrast to the garish vulgarity of the big American one. Money was not plentiful. Father had his army pension and we had the free use of the property with its produce for the household. The electricity was free, wood and turf was cut for fires, there was milk, eggs and poultry from the farm and all the products of orchard and garden. Occasionally we would eat rabbit; there was no shortage of these, and very occasionally there would be game in the winter. There were plenty of hares on the mountain and woodcock in the thickly timbered glens.

Father could have buried himself at Mount Callan indefinitely; to me it was a paradise, but Mother felt too isolated being so far away from her friends and relations. Some people would come to stay, but she wanted to travel abroad, as she had been able to do in the past. The catch was the cost. She embarked on two moneymaking schemes. The first one was dogs. She bought an English setter bitch and a cocker spaniel bitch of impeccable pedigree. The setter was called Jancey, a nice though nervous dog, but she never had any pups. The spaniel however had six pups, but the problem was that we became too fond of them to sell them. They had to be sold in the end, but they had grown into full-sized dogs and would have been eating a lot. We kept two of them for a long time; one of them won a prize at the Limerick Dog Show. Overall I don't think there was any financial gain. On the other hand, the second scheme which was pigs, did well; it made a month tour of England possible. The scheme started with two bonams – as piglets are called in Clare. The male pig grew up to be eaten by us, but the female grew into an enormous sow (her name was Scarlett O'Hara) who had numerous progeny destined for Denny's Limerick bacon factory in return for sizeable cheques. The tour was already being planned early in 1948 when it was decided that we were to leave and move to Annaghmakerrig. Father was to take on a similar role there to the one he had at Mount Callan. We could have stayed a year longer, until Robert Tottenham was ready to take over, however mother was getting fairly desperate, and apart from being back more in her home ground in Monaghan, she learnt that two of her friends had recently returned to settle there. As well as this, her health was deteriorating. She had a duodenal ulcer and had had a spell in Barrington's Hospital in Limerick. Another retired lieutenant colonel was found to fill in at Mount Callan.

During the Easter holidays we left driving in the Ford Prefect to Co. Monaghan. Christopher and I were very sad to be leaving. As the car proceeded northwards, through Gort, across Co. Galway, we kept looking out the back window to catch the last glimpse of Slieve Callan before it receded below the horizon. Throughout the period when Mount Callan was home, Christopher and I had stayed on at Garth House as boarders, so Mount Callan might have been looked at as only a holiday home; after all, school terms were twice as long as school holidays. It did not feel like this; short though the stays were, the environment of the farm and mountain, the friendliness of the people, the comfort of the house, and being part of a fully functioning family for a change, were much more important than the routine in the suburban boarding school.

It was an odd situation, having one's school in one corner of the country and one's house at the extreme opposite one. Further, the contrast between the two locations could hardly have been greater in Ireland. The school in the north-east, was in a wealthy middle-class dormitory extension of the most industrialized and technologically advanced city on the island. Mount Callan in the south-west was in an area which was as close an example of the survival of an ancient pre-industrial rural culture as one could find anywhere in Europe. The reason we stayed on at Garth House was my mother's high regard for Captain Hutton. The geographical anomaly was not as odd as meets the eye. Given that were we to go to something better than the little one room school on the road to Inagh, with its limited curriculum, and all in the Irish language, for which my mother had no time at all, the alternatives to Garth House were limited. There were no boarding prep schools closer than Dublin, and that was almost as far as Bangor. It took two days to get to Bangor, but it took a whole day to get to Dublin. Before we had the big car, we would go on the train from Ennis to Athenry where, after an interminable wait, one would get a train coming from Galway to Dublin. The night would be spent with the FitzSimon grandparents at Kilgobbin, and then on to Belfast and Bangor. Mother came with us on one or two early occasions, and would meet up with my other grandmother in Belfast. When we had the big car, Father would drive it to Dublin or Monaghan. Once, he drove up all the way to Bangor with stops in Monaghan coming and going. I have visited Mount Callan many years, indeed decades later. The familiar families were still represented, but the work on the property is now all to do with trees. Robert Tottenham planted many hundreds of acres of trees and his success as a forester has attracted interest from tree growers all over Europe. The rain and the mist were still coming, and the trees like it. People used to talk about the constant damp, but it had never bothered me as a child. Mount Callan was all good.

CHAPTER NINE

Annaghmakerrig, Garth House, London

We had visited Annaghmakerrig from time to time over the intervening years, for a day or a night or two; it was neutral ground. Going back to live there permanently did not fill me with immediate enthusiasm. It was now to be home for the next five years, but still only during the school holidays. The boarding at Garth House was to continue. By now I had come to terms with boarding school; it was not mere resignation: I actually enjoyed it. Living at Annaghmakerrig did have a lot of positive aspects, but a measure of my response was that I was happy when it was time to go back to school, and at the end of term was not always as enthusiastic about going home as might be expected. I don't know if any others of my peers ever had similar feelings for I never dared to vent my own; it would have been too galling to reveal such thoughts.

This time at Annaghmakerrig we were not just transit guests fitting into the ways of the existing household. We had our own wing of sitting room, dining room, kitchen and about four bedrooms. I say about four bedrooms, because it was not a self-contained apartment. It was the upstairs of the back of the house and contained the bathroom used by the rest of the house, and one had to go through our part to get to the four rooms on the top floor, where the maids slept. We had our own maid, who was called Dympna – a common name in Co. Monaghan on account of the saint of that name having been a local. Sometimes guests of the main house would be allotted rooms in our part and vice versa; we might have our guests in the main area. We functioned quite separately, if not with complete privacy, yet there was no restriction to prevent me going into the main house to the library or study or anywhere else. The arrangement worked well for all of us. There wouldn't want to have been confrontations or disagreements between the parties and I am sure there never were any. I can remember only one confrontation, and it was nothing to do with encroaching on privacy. There was a greenhouse in the garden in which there was a peach tree. There were not many peaches on it, but I watched them as they ripened, and then the temptation became too great; St Patrick must have missed the serpent when he passed through Co. Monaghan, for it whispered in my ear, and I ate one of the peaches. My expulsion from the Eden of the greenhouse was by Bunty, for she had counted the peaches and guessed well who the thief was. Bunty was still her organizing and bossy self, and along with Mrs G. was the only normally permanent resident in the main part of the house. As I became more civilized and Bunty mellowed with age I remember her with affection.

The Daly family was still there in full force, as was Eugene Maguire in the garden and Bob Burns everywhere else. Brian McGoldrick had retired and Seamus McGorman had gone to his own small farm and also gone into business driving a taxi. Alec Watson and Bob Robinson helped Eddie Daly about the farm. I had quite a bit to do with Eddie in these later years; it was then that I learnt the round of the farming tasks, becoming skilled with the spade, the axe, the shovel and the crowbar, various forks, the scythe, the turnip grinder, the driving of the horse and cart, the feeding of pigs, the herding of cattle, and much more. This would have been a progressive apprenticeship. I was 16½ when we left Annaghmakerrig for good, by which time I am sure I was as well trained in farm work as anyone who was less privileged than me, but had no choice other than to earn a living at farming at that age.

My formal education at school at that point, (with Christopher as well), must have been costing about half my parents' gross income. Garth House was as good a school as one could find in Ireland. The privately owned prep school is a curious phenomenon and being small, the quality is a reflection entirely of the person who runs it. I would rank our mentor, the owner and headmaster, Captain Hutton, for better or worse, ahead of all other men, to the extent of how I was influenced while growing up: Davy McMahon at Eldron, Eddie Daly at Annaghmakerrig, my uncle, any other and subsequent teachers and perhaps even my father.

I did not have much to do with the headmaster, Captain Hutton, in my early years, but for the final two or three, his immediate influence was pervasive. The younger boys were taught in class by assistants; generally there were about four of them. There was quite a turnover; in my time, one or two of them were women. George Smith, who taught everyone Maths, was there the whole time I was, but the best teachers were unqualified men who would be filling in a year or two after leaving secondary schools. One of the worst was also such a one. He was fired. This, I later heard, was for the crime of lying in bed in the morning and not showing up for the assembly. I once saw him hit a boy on the head with a book so hard that the boy was felled. This boy was a particularly thick-skulled fellow, figuratively and literally; his stupidity exasperated the teacher beyond endurance which prompted the attack that would probably have killed a boy of a more normal physical constitution. I never saw or heard of any other abuse of boys by staff. Captain Hutton was the only one to use the cane – three or four sharp strokes across the backside. It was the boarders who got most of the beatings, which were administered as a means to keep us quiet and in order, when we should otherwise have been in bed or would stray out of bounds, rather than for more heinous offences. One could expect to be caught and caned a couple of times a term. It wasn't too painful when one was wearing trousers, but through light pyjamas it was.

My early stages of boarding were not much fun; the contrast with the free and diverse life of Mount Callan was great. One had little time to oneself in the day with the classes and games, little let up until bedtime, which was at about nine o'clock. Every week day in winter we had football, in summer cricket and swimming. I liked all games, but there was a great deal of time spent getting ready, changing, going to the football field, washing off mud in showers, cleaning one's boots and oiling one's cricket bat, which took away some of the enjoyment. On Saturday there were classes in the morning. Then one had to amuse oneself with one's friends when not on a "walk". The walk consisted of proceeding through the outskirts of Bangor in crocodile to the park or to the seashore, where we were allowed to break ranks for a while, before being marched back. We wore our school uniform with our red caps which we were taught to doff when we met an adult we knew. Sunday afternoon was the same. On Sunday morning we would dress in herringbone suits kept for the occasion and proceed in crocodile to the parish church. We younger ones were let out early so we did not have to sit through the sermon, which, as it was always morning prayer, came at the end. We would be walked back to school a long way round by the seafront, and get a newspaper to see the football results. Everyone had their own team; we were only partisan about the Northern Ireland League: my team was Portadown, as the nearest one to home. For the same reason I backed Limerick and later Dundalk in the League of Ireland, which was of no interest to my northern peers. It was always a relief to get out of the Sunday suit which was hairy, scratchy and uncomfortable.

While we were living at Mount Callan, Chrisopher and I, and sometimes one or two others, were left high and dry at the mid-term exeat, when all the boarders would go home for three days. Twice I was rescued and taken to the home of a friend, once with Hamish Neil to his big house in Malone Park, Belfast and once with Bill Meek to his cottage on Strangford Lough, where we went out in a boat, and I got an earache the severity of which has never been repeated. It was during such a mid-term break that the King and Queen came to Belfast, and as a treat Nellie Swanson took us to see them. We had an upstairs window in Anderson and MacAulay's shop in Royal Avenue from which to see the car go past through a great crowd below. I saw the King for about four seconds, the Queen not at all.

Nellie was as important an institution in the school as Captain Hutton. It had been her brother who had founded the school, and she remained after his death in some sort of business partnership with Captain Hutton. She came from York and it was believed that she had been a warden in a women's prison. She took a class of the youngest boys, which I had been lucky enough to escape, having started in a class higher up, lucky to escape her draconian methods, bordering on cruelty. She was in charge of the school library which was in her bedroom, and presided at table heads at meals. She wore a green knitted woollen dress, except for some days when she had a red one. Her wizened face and hooked nose were the caricature of a witch – hence her being referred to as Greenwich, when not Redditch – and could terrify all of us. She had an uncanny sense of coming to a window and knocking on it and waving crossly whenever anyone was at mischief outside and in view of a window. The Royal Family was of such importance to her that she had framed pictures of all of them cut from the *Illustrated London News*, and hung all over the hall and the dining room. On a Sunday during the exeats, she took us to the Abbey church where she went every morning, rather than the parish church. It suited her English High Churchmanship – she would always cross herself during grace at meals, an odd thing for ultra-Protestants to see. When we were left alone with her during those exeats, she did however become quite human.

The summer of 1948 was something of a watershed. Three things were afoot. First there was the move from Mount Callan to Annaghmakerrig, then there was my first visit outside Ireland, and on going back to Garth House in the September term I would be travelling on my own, all a phase of moving into a wider world.

At the end of the Summer Term we had the sports and the prize giving. Mother came up as she had the honour of giving out the prizes. It was a custom for the mother of the head boy to do this and Christopher was the head boy that year. He had made a recovery having come down with pleurisy the year before, and as well as being sick for half a term, had been kept at home for the whole of the term following. We both had been put down to go on to Wellington, an English public school with military orientation. His illness was said to be a reason not to follow on to Wellington. The doctor said that the cross-channel travel and the poor post-war food in England would be injurious to his health, so he was to proceed to St Columba's, near Dublin.

Mother gave out the prizes from a table on the front steps. It was windy and she had trouble with her hat, and some of the prizes were blown off the table. Like in *Alice in Wonderland*, just about everyone at Garth House got prizes for the sports. There was first, second and third for every event in every age group, and of course there were prizes for the swimming sports as well. Alas, I got no prize, but that was because I had been unable to take part. One evening I had tried to jump over the cricket net, fallen and dislocated my arm at the elbow. It was frightening to see the forearm sticking out the wrong way, but worse was to come. The doctor came, and in course of setting it, pulled so long and hard that my screams of pain brought half the school to the dormitory where I had been put. I well remember the looks of fear in the eyes of those who got to look in the door at the site of the slaughter. I was taken later on the bus to Newtownards Hospital for x-rays. The people there weren't gentle either.

The term then ended and we set off on the boat from Belfast to Heysham, from where it is a short distance to Lancaster. My parents had many friends in the area. It is where they lived when they were first married. We went on to the Lake District to Grasmere to stay with Cousin Eleanor Rawnsley. She had a fairly grand house looking over Grasmere Lake, beside which the poet Wordsworth had lived. I noted that beneath some trees, beside the lake, there was evidence of a lot of daffodils. She was descended from mother's great-uncle William, the clergyman who had a connection with the Duke of Westminster, and it had been her husband Canon Rawnsley who, with Octavia Hill and under the Duke's patronage, had founded the National Trust. It was Canon Rawnsley who had persuaded Beatrix Potter (who lived nearby), to persist with efforts to have her first book *The Tale of Peter Rabbit* published. The National Trust and a Beatrix Potter Trust were very much the essence of Cousin Eleanor's activity. Her household must have been one of the last Victorian establishments in existence. The day started with morning prayers, which Eleanor would read. They took place sharp at 8 a.m. in the dining room before breakfast, with the servants present. My parents were most adamant that Christopher and I would be on time for morning prayers, but my mother with her Irish habits had difficulty in meeting the time precisely.

We were to go on the train to London having collected mother's friend Consie in Lancaster. There was an interruption to plans, as Father had to fly over to Dublin because my grandfather FitzSimon had died. Father went by plane, which could now be done, though it was expensive; it would be another ten years before I flew in a plane. He was to join us in London a couple of weeks later.

CHAPTER TEN

Annaghmakerrig, Garth House, Europe

I would now go back to school on my own. I would be driven to one of the stations on the Cavan to Belfast line, most likely Smithboro, with a visit to Eldron, or Monaghan to visit the Killens at Aviemore. I would have to cross Belfast from Great Victoria Street Station to the Queen's Quay Station. A bonus with this trip, with the time gap between trains, was the chance to go to a cinema on the way. It was on one of these excursions that I first was entertained by John Wayne and a long lasting appreciation of the Western began.

By the autumn of 1948, I had been at Garth House nearly four years, three years as a boarder. I was going on 12. I was by the standards there one of the big boys, well assured of my place in the hierarchies, ready to participate in whatever was going on. I held the rank of corporal and was in charge of a dormitory called Montgomery. There were about seven younger boys in the dormitory, and as head, one was to see that they stayed quiet at night, got up washed and dressed properly for breakfast, made their beds and kept the place tidy. The power went to my head, and I carried out my duties so assiduously that I became a favourite of old Nellie. I was also high in her esteem as a principal patron of her library. I had been through Arthur Ransome, Richmal Crompton's William books, all of Biggles and was working my way through G.A. Henty. Despite being Nellie's "trusty", at 12 one could still have lapses like attacking other dormitories with pillow fights and risk a painful caning through the pyjamas from Captain Hutton.

Apart from Maths and Latin, all classes for us bigger boys were run by Captain Hutton. He taught us French, not too well, but not too badly either, and what was called English. English included everything which was not Latin, French or Maths. He did make a stab at English grammar, but was obviously as bored as the rest of us, and poetry was not very evident; however, where he excelled was in History, Geography, Politics and World Affairs generally. I do not remember too many formal exercises but we did have our dates in History precisely and extensively drilled into us, and in Geography we would have to know just about where every place on earth was and what went on there. We had to draw all sorts of maps. This was probably something which came from his own education. His degree was in Civil Engineering, but he had had little if any practical experience of the science of it, having worked in his family firm of Dublin hardware merchants before taking up teaching. One might have expected more than the little bit of Physics he gave us. Even in his day, an Engineering degree required quite a high level of Applied Science.

His classes were more like university tutorials. No rows of desks or blackboards. We all sat around the big table in what was called the study, in which also the senior boys had their lunch. There would normally be about ten in the class at any one time. We would have debates on all sorts of topics. He particularly liked the balloon debate, where each participant would be a person in history or politics and would have to make a defence as to why he should not be thrown out of the basket of a balloon we were all travelling in, and the others would vote at the end who should be thrown out of the basket.

Whatever political parties he may have favoured, he never said. His underlying philosophy was of the liberal-conservative middle-of-the-road type, which drove a strong belief in the need always to hear both sides of an argument, which should be strongly, rationally and truthfully put, and rational decisions taken, and that the people in power must always be fair. His background was among the pre-independence Unionist Dublin bourgeoisie – his mother still lived in an Edwardian Tudor villa on Brighton Road, Foxrock. He said that when young, he followed the elections and applauded the success of Unionist candidates, but later had decided that British policy in Ireland was wrong; he was a Home Ruler in hindsight. He was, I should think, against the Irish Republicanism of De Valera, but I also think that he didn't have much respect for Northern Unionists either. In our debates we never took up Irish politics: it was all British and International. History also avoided Ireland. Captain Hutton had been to school at Shrewsbury, a prominent English public school, and he was, I guess, passing on a tradition from there. He approved of the British Empire and favoured capitalism; he was decidedly anti-communist and anti-socialist and didn't think highly of the Attlee government of the day. When the formalizing of the Republic and the leaving of the Commonwealth was being enacted in the twenty-six counties of Eire, we heard hardly a word from him about it. At that time, the Captain was quite scathing about the British Labour government's attempts to grow peanuts in East Africa by Russian-style collective farming methods. It would be far better, he argued, to encourage West African farmers who owned their own land, to grow the peanuts on a free enterprise basis. This was the capitalist anti-socialist British Imperialist talking, while avoiding Irish issues.

His position may also have been contributed to by his religious background. His family was of the Unitarian denomination; they supported the Unitarian Church which is still there in St Stephens Green in Dublin. Religious education was not one of his subjects, but for a time when we were not having visits from the local clergy, he guided us through the scriptures. His Unitarian rationalizing was evident when he made a valiant attempt to explain Moses's crossing the Red Sea as something to do with low tides; it was proper to accept the literal account of scripture, even if it did not make rational sense from experience. He was fully respectful of religious practice and always read the prayers at the morning assembly. That he read the collects from the *Book of Common Prayer* at assembly and that he marched us every Sunday to the parish church, no matter what one's denomination, was no doubt following a pattern set by his predecessor Captain Swanson, and watched over by old Nellie, a reflection of their English Anglican Catholicism.

In my last year we were visited every week by the local curate, a Mr Ingram. He wanted to teach us and explain texts from the Epistle to the Romans and the prophet Hosea. In hindsight, it was an incredibly abstruse curriculum, more fitting for a graduate theological college. It is no wonder that most of the class sat as far from the front as possible and quietly talked among themselves. I was one of the few who sat at the front and took an interest in the class, but all the same, we liked to bring in red herrings and would draw Mr Ingram into discussion about the errors of Rome, a topic not far beneath his skin. He had previously been the curate in the parish of Maynooth, which could hardly have failed to alert his focus onto the Roman Magisterium. We liked Mr Ingram, who came on a bicycle as one would expect a curate to do in those days. The rector who had attended Garth House previously, before my time, would sometimes preach in church on Sunday. He was our favourite preacher; his rhetoric was powerful, bordering on the histrionic. His most powerful pronouncements were directed not at the errors of Rome, but at abuses in life which he could abide much less, particularly greyhound racing, and not much worse, the Jehovah's Witnesses.

Religious sectarianism was not countenanced by the school authorities. In Northern Ireland the underlying ethos of sectarianism can very quickly manifest itself among the young. If when we were proceeding in crocodile on a "walk", and we should come across a similar group from St Comgalls, the Roman Catholic primary school, epithets would be let fly, and the teacher with us would have to steer us away and calm us down. We liked the glamour of the Orangemen in their regalia with their drums and bands. The staff would always belittle the Orangemen, but I don't remember out and out condemnation. The vast majority of the pupils' parents were Unionist, and probably some were Orange as well. On one famous occasion, two boys sang an Orange song at the maids in the kitchen. The Catholic maids promptly left. As a practical punishment the disgraced culprits were made to help in the kitchen and wait at table until new maids could be found.

Captain Hutton had many strings to his bow. He coached us at cricket, a game he had played himself for many years at a senior level, and took us to play matches at the four other prep schools in the province. As with the football team, these excursions were always enjoyed. These schools also came to play us. The tea for the team accompanying the match was as important as the game itself. I remember the teas with cakes and such, better than I do the games. These teas were important, as they contrasted with the dull and sometimes only barely edible ordinary meals. Post-war rationing and financial control may have been an excuse for the poor menu, but it was undoubtedly adequate – it bears no thinking about how scrumptious it was compared with what most children in the world had. The Captain didn't involve himself with the kitchen, but he was involved with everything else. He would personally telephone for the carpenter when someone broke a window or when some of the other things which sixty boys would be continuously damaging needed to be mended. Reports and accounts he wrote out meticulously in longhand, a shilling for a bus fare here or two and seven pence halfpenny there for some medicine. He must have spent hours on such mundane tasks; there was no secretarial assistance. At the end of the day, before we senior boys went to bed, we would come down to the study in our dressing gowns and make toast at the fire, while the Captain would read to us; he liked detective stories and historical novels.

Captain Hutton did not take us for football. That was left to Mr Smith. I learned later that Mr Smith did not know anything about football, and was not much interested anyway, yet we could beat the best of them among the other schools we played against. Football was my favourite sport, and I had been put on the school team at an early age, when we had a star player in Cecil Pedlow who later became a star player as an International, though at rugby. I was really too young and was dropped until older, during my final two years. Just about everyone played football; the teams for the day's game were picked at lunch every day by appointed captains from among those who were not sick. The roll was called to which one replied "All right, Sir" and was allotted to play for the whites or the colours, or one said "Cold, Sir" or "Cough, Sir", so one was excused from playing. The large number who had colds or coughs was an indicator of the climate, genuine excuses rather than antipathy to the sport.

To make up for the bad winters, the summer of 1949 was a hot one. I was sunburned for the first time. The holidays started at Annaghmakerrig as normal. I had come on the train to Smithboro, and I waited at Eldron where Aunt Jane had a supply of raspberries from a neighbouring farmer who had gone into commercial fruit growing. The local rector, known as Precentor Robinson, also came to eat raspberries and chatted to Lizzie about the Twelfth of July celebrations. "Did you go away for the Twelfth, Lizzie?" "How would I get away anywhere", she answered with her face sour. In contrast, I was inwardly very pleased with myself, as I had just won the school prize for being the best boy of the year all round, sports, work, and general conduct, but I didn't tell anyone. Father came and collected me in the car to go on to Annaghmakerrig.

We had a visit from some Australian Killen cousins, who stayed with us at the beginning of the holidays. It was this family's first post-war visit "home", as they called it, to spend some money. Australia was then having a wool boom, and Harold Killen was the head of the family company which had a quarter of a million sheep. He had bought a Rolls Royce in London for £7,000, which in those days would have bought a fairly large farm or paid the fees at Garth House for fifty years. Harold, and his daughter Judith, then 19, were nevertheless very pleasant and unassuming people. Marion, Harold's wife, gave me a box camera, a present of undreamt magnificence.

The camera was soon put to work when we went on our second tour of England. The car (the Ford Prefect had been exchanged for a Vauxhall) went with us this time. It had to be lifted onto the boat by a crane, as there were no proper ferries then. My parents had decided that we would have two weeks holiday in North Devon in a hotel. The hotel was a large Jacobean mansion run by the aristocratic family who had owned it since taking it from the monks in the sixteenth century, and were trying desperately to hang on to it. It was sold later, and the worm turned, for it eventually ended up in the hands of a religious order. We had crossed over to Liverpool and had driven down, spending a night in Malvern, and another one in Somerset. Father had, with the aid of the Automobile Association, prepared a military type plan with each town to be passed through, and all the roads with their numbers and distances marked. We came back via Stonehenge and Reading, where there were people to stay with. We thought that we might get a glimpse of a television set. Mother said that the people in Reading were the sort who might have one, but they didn't. Television was just starting in England, but there was to be no sign of it in Ireland for another few years. In 1953 when Queen Elizabeth was crowned, the few who had sets and could pick up the English telecasts of the event, were considered privileged by Mother, who then, but only then, conceded that the new medium might have some merit.

The following year, that is 1950, we went on a much more ambitious trip. We went for a month to France. The car was again put on board ship by crane, first to Liverpool and then from Southampton to Cherbourg. The first night out from Cherbourg was spent at Nantes, having stopped at Avranches in Normandy for lunch with the delicious novelty of French bread. The founders of the FitzSimon family had been Counts of Avranches prior to 1066. Father wanted to look at the place, though I am sure he wasn't expecting to see relatives walking about in the street. We proceeded to St Palais sur Mer, a small beach resort on the mouth of the Gironde where we stayed in a sort of boarding house. The dinner, which was a good one, was served each evening outside, under a tree. The beach was hot and the sea was warm. A very far cry indeed it was from the summers at Bundoran. A highlight was a visit to the Chateau de Valois at Cognac, where Otard makes the brandy; we all got little sample bottles. A lower light was that a lady was found to give Christopher and me French lessons for an hour or two each day. It may have done us some good, but one cannot learn much in a week, especially if one is not very interested. We had a few more days further down the coast near Arcachon, and then winding up through the Pyrenees to Andorra.

I had read about Andorra in the *National Geographic* and it was one place I wanted to see. My parents didn't enjoy the trip. To Father it was a bore and Mother hated the precipitous mountain passes; she would sit in the car with her head in a book. Andorra was then small and primitive, not the international resort it was to become. There was one big hotel where we stayed, hardly anyone else being there, but there was a strong and pervasive stench of lavatory drains which took the edge off an otherwise excellent steak. It was on this French trip that I first experienced eating good steak. There was plenty of good meat in Ireland, during and after the war, unlike Britain, but in our household, let alone in Garth House, good steak must have been considered too extravagant. All one ever saw, and even that was infrequent, were little thin overdone pieces. On two occasions on this holiday I was to become ill due to my unfamiliarity with the luxurious food.

We then had a week in the Mediterranean at Collioure with more swimming and then started back. We went via Les Eyzies to see the prehistoric rock paintings, to Versailles for a few days to see the standard sights of Paris like going up the Eiffel Tower, and seeing around the palace.

We saw a lot of large dark gloomy cathedrals as we proceeded down and then back up through the country. It seemed to be the thing to do, to look at the cathedral in each town; they all had one. Christopher had a narrow escape at one when a scaffold clip was dropped off a spire hundreds of feet up, hitting the pavement right beside him, and bouncing with a terrific clang. That was somewhere near Boulogne, where the car was again lifted onto a ship. As we waited a young man, who had spotted our car registration, came across and said "How's County Monaghan? I am your neighbour". He was from Dundalk. Tourism was rare in those days. He said he had been to Spain to see the bullfights. Mother smiled at him politely, but there would be no fraternization. She had started to seethe at the idea of supporting bullfighting.

The trip at least confirmed to me what the French language was supposed to sound like. I had had some exposure to spoken French before, but when back at school in French class I had tried to speak with a French accent, Captain Hutton, who was like the lady in Chaucer who spoke the "French of Stratford atte Bow rather than of Paris" told me to stop trying to be funny.

Back from France, I was now to go on to school at St Columba's. I had been destined initially for Wellington in England, as Christopher had been until he was diverted on account of his illness; but now he was so enthusiastic about his life at St Columba's that I was to follow him there. There was also a sign of financial reality. St Columba's was a good deal less expensive than Wellington. It was even possible that St Columba's would be too expensive. I was threatened with being sent to Campbell College in Belfast where the fees were less again. Christopher had enthused me with the idea of St Columba's; the idea of going to Campbell seemed to be appalling. I was entered for the scholarship exam and was awarded an exhibition, which bought the fees down below the Campbell ones. It was reported that, though my work was messy, I had made a good attempt, especially in the Greek paper. It was the Greek which got me through and so stamped my subsequent career. This was ironic for I never tried a word of Greek again. I did not really like Greek, but had taken it up for another reason, a political move. I had discovered that if I was to do Greek as an extra option, I would get out of the otherwise compulsory music class. I did not like the music teacher, a baldheaded man with a squeaky Cork accent and an umbrella, who came some days from Belfast on the train. These attributes on their own would not have upset me, I can't remember why I didn't like him or he me. The price of my exhibition was that though I later realized that I liked music, I had foregone any formal musical education.

It was a practice for Captain Hutton to tell the leavers, as they left, the "facts of life". Needless to say, at 13 or 14 we knew a good amount of them already and knew about the coming lecture. For some reason, perhaps the rush to France, I left Garth House a day early at the end of the final term. So I was to get the lecture on my own. The Captain started by saying that he was not telling me about what to do when I was married, but to warn me of what could happen at my next school. The issue was about buggery. It has been suggested he may have told the story because he was severely buggered himself at Shrewsbury. If my friends had been at his lecture, we would have been sniggering and giggling, but on my own I had to take it as an adult. But when he said he would give me some definitions, and pretentiously said "there are the testicles which you would know as the balls" spoken as if it was the revelation of the world's ultimate secret I was, even though present on my own, crippled with laughter.

The Captain was a remarkable man. Although he was somewhat eccentric, rather dour, occasionally irascible, and probably not greatly liked, he was prepared to give a lot of himself, and we gained a lot from him, for better or worse. He married some years later when he was in his fifties, and when he retired in the mid 1960s, the school was closed down and he went to live in Cork, where he played golf every day. He died in the middle of a game, on the golf course, at an advanced age.

CHAPTER ELEVEN

St Columba's College

St Columba's College is 6 miles south of Dublin city centre. The northern boundary of the grounds has been the South Ring motorway since 2000, the southern boundary is still, as it always was, the almost pristine expanse of the Dublin Mountains. Garth House had a life of a mere thirty years; St Columba's was founded in 1843 and is still going strong.

Unlike Garth House, St Columba's is big enough and has lasted long enough to appear in some literature. G.K. White wrote its history as well as his personal experiences there in *The Last Word*; Michael Campbell's *Lord Dismiss Us* is a novel based on his own time at the school, which greatly annoyed a few people who were not disguised enough, and so recognizable to anyone familiar with the place; William Trevor has written his about his experiences at the school in his memoir *Excursions in the Real World*.

The school catered to a clientele largely drawn from the Dublin and Northern Irish middle classes. In addition, however, it had a wide sprinkling of others, rural southerners, a few of an old aristocratic background, quite a number of English, Lancashire and Cheshire in the main, a couple of Dublin's Jews and a contingent of Iranian Muslims. There were in my day no Roman Catholics, but at other times there were. Roman Catholics would have been required to attend Mass at Rathfarnham on Sundays. Everyone except the Jews and Muslims had to attend chapel services, which were twice a day. If one missed chapel, one had to explain oneself to the headmaster, whose title was the Warden. The chapel was supposed to be at the core of the school's purpose, and being attended twice a day, with a good deal of ritual, certainly had its emphasis, but it did not mark the ethos of the school with much in the way of any bent for theological enquiry or disputation. The school had been founded as a by-product of the English Oxford Movement of the 1830s and 1840s. This movement was a revival, and attempt to rediscover, the Church of England's roots and ancient practices at the expense of some of the excesses of the sixteenth and seventeenth-century Reformation. Some of the movement's leaders eventually converted to Roman Catholicism, including two of St Columba's founders. The movement had a large effect in redirecting the ways and thinking of a great part of the Church of England, but apart from the foundation of St Columba's, which had a very shaky start at that, generally passed the Church of Ireland by.

There were very few prizes given at Columba's. Four or five individuals would get a prize at the annual speech day. These prizes, such few that there were, were likely to be a two guinea book or ancient endowments such as "The Sykes Divinity Prize" or "The Earl of Meath's Prize for Art". This was a significant difference from Garth. Garth had an ethos of competition. At St Columba's, if anything, it was the reverse. At Garth there were prizes for everything, but especially for sport. I had been unfortunate in that twice I missed the sports having broken bones, but on one occasion I won the Junior Diving Prize, and another time I won the Drawing Prize and one prize for being just very good. It was important at Garth to win a football match. At Columba's, it was correct behaviour not to know which side had won a match. At Garth, Captain Hutton would publish a big chart which showed one's position in the school by age and one's rank by class. If one was, say, twentieth by age and thirtieth in class one was obviously not as good as someone thirtieth by age and twentieth by class. Columba's would never have published such a table. A high achiever at Columba's might be respected, but a go-getting pushy type could hardly expect to be popular. Some years after I left Columba's, I ran into Douglas Slator on a train on the way to London. He had been the chaplain and a teacher of English. I remarked that I had seen that Columba's had done exceptionally well in the schools' cup rugby, in a game I had been to see at Lansdowne Road. They had twice drawn in the semi-final with Belvedere, the ultimate winner. Slator did not say "Yes, it was a great achievement." He said, "Oh, that was Greene and his training." He said it with a sort of patronizing smile; he was saying that Greene, who was the captain, had made the team train far harder than normal, and that this was perhaps not a very gentlemanly thing to do, and if they won, it was not at all that important.

During my first year at Columba's all the newcomers, about forty or so, were in a house presided over by an elderly bachelor who was rather a sad case. He was greatly liked by most, as he was kind and unusually gentle. It was said he was paid only £3 a week and not long after I arrived he was "let go", after forty or more years as a teacher. It was rumoured that he would make sexual advances to boys, which seemed to me to be quite unbelievable until he came to try me out. I was shocked, and rejected the advance. He shambled off muttering and never came near me again. He was let go I think for his general indulgence. My real problem with him was that he was the teacher in my first year for History and Geography, and coming straight from Captain Hutton, these were my strongest and favourite subjects. I don't believe he ever tried to teach us anything. He just sat somewhere in the room chatting to someone while we might be dutifully reading or more likely chatting ourselves. My enthusiasm for work was rejected.

Teaching generally was very patchy. There were some very good teachers, but by and large there was a tendency to leave one's progress to oneself. If one was interested and wanted to work, one might get assistance, but not always. My housemaster's approach to the teaching of History and Geography was perhaps the worst, as there was no sign whatever from him of any academic support to a pupil. A new subject was Irish. The teacher, Brooks, was very good at his job. He had the disadvantage of having a client body, the pupils, who saw little use for the subject, and a high proportion, if not the majority, came from families wherein the Irish revival was seen as enemy territory. My mother was quite contemptuous of the Irish language, but it was not long before I was won over to the merits of learning the language. This was the first sign of my Bangor Co. Down Orange indoctrination giving way. We would soon be quoting Gaelic phrases in outside hours and singing snatches of Gaelic poems in the showers, something one would never do with French or Latin, which received much more emphasis, and which boys who had been at prep schools, had been learning for years.

I got off to a good start generally. There was no one from Garth House starting at the same time as me, though there was a sizeable number from Garth at Columba's. However, John Killen, my cousin from Monaghan, who I was seeing a lot during the holidays now that we were living at Annaghmakerrig, started at the same time as me. He provided initial social entrée to his friends coming in from Castlepark, a Dublin prep school which, incidentally, was owned and run by a cousin of his mother; a man who appears to have been as unique as Captain Hutton, though of quite different character.

Another new departure was that the main game was rugby instead of soccer. I took to it quickly, but was disadvantaged against those who had played it before. That summer was my last at cricket, a game I loved, but my eyesight was changing and I gave the game up in despair. If anyone had thought of giving me an eye test and a pair of spectacles then, I am sure I would have continued. So in the summer it had to be track and field only; however my ego was much enhanced, when at the school sports, with, a leap of nearly 5 feet, I won the junior high jump. I did not this time break an arm, as previously I had, on two occasions, at Garth House when attempting to leap over an obstacle.

I don't believe that Captain Hutton ever made us learn poetry, but during my first year at Columba's I had to, both in French and English, as well as Irish (the latter was more enjoyable). I found this very tough, but I am sure it was good for us. I am sure that learning Latin was good for us too; as both Latin and learning poetry have disappeared from most curricula, life must now be easier for students, but I doubt that it is better for them.

In the second year our English teacher was Oisin Kelly and what a breath of fresh air that was. I had already met him as the Art teacher. Art was his real subject and when eventually he became recognized as the most talented sculptor in the country, he left teaching for full-time work in that profession. Art could have been an important direction for me, but it never took off. I took up sculpture, or rather wood carving, but had a great setback when a slip of the chisel took off the nose of an otherwise very excellent head I had made. I don't think I ever recovered. It was a repeat of an unsuccessful foray into carpentry at Garth House. One term Captain Hutton had introduced carpentry as an extra subject, supervised by the carpenter who was always coming to mend the broken windows. I made a cigarette box with a sliding lid. When I had finished it, the Captain lent me his packet of cigarettes to try it out, but it mangled beyond use all twenty of them. He was annoyed to the point that I rather think that I was expelled from the class rather than voluntarily resigning.

When I cut the nose off the head I was not sacked from the Art class. I found the Art class disappointing because Kelly, like the History teacher, didn't seem to take any interest in what one did. Unlike the History teacher this was not indolence – he was as likely as not absorbed in making something himself. Maybe, as is sometimes the case, he was too good at his subject to be a good teacher of it. His English classes however, were brilliant. Most of our teachers tended to treat us 15 year olds as children and avoided anything controversial, such as the topics barred from an officers' mess, like Sex, Politics and Religion. Kelly would insist that we behave like adults, no sniggering or giggling at the dirty bits, and introduced lecture and debate on all topics from all angles. He could sometimes shock the more strait-laced and conservative, and most of us were that to some extent. He was not radical or nihilist, but with patience and forbearance, he was, in fact, a supporter of the Church of Ireland, and to the mystification of the northern Unionists, favoured Irish independence. Any institution or any ideas would be subject to analysis and criticism. His wit was often evident, complex and ironical. Appreciating Kelly and his classes was a breakthrough in intellectual development; I see this in my own case as to have been a privilege, but that may have been the contrast with most of the rest of the class work. There were of course pupils who remained impervious to Kelly.

My second year intellectual development was patchy; Kelly's contribution was on the plus side, but on the minus side I lost interest in Latin, and that was to wither away. I had taken to smoking a pipe with plug tobacco, and during the Latin class, which was the class before morning break, I devoted my time to cutting my plug and filling the pipe, quite an intricate operation.

Smoking the pipe was a symptom of another development, the teenage rebellion. Smoking was the most heinous of common misdemeanours and was automatically punishable with a severe beating. It was known even in those days that smoking was no good for one's health, though direct links with lung cancer and heart disease were not well established and were not known at all to the public at large. There was however a curious hypocrisy around the habit of smoking and social control. Many of the staff, including the Warden, were smokers. Smoking was still a mark of the sophisticated adult. In those days, before stepping into polite society, one had to learn the proper etiquette of offering a cigarette from a silver cigarette case, preferably with one's crest on it, never from a packet. Rebellious teenagers were only trying to become adults and were set on for committing the impertinence. I was caught smoking only once, and that was by no less a person than the Warden himself. A number of us were in a garden shed near the sports fields, puffing away, when we heard the Warden's voice outside. We froze in fear and stubbed out our butts lest he should look inside and that is what he did. He was quite surprised, looking at us sitting silently in the shed, and looked from one to the other of us saying our names "Lee, Scott, Killen, FitzSimon", and then it dawned on him what we were up to "and a fine smell of tobacco smoke too" he said. We were then sent to our housemasters for the due chastisement. My housemaster, G.K. White, who himself smoked, and with a long cigarette holder at that, similar to those used by ladies in films about 1930s salons, set about to give me six strokes, the maximum, but he miscounted and gave me seven. "Horse" Scott who was waiting outside for his turn had a look of horror on his face when I came out, for he had counted the strokes and could hardly believe it. Perhaps I should have complained at the excessive punishment, but I was really rather pleased, as to have had "seven" was a unique distinction. It didn't stop me from smoking; it would be many years before I gave it up.

That year in the school was a tough one for the authorities. Smoking was deemed to be bad enough, but an epidemic of lawlessness broke out, and if it hadn't been contained, control might have been lost totally. The containment was effective, the end was good for most of us and especially the school, but the means in obtaining the end was not an honourable one. One of the boys who had been a partaker in much of the mischief and who knew about a lot more, wrote it all up in a diary which he lost, and which found its way into the hands of one of the masters. The dishonour was not that action should have been taken, but it was the technique of interrogation which would have done justice to the Gestapo. One by one, individuals mentioned in the diary were faced with allegations of misdemeanours without knowing where the allegations had come from and hence they had no means of defence.

The misdemeanours worse than smoking included going out from the dormitory and roaming around the district in the middle of the night. Though I was invited on such adventures I never partook: once in bed I wouldn't want to get out of it until I had to. Going to pubs was another. I had been to Lamb Doyles and Rockbrook, a mile or so from the gate, and had on such occasions a portion of a bottle of Macardles or Cairnes ales, which was actually more than just an offence against school rules, but illegal underage drinking. I was not accused of this; I was however taken to task for going to the cinema. It cost only a few pence on Sunday afternoon at the Odeon in Dundrum, and it had become a regular expedition by the time we were caught. Apart from the feature, there was an exciting serial – "Flash Gordon and Ming the Merciless" – so we couldn't miss the next episode. One time when the lights were on I counted twenty-eight naughty Columbans present. There were cases reported in the diary of boys who had "borrowed" cars in the middle of the night for joy riding and pilfering from surrounding estates; there were tomatoes from Mr Love of Marley's greenhouses. One boy came back the proud possessor of a fireman's axe, and another with an electric motor, whatever they intended to do with them.

The witch hunts led to a number of expulsions, and some boys, though not thrown out on the spot, were told not to come back the next term. I was one of several who were "gated"; that is we were not allowed beyond the school boundary for the whole of the Summer Term and had to attend special roll calls. I suffered from my punishment, and though I never forgave the Warden for the way he made use of the diary, I was I believe deflected from a downward direction in delinquency with whatever dire consequences that might have had.

My third year at Columba's had a traumatic start. The first game of rugby of the season put me out of all sport for the next two terms. A large and plump boy tackled me from behind just as I was about to score. He landed on my foot such as to twist it at right angles to my leg which was given a very nasty break. I was carried away to a shed and then an ambulance brought me to the Adelaide Hospital. I was sedated and it was hours later when I woke up in a ward bed with my leg in plaster. It turned out that I had a friend in the ward, one of my comrades in crime of the previous year. I don't know what he was there for, but he was mobile and able to run messages which he did for me and the other inmates who were all old men: farmers with hernias were the most common. He even had some whiskey, which was of great comfort. How or where he got it from I cannot think; it would have been every bit as illicit in the hospital ward as at school. I was in the hospital for a week and I think quite happy there. I can only remember the visitors, apart from a nice nurse called Nurse Mansfield. The school chaplain Slator came to visit, as did the housemasters White and Hutchinson, and my grandmother FitzSimon, who would have been 81 that year, came on the 44 Bus with her hair freshly dyed. There was a visit from the rector of St Peter's, one Revd Dowse, the local clergyman. He told me that he had been at school at St Columba's but had sent his sons to Portora because the Warden, the one before my time, had been so dreadful. We also had for our spiritual sustenance a visit from a group or choir of evangelicals (the Adelaide was a Protestant hospital), who sang hymns one of which went "Heavenly Sunshine, Heavenly Sunshine, Heavenly Sunshine, Jesus is Mine".

I went back to school with crutches and didn't have the plaster taken off until the end of term just before Christmas. The cast of the plaster gave me two privileges: one was that as I couldn't have showers, I could use the masters' bathroom with its bath. I took pleasure in wallowing in the bath, the door being locked so that occasional masters who tried, failed to get in. The other privilege, though it was not meant to be a privilege, was that I didn't have to line up with the mob in the cloisters to march into Chapel. I would hobble in advance in my own time to a place a bit out of the way, near the organ and the choir, and hobble out in my own time. It was then and only then that my musical education slowly started. I discovered that I liked the sound of the organ and even more so the choir.

One couldn't avoid exposure to pop music and I remember snatches of songs of the day, but it was at this same time I had the opportunity by way of the radio, that I developed a love affair with the Irish ballad. McCoy, who came from Tyrone, and I would listen regularly to "The Ballad Makers' Saturday Night" on Radio Eireann.

Immobilized by the plaster for a whole term, and for the following term going about with a walking stick, apart from having uncomfortable sessions of physiotherapy, there was plenty of time to read and study in the library, when everyone else was doing something physical and strenuous. I tried hard with my History but the odds were against it. The first year, History had been so non-existent that I do not remember what sort of History it was. In the second year it was more rigorous, but I found it somewhat trying. After I had left school, the teacher told me that he had made a point of making the classes interesting and not to fill our minds with ancient battles, as had happened to him when young. He went on to become a successful barrister, and his classes may have been interesting to him, but I am sure I would have preferred to hear about the battles of Clontarf and the Yellow Ford and the Heights of Abraham, than about Praemunire and Acts of Attainder.

By the Summer Term, I was out of the plaster, but not up to taking much part in games. One had, however, the Dublin Mountains rising up from the back boundary to roam around. The school rules were that one was not allowed out of the grounds northward towards the city, but one could go as far as one liked into the mountains, theoretically all the way to Wexford. Usually one had the mountains to oneself, the whins, the heather and the views over the city and beyond. There was a stream in a hidden glen with a deep pool in it, known to us as Damnation where one could swim. There, a group of us ran into politics in the making. We came across a number of men in a quarry, who appeared to have rifles and were performing a military drill, left turns, right turns, shoulder arms to the commands of their officer. We watched in amazement from the cover of some whins at the extraordinary scene; nobody could guess who these people were. Then one of our group stood up and shouted some wisecracks which caused the troops to break ranks, and some of them to start to run in our direction. We scattered and ran as if for our lives, but found it was more than just a game when we heard shots fired behind us and what sounded like bees over our heads as the bullets flew past us. We retreated to the college, but having come across where the troops had left their bicycles, we let the air out of all the tyres and considered we had won the battle. One of us reported the incident to the authorities, and a car load of Gardai came up to take notes. They said that they knew who the troops were. This was not the only time we came across men doing manoeuvres on the mountain, but I do not remember thinking of it again until the following year, when a raid on a police barracks in Fermanagh resulted in the death of a man from Monaghan and another from Limerick. This was the start of a revived IRA campaign after a long quiet period. The campaign was to go on for several years until De Valera was re-elected in 1957, and shut most of them up in Portlaoise Jail.

In my third year, my own reading was supplementary to the classes of Mr Hutchinson, an Englishman and former cavalry officer, who went on to become a clergyman. He was also an assistant housemaster and ran the debating society to which he introduced me that year. The problem was that History was only a half subject. The high flyers went to study Physics and Chemistry or German. Those people who were not up to such rigours, could do an easier course in General Science along with a little History. I chose the latter, not for the ease of the science, but so that I could stand my ground in History. Geography had disappeared entirely, though that year the Warden taught it to some, so as to keep in his hand at teaching. I think he admitted that he didn't know very much himself. I couldn't go to his classes because of clashes, but I was allowed to sit the GCE and Intermediate exams nevertheless, and got one up on the Warden by getting the highest marks in the school, without the benefits of his tutelage.

At the end of the year we did two sets of exams, the Irish Intermediate and the English GCE "O" Levels. We were really a year late doing these exams. This was because, for the Irish Intermediate, the Irish Language had to be passed if one was to get a certificate; we were coming from behind. Most candidates in the Republic would have been learning Irish for eight or nine years. Very few at Columba's would have had more than three years. The GCE had a more flexible arrangement. One passed individual subjects any of which theoretically could be done any year. If one was to proceed to an English university, one needed a certain number of subjects at Ordinary Level, and some, usually two, at Advanced Level. In those days one could get into Trinity College Dublin with "O" Levels only. Trinity was where most of us who were to go on to tertiary studies would go. There were always a few who went to Queen's in Belfast and of my contemporaries, only a few went anywhere else. Cambridge, Edinburgh, Paris and Cork were represented however with one each. Over half the leavers would not go to university. Articles with a firm of accountants were common and for some reason I do not know what, we were a supplier of officers to the Rhodesian police. There were several who would put in a couple of years in the British Army or the Royal Air Force, but only one or two from my time made a career of it. One boy joined the Irish Navy.

Many of us came back for another year, even having finished with exams. The idea that a school education had more to it than the passing of exams was, if not prevalent, quite common. I came back as a "house captain". The Warden had cynically said to me, "I see that Mr White (my housemaster) is taking a bit of a risk making you a house captain". He, the Warden, had little respect for me and I, for that matter, did not have too much respect for him.

If Columba's was not a power house of academic or sporting achievement, or an institution of discipline and hard work, it had other beneficial attributes. From time to time a scholar or artist of distinction came out of it. Even an occasional sporting hero, and in recent years a pop star of world standing, came forth, but generally it was a place of mediocrity. This mediocrity was however qualified by a general decency in the way people treated each other which is not always universal in such institutions or amongst their alumni. The school had been founded as a religious institution, but very quickly took on the form of the English public school, and never could quite make up its mind that that was what it wanted to be. There were times when it almost collapsed and disappeared altogether. There was a conflict between a pretension to greatness and an underlying tendency to extreme inefficiency; indeed it could be quite lackadaisical. Apart from my experience of the dishonorable behaviour of the Warden in the Diary Scandal of 1952, my abiding experience was that it was a friendly place for staff and pupils alike. I never came across a case of physical bullying, but though rare, there were instances of a more subtle psychological bullying, when an individual would be picked on by a group. My first year, I suffered a bit of that, but not for long, though that year some boys mocked a rather effeminate newcomer to the point where his parents found that they had to take him away. When it became known what had happened, the mockers were quite contrite.

The prefectorial system, whereby much of the day to day organization and supervision was in the hands of senior boys, worked well. I have heard it said in other schools that senior boys could not be trusted to supervise juniors. The ethos at Columba's was such that the idea of seniors abusing juniors was hardly thinkable. The role of the house captain was to think first of his charges' welfare. If his charges were to behave too badly, he would send them to the school prefect who, as he had a higher rank in the hierarchy, had the authority to use the cane, or to the housemaster. I only once had occasion to refer a recalcitrant for punishment; I had become exasperated with a boy who refused to take notice of my request to stop throwing butter at other boys at the tea table. The prefect, in his wisdom, decided that throwing butter or upsetting my equilibrium didn't warrant punishment more than a little talking to, so I finished my year with a clean slate, by serendipity, never having been instrumental in having a boy beaten.

There was legitimate enjoyment in my last year, especially of sport: I was on the rugby, swimming and athletic teams. The away matches, where one would stay overnight at another school, were always highlights. Normally we played against other Dublin schools, but the first teams would go as far as Belfast, Dungannon and Enniskillen. I particularly liked going to Campbell College in Belfast where I saw many of my old friends from Garth House. We all liked Dungannon, which seemed to be rather rowdy and irreverent and after our own hearts. Portora in Enniskillen we thought to be a bit stuck up, and we were genuinely surprised to find Portorans thinking that their school was the best one in Ireland. Surely everyone knew that Columba's was? Coming back from Enniskillen on the train was the last time I was to travel on that railway line, now that we were no longer living at Annaghmakerrig. The line was to close a few years later. We stopped in Clones for at least an hour, so I was able to direct some of the team onto my home ground, up Fermanagh Street, to a suitable pub. Coming back from Belfast on the train one time, was the night after the last international rugby match played at Ravenhill until recent world championships. There was much drinking and singing by all on the train from one end of it to the other. We were accompanied by a new rugby master, Mr Dibdin, recently arrived from Oxford, who became quite agitated when he couldn't stop his charges from mingling freely with the revelling stout-swilling football supporters.

There were some quite illegal expeditions at the end of the third term, which involved driving cars. Among those of us about to leave was Dan Brownlow. Dan was a proud fellow and not always the most diplomatic. He liked to cut some style. We had both been in London during the Easter holidays: he was staying in the Cumberland Hotel, and when he was about to go home, a coloured waistcoat he had ordered from a tailor in Savile Row, was not ready. I was ordered to collect it when it was ready. The tailor asked me if I would like it delivered to my hotel, but I said that I preferred to collect it myself; I did not want to admit to this "By appointment to the Royal Family" tailor that I was staying in a communist hostel in Paddington which cost me 35 shillings a week, breakfast included. The waistcoat cost what would have been for me two weeks wages.

Dan's father had died recently, and had left him with a business which he would very soon have to attend to, but in the meantime he had a large and powerful car. It was a school rule that even if one had a driving licence, one was not allowed to drive during term time. Normally this rule was irrelevant, as so few would have access to a car anyway. Dan kept his car in the yard along with other staff and visitors' cars for the last few weeks of term. Though some suspicions were aroused, it wasn't until after we had left that the adults grasped the enormity of the impertinence, that the car belonged to a pupil, and was in frequent use for driving his friends into town and elsewhere.

There were only two places where one could get something to eat in Dublin after about 1.00 a.m. We got to know them, for that was the adventure. The adventures were kept sufficiently secret, not only to avoid the authorities, but also to avoid the undermining (by such contemptuous example) of our own authority in carrying out our prefectorial duties. Most of the adventurers were house captains or prefects.

Despite my final couple of weeks at school, during which I regressed towards earlier delinquency, I got away with a clean sheet. The Warden made a little speech to us leavers to the effect it was the first time since he had arrived five years before, that there was no one who he was glad to see the back of at the year end. I had never really come to terms with the man, but this admission mollified me somewhat. It was with my housemaster G.K. White that I made a point of keeping in touch with for the next thirty years, until he died.

CHAPTER TWELVE

Holidays

My last family summer holiday was in 1951. It was really only a half family holiday. Father did not come and Christopher went on to France, where he was to spend a month learning French as an exchange student. Mother drove down to Dunmore East in Co. Waterford. We had with us the dog and a French girl, who was staying with us at Annaghmakerrig. Dunmore had been chosen because the Butlers had a cottage there, a sort of prefab called Crab Cottage, and Mother took a small terraced house nearby for a week or two. Peggy and Julia were at Crab and had with them the Perrys from Offaly. Phil Perry, Hubert Butler and Father were absent, whatever their excuses, but Hubert did come down for at least a day or two. Maiden Hall in Kilkenny was not far away. One day we went with Hubert to Passage where he gave a lecture (in a wet and windswept field) to a few local historians with their family and friends in attendance, about the Swiss Colony of New Geneva, established there in the eighteenth century. It wasn't all wind and rain at Dunmore, and there was plenty of sea bathing, but one wet day I went on the bus to Waterford with Julia to the cinema; it was a film about the dog "Lassie". Back at Annaghmakerrig, it must have been another hot summer, for the lake that year was unusually warm.

We were back in August, for that is when the Royal Black Preceptory, the higher order of Orangemen, has its parade. We went to the parade at Aghabog Church. The French girl, Monique, said she shouldn't go to a non-Catholic religious event, but Mother said there was nothing much religious about Orangemen, so Monique came. Somehow or other she became entangled in the ranks of marching men and couldn't get out from among them until these serious besuited men, with their splendid sashes, had marched into the church, with her in the middle of them. Their strong faces said nothing, but inwardly they would have seethed at the indignity. Would it have improved their humour if they had known that this female interloper in their ritual was also a Papist?

The following Christmas there were two weddings, one in London and one in Edinburgh. The London one was in Westminster Abbey: the bride, a cousin on the Elliot side, had been one of Mother's bridesmaids. At the Edinburgh one, the bride was one of the Australian Killens. Mother, Father, Christopher and I went over by way of the boat from Belfast and the train to Euston. The wedding in the abbey was not a case of marrying into the Royal Family, but the groom was a master at Westminster School, so the privilege was extended. We didn't have carriages or the Household Cavalry, but we did have the abbey choir. Christopher was left in London to attend some academy for the rest of the vacation. There were aspirations of sending him to Cambridge, but it was recognized at St Columba's that he wouldn't get enough marks to pass in there. The rest of us went on the very long train journey to Edinburgh via Lancaster. Whereas I remember the Westminster Abbey wedding, I don't remember the actual ceremony in Edinburgh, but I do remember the reception in the George Hotel. There were a lot of tall men in kilts, who would no doubt have consumed whisky; as they carried out Donald, the groom, they jammed him in the revolving doors, which did enough damage to his back for him to have trouble with it for a long time after. Diana, the bride, was the daughter of Eric Killen who bred shorthorn cattle in New South Wales. She had been sent by him to the Perth Show to buy a bull, and there met Donald who was to sell her one. Eric made a long speech, extolling the virtues of the Empire and of shorthorn cattle; it was not always clear which he was talking about. We came home by way of the Glasgow boat. The Clyde was still in the post-war shipbuilding frenzy and it was a sight to see all this activity mile after mile along the river.

The next summer I was to set off without any of the family. The idea of going to the Gaeltacht to improve upon one's Irish was not common among Columbans, but somehow my friend Noel Hamilton and I had it in our heads that it was a thing to do. Hamilton came from Co. Donegal: his parents ran the Hamilton Hotel in Bundoran, so the Donegal Gaeltacht was in our sights, though it is nowhere near Bundoran. Mr Brooks (the Irish teacher) put us in touch with a clergyman, the Revd Coslett Quinn, who was a Gaelic scholar with contacts in Donegal, who in turn gave us the address of Big Nora McGinley on Gola Island. Mr Brooks wrote a letter in Irish to Big Nora, who replied in English saying that we could stay with her for £3 a week each, but please write in English, for though they spoke Irish on Gola, they weren't too good at reading or writing it.

Father took me and my bicycle to Clones where I took the train to Enniskillen. I then rode the bicycle along the south shore of Lough Erne to Bundoran. The journey took most of the day. The next week was spent in the luxury of the Hamilton Hotel, treated not only as a family guest, but as a hotel guest able to choose my breakfast from the menu and having it sent up to my bedroom. Other decadent activities included playing slot machines in the Fun Parlour across the road.

It was another full-day trip the length of Donegal from Bundoran to Gola; actually it took us two days. We were dropped off by car at Ballyshannon, a bus took us to Donegal Town, a little diesel railcar took us over Barnes gap to Stranorlar where, after a long wait, there was another bus trip to Letterkenny, and then the final bus ride through the mountains to Bunbeg. In the evening, when we arrived at Bunbeg harbour, the weather was too bad for the boat to come over from the island. Next day Joe McGinley, Big Nora's son, tracked us down to the B&B where we had stayed the night, and we were off to the island in his motorboat. He said that the waves had been too big for the motorboat the day before, and he could have come over in a curragh, but thought that we might be nervous in it.

There were fifty families living on the island then, but it is now uninhabited. The houses were clustered on one corner, with fields of potatoes and oats and grass laid out on a rundale system covering about half the island, the rest being bog and mountain. The McGinleys were one of a half dozen families who had two-storey houses and were also owners of a big motor boat which would go out fishing into the deep sea. Big Nora told me the house was built in 1910, and that she had carried the planks on her back from the beach. Joe had just finished helping build a concrete jetty paid for by the council. He, like most on the island, had put in years of labouring work in Scotland. The daughter of the house, Eileen, had also worked in Scotland for a Jewish family, and she knew all about Jewish food. Hamilton and I were well fed, and thought that the islanders had a high standard of living, but Eileen eventually said that it was our presence which accounted for the meat and other luxuries. There was no electricity, but at that time there was none at Annaghmakerrig either. The population was not big enough to warrant the presence of a doctor, but there was a little school. It was about 3 miles in the boat to Bunbeg Harbour, so the islanders had to be fairly self-contained. Quite a few boats would go over on Sunday for Mass, but I had the impression that it was a minority of the population which did so.

The original idea that we would improve our Irish was wishful thinking. A couple of weeks in a household where English was fully understood would hardly have been effective. The only real attempts I made at communication in Irish were with a 5 year old grandson of Big Nora known as "Thady Beag" (little Thady) who I would chase and play hide and seek with. Only a few old people and the very young were not bilingual. I did at least learn to distinguish the Donegal Irish accent, along with a few phrases, from that of Munster which was the one Mr Brooks taught. I doubt that the trip improved my exam marks, but living among these people certainly widened my view on the world. One might think that going to Gola in 1952 would have been a step into earlier times, but it was nothing like the going back in time of the move to Mount Callan in 1948. Gola was too tied to Glasgow to be as culturally remote as pre-industrial West Clare, despite the language difference.

The next summer, rather than an expedition to explore isolated Gaelic roots, the net would be cast further afield into quite a different world of international and continental culture by way of an expedition to a work camp in Holland. In the winter of 1953, catastrophic storms and high tides burst the dykes along the Dutch coast, inundating great areas of the land which was below sea level, causing millions of pounds worth of damage, and quite a lot of lives were lost. The family of my school friend Jeremy Taylor knew Terry Trench, who was a friend of the Butlers and who I had met at Annaghmakerrig, and who was a founder of, and power in, An Oige, the Irish Youth Hostel Association. Trench set out to recruit volunteers from An Oige to go to help the Dutch rebuild a youth hostel which had been washed away. Jeremy recruited me. The deal was that we would get free bed and board and that the return fare from Dublin to Rotterdam was only £8. A normal fare would have been three times that, but what we had were the drovers' quarters in a cattle boat. This travel deal was available to people in the know who would be discreet. It was due to a union feather-bedding practice. The union rule was that there would be so many drovers on the ship, but as there was no need for them – the crew considered that they were in the way – the drovers were quite content to draw their wages and stay at home.

There were four lads or rather grown men, from Drogheda, which is where Trench lived. Jeremy and I were the only teenagers. We were all taken in hand by the ship's steward, who must have appreciated our company, for he served us out all the beer and gin available. At some point in the evening's drinking, he was explaining how in Holland a man wears his engagement ring on one hand and shifts it to the other when he marries, Catholics go right hand to left hand, Protestants left to right, or perhaps it is vice versa. One of the Drogheda lads said "What about Presbyterians?" whereupon I gave an explanation that Presbyterians were a class of Protestant. I noticed that the Drogheda lads seemed to hang very respectfully on my explanation. It came to light as the drinking proceeded that their respect for my ecclesiastical knowledge stemmed from their belief that we were not from St Columba's, of which they hadn't heard, but from St Columban's, a seminary near Drogheda run by the Maynooth Mission to China. Indeed one of the lads had enjoined the others to mind their language, so as not to upset the young missionaries. All the drink on the ship was finished somewhere off the Isle of Wight. I was quite ill, despite the sea being as calm as a millpond, but the nauseous smell of the cattle was as much the cause as the drink.

After we landed at Rotterdam, the steward led us all out on a tour, which included a couple of pubs. A lot of Rotterdam was still flat from the wartime bombing, but it was still an impressive and lively place compared to Dublin, let alone Drogheda. How could he return the stewards' hospitality moaned one of the lads "What could I show him in Drogheda? St Mary's Arches?"

We split up. Jeremy and I and one of the Drogheda contingent, Pat Walsh, a carpenter who was going to emigrate to New Zealand, were destined for a camp in Zeeland in the south. The Youth Hostel had enough volunteers, so we went to a camp run by SCI (Service Civil International). This body, which had an English branch called IVSP (International Voluntary Service for Peace), was founded by a Swiss called Ralph Hagenauer, and organized work camps all over Europe and beyond to house volunteers to do worthy work. The emphasis was not so much to get work done but to collect people from different countries to work together. Facilities at our camp were fairly basic. There were dormitories with bunks in a very limited space, not much in the way of hot water and we were up for breakfast at six o'clock. For breakfast we had hot black tea and cold porridge, and for supper it was cold black tea and hot porridge. We did get more than this, such as black bread and sausage. It was nevertheless a fun place. There was singing and folk dancing in the evening. An American girl tried to teach me the Virginia Reel, but I never could get the hang of it. It so happened that Ralph Hagenauer himself had elected to stay at this particular camp while we were there, and there were a number of visitors like himself, who gave lectures and led discussions on such topics as apartheid in South Africa and trade unions in East Germany. The work, though not heavy, could be monotonous. I was first set to work to paint the steel sheet piles driven into the gaps in the dyke with bitumen. In the wind, I had bitumen blown into my eyes one day, so I was taken off that and spent the rest of the time in a garage cleaning the mud and rust off agricultural implements which had been salvaged from the flood. This was not much fun, but as there were always several of the volunteers working there, there was plenty of opportunity for chat, which was not possible on the sea wall. I remember a pair of Algerians, an Austrian and a Norwegian, probably the first of those nationalities I had ever met.

One day the Queen of the Netherlands came to visit and flags were waved at her car. She pronounced the gap in the dyke on which I had been painting the sheet piles, officially closed. There were a lot of reporters following the Queen, and Jeremy and I were singled out for interview, maybe because we were the youngest in the camp, and duly written about in the main Rotterdam newspaper. We were asked something silly and gave equally silly replies. One theme was whether a pair of teenagers thought that they could come across the sea and save the world. I don't remember our replies. Perhaps it wasn't such a silly question and I was just too young to appreciate it, or appreciate how SCI was an idealistic pacifist movement. I hadn't come to save the world, only to help fix a youth hostel and have a holiday at the same time.

Our planned time at the camp was cut short by a week. Pat Walsh had heard from the other Drogheda lads that the ship was to sail a week early. Jeremy and I had always intended to spend a couple of days in Amsterdam, so we left immediately and after Amsterdam, went to the shipping company office in Rotterdam. We found out that the ship was not to leave early, and later, when they showed up, we were to learn that the Drogheda lads had had enough of their camp and gone off to drink in Dusseldorf. They invented the early departure of the ship to save themselves embarrassment, but it was inconvenient for Jeremy and me. Not that I minded as it was all part of the adventure, but we were seriously short of funds and had to sleep out in a wood for some nights and live off dry bread and sausage. We did however manage quite a bit of sightseeing which we would not have done if we had stayed in the camp.

On the trip back, there was the worst storm of the season in the English Channel. I didn't need any drink or smelly cattle to be sick all the way. The worst thing was that the drovers' cabins were right in the bow, where the anchor hung, and as we plunged over each wave, the anchor would clang into the side of the ship just near my head.

Oddly enough, I had learned quite a bit of Dutch in the short time. I also learned quite a lot about conscientious objection and peace movements, which, though never converting me to pacifism, would give me a lean in that direction from time to time.

Towards the end of my last Easter Term at school, I was in conversation one day with two of my schoolmates, Mather and Graham, who lived in England, and learned how they had been looking at the idea of working during the vacation. The idea of working in a menial job and being paid was a new concept; I had never heard of it among any of my other associates, especially because we were in Ireland where if there was any work available, it was for those who would need it. One had only come across the idea of working one's way through college from American films. Mather and Graham talked about Lyons Corner Houses, whose main business was cheap self-service restaurants in London, as a place where one could get a vacation job. Oddly enough, when I spoke to Father about it, it turned out that he knew one of the Lyons directors, who had been in his regiment during the war. Father wrote to this man, who wrote back saying I should report in to the Lyons Head Office near Oxford Street.

My parents had paid for my trip to Holland the year before. This time I did my own financing by way of selling my bicycle. I sold it to Fred Farmer who was a groundsman at the school, for the fare to London via Holyhead, which was less than £2. I had a place to stay at Notting Hill Gate, thanks to Edward Fitzgerald, the last of the line of Fighting Fitzgerald of Turlough in Co. Mayo; he referred to it as his communist hostel, and it would cost only 5 shillings for bed and breakfast. When I arrived there, I discovered it was run, not by the communists, but by the same organization of peace activists that I had been with in Holland. It was quite comfortable and quite a fun place, and it would serve me as my London club on subsequent visits.

I reported in to Lyons Head Office and was straightaway put into their training school in the same building. The class for the two-day course in learning how to use the commercial cooking machines (there was something called a bain-marie), was made up of a few young women who were embarking on permanent employment, and three youths of my age, who like me, were just there for the school vacation. They were from Dulwich College, which is a public school and it was important for them to know if I was from a public school or a grammar school. Coming from Ireland, I didn't know the difference, but when I said public school, they were quite content to accept me.

After my training I was sent to work at the Lyons self-service restaurant in the Strand. Having been brought into the company by a director rather than from the Labour Exchange, I was to start a step up the ladder, earning £4 5*s*. per week instead of £4 – the extra 5 shillings was for the responsibility of working the till. Being under eighteen, I had to have a special statutory break with a glass of milk; the manageress would hound me to make sure I had it. She may have been concerned about my welfare, but maybe it was fear of the union if she didn't see to it. Besides me, the staff was all female except for one Australian who had been drifting about Europe since the end of the war. He was the kitchen porter and the two of us would retreat to the male locker room, where the female management dare not intrude, to eat odd bits of pilfered food, and to smoke. His best time, he said was in the war in Italy, where a woman could be had for a packet of cigarettes or a tin of corn beef. Pilfering food was not really necessary, as one was entitled to a full meal, two if one's shift spanned the meal times.

The only onerous task was cleaning out, every day, a machine with little intricate tubes which made the coffee. Otherwise it was an enjoyable job; one got to know regular customers who were terribly pleased when one remembered what they liked "The usual today, Sir?" Once, Father's friend the director, called to see how I was getting on. I think I may have been there under false pretences, since he had it in his head that he was starting me on a permanent career. The manageress was very impressed and wanted to know why Mr Lindsay had come to see me.

Dan Brownlow and Alec Johnston, close friends from school, also came in to mock and laugh at me. Alec was over with his parents and sister from Derry staying in a hotel and, by chance, staying in the same one, was Dan in his own solitary glory. Alec and I would go to Hyde Park Corner where we were greatly taken with the speakers, and would heckle a couple of them with whom we profoundly disagreed. Dan would not lower himself to such behaviour. I would also see quite a lot of Joe Hone, who had left school and was working in his uncle's bookshop in South Kensington, and once I dined in Soho with Tony Guthrie who lived in London. He didn't live in Annaghmakerrig until some time after his mother died. He asked me if there was an *esprit de corps* amongst the ladies in Lyons, and I was embarrassed because I did not know what the phrase meant. In all there was a lot fitted into the month long vacation and the trip even showed a financial profit, enough to start the next excursion at the end of the Summer Term.

John Corbett, our neighbour in Glencullen (we had moved there from Annaghmakerrig the previous year), knew a vet in Herefordshire who would canvas his clients, the farmers of the area, for offers of work for a few of us. By the end of term there was a firm offer from a Mr Edmonds of Upper Wick, Worcester.

I recruited David Nowlan, David Blackwell, and Michael Morgan, all from my house, and all leaving school that year. Nowlan and I set off together on the Liverpool boat. It was so crowded there was nowhere to sit down, even on the deck. The only place I could find to sit was on a winch, which was hard to stay on when one nodded off to sleep. Next day we set off to hitch-hike to Worcester, but started by bus to Chester to get clear of the city, and were then lucky enough to get a ride in a van to Birmingham. It was getting late so we did the last leg to Worcester by train. Blackwell and Morgan came later. We all left at different times, and I stayed for more than two months.

We stayed in an annexe of the farmhouse and were fed in the kitchen. We were well looked after. Mrs Edmonds cooked the meals which were good and varied, apart from the breakfast which was good but never varied, as it was always based on ham. One could have as much ham as one wanted. It all came from the farm pigs, which one sometimes had the great privilege to feed and the lesser privilege to clean out when the full-time pig man was not there. There was to be a harvest of barley later, and a few cattle grazed down near the river, and of course there were the pigs, but the main business of the farm was growing fruit and vegetables. There were five men, full-time workers, but the fruit harvest needed many more; the four of us made a significant contribution; it was obvious that it was difficult to get casual labour. Besides us there was a stream of various harvesters passing through.

The first harvest was that of the broad beans. Blackwell proved to be the most efficient at that: he could fill the boxes quicker than anyone else. We were paid piece work. Next came plums, a trickier exercise – the skill was in moving one's ladder to the right places. There were a lot of plum trees and the plum harvest went on for a long time. One occasionally had a break from picking if one was detailed to go with the truck to the cannery at Pershore. There should have been a good harvest of blackberries, but a rumour was going around Liverpool, the main market, that humans could get myxomatosis from blackberries. This was a disease which had been introduced to wipe out rabbits. There was a good harvest of damsons, and then it was general work until hop-picking started. As well as Upper Wick Farm, which was just beyond the Worcester city limits (one could walk into the city if one missed the bus), the Edmonds had another farm over the border in Herefordshire, where occasionally we went to do something or other. When hop-picking started, an encampment of gypsies sprang up beside the Herefordshire farm. They had come to do the picking. Mr Edmonds was glad to have them, but was always worried that something would go wrong. He had stories of fights in the camp, and how just about anything within miles could disappear in the night, with the consequence that the police were continual visitors. Once they found in the camp a roll of telephone wire, 3 miles of which had disappeared from a nearby roadway during the night.

At Upper Wick we managed without gypsies. Hops were the most important business of the farm. In earlier times people had to pick the little green buds off the vines, a very labour-intensive exercise. Thousands of families would migrate for the season from the congestion of London to the hopyards of Kent to get some fresh air as well as make a bit of money. It is only in Kent and around Worcester that the climate is right for hops. Attempts to grow them in Ireland have failed. Hops act as a preservative in the beer and also help the flavour. It first was introduced into England in the early sixteenth century. It is said "Hops and Heresie came in a Yere."

Never had I been, and never have been since, as physically fit as I was at the end of the hop-picking. The harvesting was now mechanized to an extent; my job was to stand on the trailer as it drove along the rows of vines pulling them down and stacking them. The vines were then taken into a shed where they were hung on hoops which carried them through a big threshing machine. It still needed a bevy of ladies in turbans to separate good hops from bad ones, as the buds proceeded along a conveyor belt to the drying floor in the kilns.

David Nowlan left before the end of hop-picking, but before he left, he had made contact with Canon C.B. Armstrong who lived in the Worcester Cathedral close. Canon Armstrong had been Warden of St Columba's in the 1920s and 1930s, before our time. Armstrong sent a card with an invitation to "tea, after evensong one Sunday". Perhaps Blackwell and Morgan had also left – at any rate I was the only one to go. While we were at Upper Wick, it was quite common for us to go to church. The two Davids were both the sons of clergymen, and it was David Blackwell's intention to proceed to the Divinity School with a view to ordination. I would go along with them, as I had nothing else to do, but I would never have dreamt of going to evensong in the cathedral on my own. However I went, and it was to be my Damascus Road. I was so affected by the singing of the choir that from that point it was inevitable that I would, though it was some years later, acknowledge that I was neither a Presbyterian nor an agnostic which I had variously considered myself to be, but an Anglican, with a High Church lean at that.

I had a very interesting chat with the Canon over tea in his house in the close. He would have been about 70 then – he lived to be over 90 – and had left St Columba's twenty years before. He gave me some historical perspective on the college, but the main impression I had was of stepping back a long way in time. He was, like Cousin Eleanor Rawnsley in the Lake District, a throwback to Victorian times, in the things he talked about and the phrases he used. When I left, as he opened the door, he said "Did you have a hat or a stick?"

We had very little extra-curricular or social activity, as the working hours were long. There was a table tennis table which had much use in the annexe where we lived, but about the only break of consequence was the regular Saturday evening trip into town to the cinema. The long hours, the piece work when picking the fruit, and the fact that we were charged only 30 shillings for our beds and most excellent board, made me by the time of my departure in October as rich as Croesus; I had all of £50. I had a couple of days in London staying at my communist hostel, and took Joe Hone to dine at the Hyde Park Hotel, where we were surrounded by a troop of wine and other waiters who were somewhat intimidating as they sensed a chance of plunder. They would have got a good bit from me. I was in a very sound financial position on my return to Ireland to start the next phase of life as an undergraduate at Dublin University, Trinity College in October 1954.

CHAPTER THIRTEEN

Glencullen

During 1952, my parents started looking for a permanent home of their own. There were a number of expeditions to see houses, from Kilkeel in Co. Down to Swords in Co. Dublin. Aunt Jane had died that year and left Eldron to my mother. Consideration was given to making some alterations to the house and going to live there, but this idea was abandoned. Late in the year it looked as if a house near the mouth of the Boyne below Drogheda was about to be settled for.

At that point, my FitzSimon grandmother, Maud, having seen that Glencullen House was for sale, put up the idea that she would sell Kilgobbin House, and we would all move to Glencullen, and that is what was done. It was just over twelve years since the mortgagees had foreclosed on Glencullen House, and it had had three owners in the meantime. Father still owned several cottages in Glencullen along with several hundred acres at the top of the mountain, which he had inherited from grandfather Dan. The purchase price was made up mainly by my mother.

My mother had inherited some money from her mother and also she had sold Eldron. She also salvaged a little from her Canadian oil well. This oil well had been a saga for some years. After my grandfather Willie Killen's brother John had emigrated to Canada and set himself up in the pioneering settlement of Edmonton, Willie had sent him some money to buy some land, and 300 acres of pristine prairie was bought about 30 miles out, at Leduc town. Nothing happened on this land for many years until John's son Allan started to farm it. Willie told my mother when she married that the land was hers, but it seems that Willie forgot this, and when, during the depression of the 1930s, Allan could not pay any rent, Willie told him that he might as well keep the land, and made it over to him. In 1947 oil was struck at Leduc. Mother seems to have thought that if she did not have legal title to the land, she had some moral right to it, and along with Cousin Bryce Mayrs, pursued Uncle John for some share in the oil money which appeared to be very substantial. Allan was able to retire from farming and pursue theological studies in a college in the USA to which he was said to be donating the oil money. Uncle John and his daughter Beth visited us at Annaghmakerrig. He was about 80 then and stone deaf. He still had a Belfast accent after more than fifty years absence, and seemed to me a decent enough old chap. In the end, he, and I think it was he himself rather than Allan, gave my mother more than what had been originally paid by my grandfather to buy the land. Also every Christmas he would send to Christopher and me £25 each, which was very useful through my college days.

My father organized an expedition, with military precision and in great detail, for the move from Annaghmakerrig to Glencullen. I went in Seamus McGorman's taxi along with Dympna, our maid and her cousin, who came as another maid, as much to keep Dympna company, as to manage the likely greater workload. The dog and cat came too.

We settled into Glencullen very quickly. As planned, Grandmother Maud joined us and was allotted her own sitting room. Also, Aunt May FitzSimon, who was then eighty-two, came. She had left Glencullen in 1914 for England. She was registered in Thom's Directory for that year as one of the Nobility, Gentry and Merchants of Dublin, a description which seems to me rather strange as I remember her as a little old lady sitting somewhere unobtrusively. She had left originally for war work as an auxiliary nurse, and later she lived as a sort of nanny assistant with cousins called Thomas in London, a family descended from her Aunt Eily, who had been married in Glencullen in 1862 to an Indian Army officer. She was particularly involved with looking after young Martin Thomas who was later to become a Jesuit priest and would suffer martyrdom in Africa, along with some other European religious in a massacre at a school, in the course of the Zimbabwean civil war. Aunt May had gone to live at Kilgobbin with Maud after Dan died. She died not long after moving to Glencullen, in the bedroom which had been hers in her youth. I also would use that bedroom, but thirty years after her death it was still known as Aunt May's room. When she died, my grandmother said that she heard the knocking ghost.

My grandmother was not the sort of person one would have expected to take much notice of a ghost. I myself do, though I admit I haven't yet seen one or heard one, and the right side of my brain tells me to discount the stories. We had several ghosts in Glencullen House. The one story which would frighten me if I was in the kitchen late at night was one of Aunt May's, who had come down at night and was heating some milk at the stove, when she heard heavy footsteps climbing down the stairs. The footsteps went round the kitchen table and then out and up the stairs again. Aunt May followed the sound of them with her eyes, but never saw a thing. The knocking ghost's most famous manifestation was in 1862. There was a full house on account of a wedding in the family. Three ladies were sleeping in what we called the white room. They were woken by a loud banging on the wall, which then moved across the ceiling and then went down another wall. One of the ladies cried out "Even if you are the Devil banging nails in our coffin, please stop." Next day she went to the priest to have him say prayers for the knocker. The other two ladies went into town, but as the coach was going over Portobello Bridge, the horses panicked and the coach toppled into the canal. All the passengers were drowned.

The child with the bleeding head was remarkable in that it was seen more than once, by several people. One time was when the cow man was driving the cows into the yard, and he saw a child sitting on the step of a building and thinking that the cows might walk on him, he said to the child to be careful. Then he saw that the child had a cut on his head so he asked could he help. The child said not to worry, he would be all right, and then disappeared. On another occasion he was seen inside the house and disappeared following a similar conversation with two ladies. Some years before, a boy in the family, Morgan FitzSimon, had died from a head injury after he fell off a wall of the priest's house while it was being built. Some theorists have suggested that the apparition of the bleeding child was him.

There were other suggestive supernatural occurrences. There was the crashing ghost; one heard a crash as if all the glass and china in the dining room had fallen and smashed, but on rushing to the scene there was nothing touched. There was once a terrible and unexplained wailing and shrieking which caused Peter Maguire's horse passing down the yard to bolt from his cart and he "wasn't caught till he got to Curtlestown". There was Anthony; the name given to the ghostly opener of doors. Anthony FitzSimon, who died in 1834, and was recorded as being somewhat nervous and wouldn't sit still for long, was singled out for special masses for the repose of his soul to be said as long as there was a priest in Glencullen. It must have been thought that he especially needed this, and later generations can't have had full confidence in the efficacy of the masses, if they thought that it was him going around opening doors.

At any rate these ghosts never caused me or anyone else any trouble. Perhaps because Tib, my Uncle Henry, had Father Curtis, the resident Glencullen curate, come down with his candle, book and bell and put all the ghosts to rest. Tib told me this shortly before he died, saying that he had never told anyone else he had done this, for fear that they would laugh at him.

There were a number of cottages in Glencullen which belonged to Father, and he was soon to sell the ones not actually on the land which was bought with the house, some 25 acres. On this land were two cottages, inhabited by bachelors Art Smith and Gerry Mayne. Art was a family retainer, brought up by the Maguires of the Crowfall, other retainers who by the time we moved back had their own farm. I had always known him as someone who came to do odd jobs for my grandparents, and during the period when the Glencullen House was in the hands of others, various things, including a lot of books, were stored in his cottage, which had been originally built as the dispensary. I soon learned that Art was a good man to talk to and would sit with him in his cottage of an evening and he would enlighten me on various topics, among other things, about what is now called the War of Independence and the Civil War – a woeful business he called the latter. Art was only a few years older than my father and they had been companions in mischief, I was told by others, during my father's youth. It never entered my head, until recently when Christopher said that he had always assumFitzSimons'sed it, that Art was an illegitimate FitzSimon. I now subscribe to that view as being quite plausible. There were at least two illegitimate relations of Grandmother Maud in the cottages around Moreen. Furthermore, Art looked like a FitzSimon. Such things were not talked about. I wonder if my father knew if Art was his cousin or perhaps half-brother.

The other cottage was a very small one, tenanted by one Gerry Mayne. Gerry had had many jobs in many countries: he was a car salesman in New Zealand at one stage. For the short time that I knew him he was the classic remittance man. He was paid to stay away from his family lest he would embarrass them with the eloquent irreverence which his partiality for drink would bring forth. He was the uncle, or to be precise, stepuncle of no less a person than John Charles McQuaid, the redoubtable and dictatorial Catholic Archbishop of Dublin. Gerry would always come down to the house to pay his rent, 12 shillings a week, immediately he got his cheque from the Archibishop's family, and then go to Foxe's pub, for, as he put it, internal lubrication. He was eventually put into a home on the Dublin north side, but managed on occasion to escape and make it back to Foxe's before his minders could retrieve him.

The first Sunday after moving to Glencullen, Christopher and I went to Mass with Father, the maids from Monaghan trailing behind us, less happy than me, as they had to sit somewhere in the back among the strange Leinster folk. We went to the front where there is a pew with a brass plate with "Mr O'Connell FitzSimon and Family" on it. I had never known my father to attend church before except on holiday in England where we went to the Church of England. There are Roman Catholics, Greek Catholics, Anglo-Catholics, but on reflection I have come to the conclusion that Father was a Glencullen Catholic. He was a regular at Mass at Glencullen till he died.

Another retainer of sorts was Pat Kenny, the gamekeeper. His father, also Pat, was gamekeeper before him, in the days when there was a lot of game to keep. The grouse had all but disappeared by 1953. Father had leased the shooting to Colonel Alexander, the brother of the Field Marshal Alexander of Tunis, but it was a losing battle for anyone to find anything to shoot. A year or so after we arrived, I walked the whole top of the mountain, and although it took all day, I didn't see a bird. Just as I was about to leave, a grouse got up and I aimed at it, but I didn't have the heart to pull the trigger; I didn't want to be the person who killed the last grouse on the mountain. There had been long periods when the shooting was let, and a limit was always put on the number of birds which could be killed in a season; 250 birds would be a typical limit. From 1842 a normal rent would be £120; there was a high figure of £200 in 1920 which reflects the post-war inflationary boom, and a low figure of £104 in 1934, a year which marked the depth of the worldwide depression and De Valera's economic war. As well as the grouse, there were always hares, which unlike their rabbit cousins are considered to be game. In one drive along with Lord Powerscourt, who owned the adjacent mountains in Co. Wicklow – the county boundary was the boundary of the FitzSimon Glencullen estate – 164 hares were shot.

In the past, there was work for the gamekeeper. He had to contend with foxes and skall crows, poachers, and on one famous occasion in 1886, a man called Rogerson pastured 200 sheep on the mountain, claiming he had the right. It took the courts a year to rule in the FitzSimons' favour, so the grouse took precedence over Rogerson and his sheep, and he had to remove them. Pat was effective at keeping off poachers as far as we know. The only poaching stories we have are of the Glencullen schoolmaster who was a shooting guest on Glencullen Mountain, but would poach on Glendoo, the Guinness estate, as did Father Curtis at a later date. During the war, and immediately after, an enormous quantity of turf was taken off the mountain. Individuals could purchase a "bank" from my grandfather: a bank was so many square feet in area and as deep as one cared to dig. The turf blanket on Glencullen – one calls such mountain bogs "blanket bogs" – is very deep and is of high quality, better than most bogs. As well as individuals, there was a contractor cutting for institutions. Over the five years 1942–1947, grandfather Dan netted £2,500 profit from turf sales, but at the expense of terrible disruption to the grouse. In 1942 some 400 acres below the bog were sold to the Forestry Department. The shooting rights on that bit of land were kept; however when the Department went about their business of planting trees, the grouse there would have fared no better than the ones above on the bog. If this was not bad enough for the birds, a terrible disease struck, decimating the grouse population across the whole British Isles. Father sold what was left of the mountain in 1957. He resented having to pay Pat, even though it was a pittance, for looking after what was really nothing, but the greater problem was that he was having to pay considerable council rates. When the mountain started to produce turf, the council had greatly increased the rates. Despite some years of correspondence, the council refused to reduce the rates, though the turf cutting had long ended. The mountain, instead of being the financial asset it had been, was now only a liability: it had been losing money for 10 years. The mountain later became part of the Powerscourt estate.

The quarries on Glencullen Mountain were no longer working, but it was only in recent years that they had been abandoned. Stone cutting was a major contributor to the local economy from the late eighteenth century onwards. The FitzSimons were never actively involved in stone cutting but were, in the early nineteenth century, drawing a rent of £31 from the stone cutters, and would stand surety for them. The portico and pillars at the front of the house were built of granite cut from the mountain in 1818 and in the following decade cills and flags were cut and taken all the way to the house at Ballinamona Co. Wicklow where Christopher, Poor Dear Fitz, lived with his wife Ellen, daughter of the Liberator O'Connell, before they moved into Glencullen House. But this was small stuff compared to the building of the GPO in Dublin with its pillars, all granite from Glencullen Mountain.

The Glencullen Ballybrack community of the valley of the Glencullen river, or rather communities (the Ballybracks would sit at one end of the bus and the Glencullens at the other), was about four or five hundred strong in 1953, not much less than it had been in the previous century. The population had actually gone up during the famine times, but suffered from heavy emigration from the 1860s to the 1890s, especially from the wilder upper end of the valley. The village had an infrastructure. The church, the school, the pub and a Carnegie library functioned, but the earlier police barracks and the dispensary had long relocated in Stepaside. There was no shop. Janey Mulvey opened a shop shortly after we arrived and it passed to Mrs Kenna, whose husband Jim supplied us with milk in return for the grazing on two of the four fields, but she gave it up soon after. I expect that the population wasn't big enough to warrant a shop, and it was becoming increasingly more inviting to shop further afield as more and more people acquired cars.

In 1953 ours was the only telephone in Glencullen, apart from one in Foxe's pub. There were people who didn't like to make private calls in the pub, because they could be heard by the drinkers. The practice developed of local people coming to use ours, and Father would not refuse anyone, but he charged them tuppence a call. If I was there, I did not make a practice of listening to conversations; however one I heard was a call to the guards for help, as a man was beating his wife, not the sort of information to have been trumpeted in the lounge bar. There was, I think only one other car in the community at the time; it was actually a pickup truck belonging to the Kennys of Boranoraltry, the little settlement on the side of Glencullen Mountain. This family of unmarried brothers and a sister, relations of our gamekeeper Pat, along with other activities grazed cattle on the lands of Moreen, which, following on the foreclosure of the mortgage, was owned by the Sisters of Charity. In the back of the truck there was always a black and white collie dog. The truck was driven by the eldest brother who had the driving licence. When he died the truck and licence passed to the next one, and so on down till they were all gone. I didn't have a car; it was an easy ride on a bicycle, down to Kilternan or even Dundrum, but a massive ordeal to ride back. The crossroads at Foxe's is over 900 feet above sea level. It would take about three quarters of an hour to walk from the cross roads to Kilternan, where one could get the number 44

Enniskerry bus to the city. There was also a single-decker bus called the 44B which wound along the side of the Two Rock Mountain to serve the stone cutters' cottages of Barnacullia, and from the Glencullen cross roads went on to Ballybrack. It did two runs in the early morning, and also in the late evening, and so served commuters to the city, and with its circuitous route, took about an hour. For my first term at Trinity College I would go in on the 7.30 bus every morning and come out on the mountain route at 5.45 p.m.; if times didn't suit it meant the walk up the hill from Kilternan.

CHAPTER FOURTEEN

Early FitzSimon history and the O'Connell connection I

The family to which I belong is a Dublin one. There is no documentary evidence of the identity of the forbears of the Thomas FitzSimon who bought Glencullen in 1672. We cannot pin down exactly who our ancestors were, but there are plenty of indications. There is a two hundred year old family tradition that the founder of the line of Dublin FitzSimons was John FitzSimon of Clondalkin whose father, Thomas arrived from Cornwall in 1323. His family had previously spread branches over the eastern counties of England since the Norman Conquest in 1066. These families are well recorded. They are descended from Toustain le Goz, Viscount of Falaise, who was a close relative of Duke William the Conqueror and was the Duke's standard bearer at the Battle of Hastings. Toustain's elder son remained in Normandy as Viscount Avranches; the younger son was Simon, Lord of St Sever, who also fought at Hastings, and was subsequently granted lands in Norfolk. It is from him that our name is derived.

By the late fifteenth century we find several FitzSimon families in Dublin and Westmeath. We find them among the principal landholders and merchants of the Pale. By 1500, the Pale, the area immediately to the north and west of Dublin, was the only part of Ireland firmly under the control of the King's government and defended against "the King's Irish Enemies".

FiTZSIMON FAMILY TREE

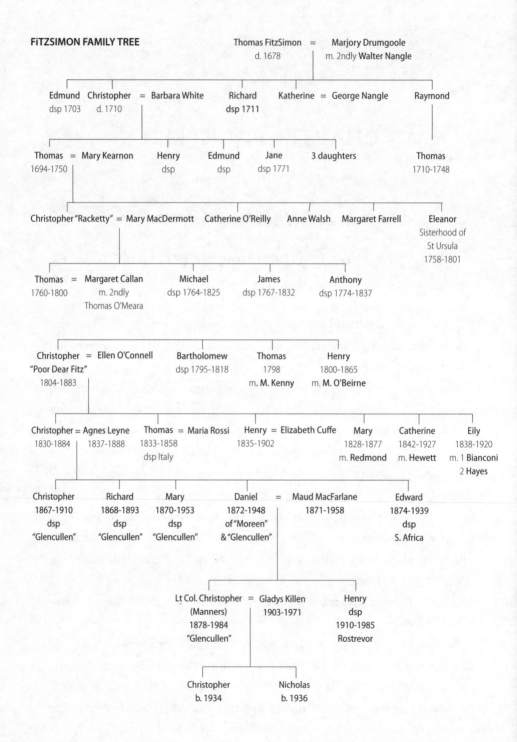

Thomas FitzSimon = Marjory Drumgoole
d. 1678   m. 2ndly **Walter Nangle**

Edmund   Christopher = Barbara White   Richard   Katherine = George Nangle   Raymond
dsp 1703 d. 1710   **dsp 1711**

Thomas = Mary Kearnon   Henry   Edmund   Jane   3 daughters   Thomas
1694-1750   dsp   dsp   dsp 1771   1710-1748

Christopher "Racketty" = Mary MacDermott   Catherine O'Reilly   Anne Walsh   Margaret Farrell   Eleanor
                                                                                                     Sisterhood of
                                                                                                     St Ursula
                                                                                                     1758-1801

Thomas = Margaret Callan   Michael   James   Anthony
1760-1800   m. 2ndly   dsp 1764-1825   dsp 1767-1832   dsp 1774-1837
            Thomas O'Meara

Christopher = Ellen O'Connell   Bartholomew   Thomas   Henry
"Poor Dear Fitz"   dsp 1795-1818 1798   1800-1865
1804-1883   m. M. Kenny   m. M. O'Beirne

Christopher = Agnes Leyne   Thomas = Maria Rossi   Henry = Elizabeth Cuffe   Mary   Catherine   Eily
1830-1884   1837-1888   1833-1858   1835-1902   1828-1877   1842-1927   1838-1920
                             dsp Italy   m. Redmond   m. Hewett   m. 1 Bianconi
                                                                                                         2 Hayes

Christopher   Richard   Mary   Daniel = Maud MacFarlane   Edward
1867-1910   1868-1893 1870-1953   1872-1948 1871-1958   1874-1939
dsp   dsp   dsp   of "Moreen"   dsp
"Glencullen"   "Glencullen" "Glencullen" & "Glencullen"   S. Africa

Lt Col. Christopher = Gladys Killen   Henry
(Manners)   1903-1971   dsp
1878-1984   1910-1985
"Glencullen"   Rostrevor

Christopher   Nicholas
b. 1934   b. 1936

Major Lennox MacFarlane

Napier MacFarlane – Army Boxing Champion

Moreen, Sandyford, Co. Dublin

Hunstown House, Mulhuddart, Co. Dublin – MacFarlane family home

Glenville, Glenwhirry, Co. Antrim – home of the Killens until 1875

Glencullen House

Glencullen House from the top garden

Stirling House, Co. Meath – early home of the MacFarlanes

Daniel O'Connell FitzSimon (1872-1948)

Author's parents' wedding photograph

Author's parents' wedding group

In 1538, Lord Deputy Grey led an army of Palesmen against such enemies, a common enough necessity. This time it was against the O'Neills of Tyrone, who had led a large force from Ulster raiding for cattle into Louth. The Dublin army routed the O'Neills at Ballyhoe where the Pale borders with Monaghan. It was reported that Thomas FitzSimon of Corduff had "fought verrie valiantly" and that James FitzSimon, the Mayor of the City of Dublin, was dubbed knight on the field. This Thomas of Corduff, who was the father-in-law of the historian Richard Stanihurst (which is probably how we come to have such a good report of his prowess on the battlefield), was the Recorder of Dublin and married a daughter of Nicholas St Lawrence, the Baron of Howth and Chief Baron of the Exchequer. He was the father of Sir Edward FitzSimon who graduated from Cambridge in 1556 and became Sergeant-at-Law. Sir Edward was tenant-in-chief of lands at Baldoyle. These rich North County lands were quite close to Corduff and to Howth. They had previously belonged to the abbey of All Hallowes in Dublin and following the dissolution of the abbey in 1539, belonged to the City Corporation. Sir Edward had a son Christopher, also a lawyer, and a grandson Thomas who was living on the Baldoyle property into the 1640s.

This Thomas had his rent set in 1637 at £240 a year. He also had to pay the Protestant curate £2 10s., though there were no Protestants in the parish, Mass being said in the FitzSimon house. The estate consisted of the lands, town, castle, grange and fisheries (fish had to be supplied to the Corporation for their feasts) of Baldoyle. Judging from the amount of rent, the whole estate must have been one thousand to two thousand acres, perhaps the whole of the parish.

The rebellion which broke out in 1641 all over Ireland was followed by continuing intermittent war until after Cromwell's arrival in 1650. North County Dublin was devastated. An army of northern Catholics under O'Neill pillaged the county in 1642, and in 1644 the Royal Army under the Duke of Ormond, laid waste anything that was still there. In the meantime there were continuous robberies and burnings of houses. Thomas, presumably because of the devastation, could not pay his rent and petitioned to have it reduced, but was unsuccessful. In 1646 we find the estate in the hands of a Protestant who was only having to pay a rent of £120 a year. Thomas disappeared from history. He had been outlawed, as no doubt, like most of the Dublin gentry, he had supported the rebels. It has been long held in my family that this Thomas was the father of the Thomas who bought Glencullen in 1672, though we have no documentary evidence to that effect.

The disappearence of Thomas of Baldoyle was not unique.

Throughout the fifteenth century, the country beyond the Pale was quite outside the control of the Dublin government, and from about 1540 it was in a state of continuing war, as the Tudor monarchs set about the conquest of all Ireland. Dublin, though the most significant city in Ireland with all the trappings of a capital since the thirteenth century, including the royal government, two cathedrals (functioning), a university (nearly all the time not functioning), courts of justice and all the officials of public office with their elaborate rituals, did not have the trade it should have had, or the wealth, or the population. The population remained, for over two hundred years, at around 10,000 to 15,000, so it is not hard to see how an oligarchy of some twenty or thirty families of merchants and local landowners could dominate the business of the city and occupy the public offices. The FitzSimons were among such families. There were at least five separate but interrelated families of FitzSimon, members of whom would marry among their peer group of the oligarchy, and between them provided, throughout the sixteenth century, several mayors, recorders, bailiffs and other lesser civic officials, as well as a Dean and a Precentor for St Patrick's Cathedral and an Archbishop of Dublin and a Lord Chancellor.

All the FitzSimon families of the influential oligarchy which controlled Dublin disappeared from the records. The so called Old English were squeezed out by new English Protestant settlers. A few of the Old English became Protestants but this alone was often not enough for them to maintain their status. It was quite common for the Old English to accept the church reforms of Henry VIII and Elizabeth, but towards the end of the sixteenth century, there was a strong revival of Roman Catholicism driven from continental Europe where many seminaries had been set up for the training of Irish priests. By and large those Old English, who had conformed to the state church, the Church of Ireland, elected to revert to Roman allegiance. FitzSimons provide an example; a letter from Christopher to his father Sir Edward in 1585 from London where he was a law student, urged his father to have no more to do with the Church of Ireland. Christopher was by then, despite being in London, quite firmly in the fold of Tridentine Catholicism. Another FitzSimon, a grandson of James the Mayor, who was knighted on the field of Ballyhoe, one Henry, returned to Ireland from France a Jesuit priest and for some years around the turn of the century was well known in Dublin as a preacher and controversialist. He was eventually forced to leave, and died in France in 1629.

Besides Thomas of Baldoyle's disappearance from history on the eve of the Cromwellian invasion, there were two other Thomas FitzSimons, landowners who were evicted under Cromwell's policy of "To Hell or to Connacht". At this point, or rather at the restoration of the monarchy in 1659, we become confused trying to identify between the Thomases.

The family of one Thomas FitzSimon, of Ballamadrought, near Swords in North County Dublin, got their property back following the restoration of King Charles. This family died out in the eighteenth century, and there is now no mystery surrounding it. Another Thomas FitzSimon was evicted from his land at Tullynally in Co. Westmeath and is not heard of again. His lands fell to a Cromwellian speculator who later sold them to another Cromwellian, one Pakenham, ancestor of the Earls of Longford, who have been there ever since. It has been suggested that this Thomas was the one who bought Glencullen in 1672, and there are certain pointers towards that possibility. We Glencullen FitzSimons have a late seventeenth-century painting of our coat of arms, under which it is written that the coat "doth properly belong to Richard FitzSimon son of Thomas FitzSimon who was descended from the antient family of that Surname of Tully Nally in ye Co.ty of Westmeath". The mystery is whether we might not be descended from Thomas of Baldoyle but rather from the Tullynally people.

FitzSimons took possession of Tullynally in 1441, forcing out the occupants who were a family of English origin. It appears that they used such a level of skullduggery against the occupants, who being under-age girls, did not have the wherewithal to defend themselves legally, or by force of arms. The latter might have been more successful. At the time Westmeath was outside the Pale. FitzSimon became a common name in the area, both in Westmeath and within the adjacent area of Meath, within the Pale, as it is to this day, and just over the border into Co. Cavan. Cavan FitzSimons in the main are descended from one Simon O'Reilly. It was not unusual for Gaelic families to occasionally adopt Norman nomenclature, Fitzpatrick was originally MacGiollaPadraig. At the time of the Cromwellian evictions, there were many FitzSimons living around Tullynally as well as Thomas the "Gentleman" in the big house. Some of these people had Gaelic forenames and some of them had English forenames. I would expect that there was a mixture of old loyalist Normans and Normans who had become "more Irish than the Irish themselves", who might have descended from the same stock as the Dublin FitzSimons, and also immigrants from Cavan, really O'Reillys.

It is unlikely that the coat of arms would have been borne in Ireland before 1482. That is the year when the FitzSimons of Suffield in Norfolk, who had previously borne the arms, became extinct and when the arms would have been available to be granted by the Garter King at Arms to some other family. The Suffield branch was remotely related to the Thomas who arrived in Ireland from Cornwall in 1323, but different arms had been borne by this Thomas's more immediate family. Given that Thomas of Glencullen had the arms from Tullynally descent, it would have to be from a post 1482 migrant from Westmeath to Dublin, most likely a sixteenth-century migrant. One could suggest that a possibly remotely connected country cousin came up to Dublin to make his fortune and in time founded one of the lines of the FitzSimon oligarchs. Such a person would not have been an ancestor of Thomas of

Baldoyle, whose forbears we can trace back through Thomas of Corduff who fought at Ballyhoe, as being resident in Dublin before 1460.

In 1672, our well-documented ancestor Thomas, well-documented that is after 1672, for that is when we first come across him, bought Glencullen from Lord Fitzwilliam of Merrion for £100. This was a very small sum even for those days; not long after the property had an annual rental of £60 which would indicate that the real capital value was upwards of ten times the sum paid for it. There must have been something more to the deal which we do not know about. It could be that Fitzwilliam and Thomas were cousins; there was a FitzSimon/ Fitzwilliam marriage at an earlier date, but it is sure that they were doing business together. Both of them were officially classed as "Irish Papists", and Fitzwilliam, rare among the large Catholic landlords in surviving the evictions intact, could have been involved in deals along with FitzSimon in efforts to avoid the Penal Laws. Apart from the Glencullen deal we find Fitzwilliam and other names of the old Catholic merchant families of the city appearing as witnesses to FitzSimon business documents. The members of the old oligarchy were still doing business, even if they were no longer influential and their activities were unrecorded in government circles. It is clear from this that Thomas of Glencullen was one of the this network, and by inference sprung from the old oligarchy.

If we accept this, our Thomas cannot have been a recent migrant from Westmeath. If his ancestors were from Westmeath, they would have to have come to Dublin well before the time of the Cromwellian eviction of Thomas of Tullynally in 1654.

Our choice as to the origins of Thomas of Glencullen comes down to accepting the old family tradition of him belonging to the Baldoyle people, with descent from Thomas of Corduff, a tradition of no determinate age and with no documentary evidence. Or if we reject this we must accept his descent from one of the other four sixteenth-century Dublin merchant families, which we can identify but cannot pin down precisely, nor in all cases relate one to the others. If the latter hypothesis is correct, there is still the intriguing suggestion that to explain the descent of our coat of arms, one of these families of the merchant oligarchy was not of long established Dublin breeding, but is an immigrant one from Westmeath.

Thomas who bought Glencullen in 1672 died in 1678. Before he died he had bought several house sites on St Stephen's Green, a very recent subdivision laid out by the City Corporation to help the city develop in a planned manner to the east. He had a house on at least one of the sites, which he appears to have been living in at the time of his death. Glencullen was then a wild and undeveloped place, a speculative investment for future improvement. He also bought land in Co. Wicklow, as did his eldest son, Edmund. Edmund who died in 1703, a bachelor, left us a quite competent love poem; perhaps he wrote others, but one is enough to establish him as the only FitzSimon to have contributed anything at all by way of such art – we have to look much later to the O'Connell connection for anything more.

When Thomas died, by request in his Will, he was buried beside his wife Marjory's grandmother in St James's churchyard. His widow Marjory remarried, her new husband being Walter Nangle of Kildalky in Co. Meath. This family provided the line of eighteen successive Barons of Trim from the twelfth century, Walter himself was MP for Trim in King James's "Patriot Parliament" of 1689, and so by being on the wrong side, had much of his land confiscated by King William. The family survived, which was just as well, because Thomas and Marjory's daughter Catherine had married Walter's heir from a previous marriage.

Besides Edmond and Catherine, Thomas and Marjory had three other sons. Richard, to whom we attribute the attestation of the coat of arms, died unmarried in 1711. Christopher and Raymond had families and subsequent descendants. Christopher and Raymond were active in Dublin business. With a partner, Captain Roche, who had learned the trade in Holland, they set up the first factory in the country to make crystal glass. The business got off to a bad start. Captain Roche on inspecting the brick glass house, poked the underside of the roof with his stick which brought the whole roof down, killing a number of workers. The Captain was lucky to be dug out alive – he was located because his stick was protruding through the rubble. The business however did prosper, and continued for over seventy years.

In 1698 Christopher FitzSimon bought some more sites on the north side of St Stephen's Green and started to build a large brick house on two of them. Before it was finished, it caught the eye of the Earl of Kerry who agreed to take it on a long lease. The Earl was just in time to specify a number of alterations to suit his own taste. Some more rooms were needed, the main staircase had to be widened, given grandeur, and the stables at the rear enlarged to accommodate more horses. The Earl took it on a long lease at a rent of £120 a year. This rent was double that of all the Glencullen land at that time. The building became known as Kerry House, and when the Earl was given the added title of Earl of Shelbourne, it became Shelbourne House. In time, much altered, it became the Shelbourne Hotel.

Christopher died in 1715, heavily in debt. This may have had an advantage, for this was the time when the Penal Laws were at their most severe. Not only were Catholics excluded from public office, but their estates had to be split up amongst all the sons, unless one of them became a Protestant in which case he got the lot. The idea was to ensure that a Catholic would not become too powerful and influential. Christopher had three sons; what they inherited to share, split up amongst them, were debts. The younger two were to die quite young and unmarried; Thomas, the eldest, was to prove himself to be an astute businessman and managed to steer himself through the system so that in time the debts had been paid off and he had the whole estate for himself. As well as having to contend with what we would consider to be the normal hazards of business, he had to contend with the Protestant discoverer. Such people made their living as freelance investigators of breaches of the Penal Laws which were not always vigorously enforced by the authorities. There were various ways of combating discoverers such as having property put in the names of Protestant friends who would later give it back when the investigations had blown over. This was a risky business and one had to trust one's Protestant friends. Thomas, son of Raymond, had one Protestant friend, a Mr Espinase of St Stephen's Green, to whom had been entrusted title to some land at Kill of the Grange. Though Espinase was a trusted friend, he unfortunately died before the deal was completed, and his son who was no friend at all, and on whom the title devolved, made off with the whole property himself.

Besides the Wicklow and Glencullen lands, which Thomas, Christopher's son, was improving, and the glassworks in which he had a half share (his uncle Raymond's family had the other half) he was frequently dealing in property both in the city and in the country. He called himself variously "of Dublin" or "of Ardinary" (one of the Wicklow properties) but never "of Glencullen". It is possible that his younger brothers may have lived in Glencullen; certainly his sister Jane who died in 1771 and was buried in Kilgobbin, lived there. There was no problem with the Penal Laws of inheritance when Thomas died in 1750, for along with his six daughters, who were not affected by the Penal Laws, he had only one son who then could legally inherit the whole estate. Three of the daughters married: one became a nun who after a novitiate in Paris, founded the Ursuline convent in Cork in 1773, and two others died unmarried.

The son Christopher, was known as "Racketty". This was because he was an extrovert and very noisy, not because, it is said, of his involvement in rackets, though he may well have been. He married Mary, the daughter of Anthony MacDermot, the richest wine merchant in Dublin, who provided a dowry of £5,000, a tidy sum in 1759. Soon after, the glassworks was failing, under competition from overseas and an adverse taxation regime. Racketty petitioned the government for assistance, but got none. The glassworks was shut down in 1759. It had been the biggest glassworks in the country for making high-quality crystal-decorated drinking glasses; in Captain Roche's day, it was even exporting glasses. Thereafter the business was to become one of importing glass only. This was to continue until 1788, by which time Racketty had given up the business completely. He spent most of the 1760s living in France: two of his younger sons were born there, in Amiens and Paris respectively. Presumably he was the buying arm of the business.

He returned to live in Dublin some time after 1770, and is thought to have lived in Glencullen. We do not hear about his business dealings except for a very large sum of money, several thousands of pounds, that he was owed. He was living as a gentleman waiting for the loan to mature and for him to be paid, but when the day came there was no money there; all of it had evaporated. The problem then was that he had made sizeable borrowings in anticipation of the repayment of the loan, and so he found himself in Queer Street; he was broke. He had nine judgements totalling £6,750 against him. Luckily for the family, he had previously made over title to the estates to his eldest son Thomas, and he was able to flee from his creditors to the Isle of Man where he lived out his days. If he had not got away he would have been put in the debtors' jail until the money was paid back, an exercise which was to take many years.

The eldest son, Thomas, had, in 1790, married Margaret, the daughter and co-heiress of another rich Catholic merchant, Bartholomew Callan. Some of the £10,000 dowry came in shares in the Grand Canal Company, in which Bartholomew was one of the original investors. Thomas spent his time between Swords House, which belonged to the Taylor family, (Callan relations), and a new terraced house which he had bought in Gardiner Place in the north city. He had a cook, housemaid, nurse, coachman and postilion. He can't have been living too badly, for his wine bill for 1797/1798 came to over £100, a sum almost double the combined wages of his five servants. Perhaps this was an exceptional year; there could have been a need to celebrate the defeat of the rebels of '98, or conversely to drown sorrows.

There is no suggestion that Thomas was active on one side or the other in the rebellion, but his brother-in-law, Margaret's sister Helen's husband was. This was Dr Esmonde, who led the rebel forces of Co. Kildare. Esmonde was defeated in an attack on Naas, captured, and taken straight away to Dublin where he was hanged on Carlisle (now O'Connell) Bridge with his coat on back to front. This was because he had been an officer in the Militia and so was seen to be a "turncoat". Helen was then to marry another '98 participant, Harvey de Montmorency

Morres. Harvey fled to Hamburg with the celebrated Napper Tandy, but came back, and was let off, only suffering loss of his estates. Helen and Harvey lived thereafter in Paris, where they were visited by later members of the family, and have descendants who live in Germany.

Some friend or associate of Thomas was still in jail, in Wicklow, in 1800, for Thomas went to visit him and there caught "a putrid fever" from which he was to die at the age of 40, leaving four young sons with the widowed Margaret. Margaret then went with her sons to the Isle of Man to live with her father-in-law, Racketty, and Racketty's sister the widowed Mrs Farrell, known as Aunt Farrell, who had lived in France, but had been left destitute after the Revolution there. Margaret sent her two oldest sons to a boarding school in London.

With the relaxation of the Penal Laws, an Act of 1792 made it possible for Catholics to practise as barristers. Michael, Racketty's second son, was, in 1795, one of the first so to be called to the Bar. He was a student in London, and while there found it necessary to write to his brother Thomas for £8, so that he could get his watch out of pawn, despite the fact that he had been left £2,000 by his grandfather Anthony MacDermot. When Racketty departed for the Isle of Man, and with Thomas dead, it was Michael who looked after the estates, which now belonged to the 7 year old Christopher, Thomas and Margaret's eldest son.

Michael managed the letting of the various lands to middle men or large farmers who then would have sublet much smaller holdings. Over the space of several years he paid out Racketty's various creditors, and sent allowances, usually several hundred pounds a year, to the household in the Isle of Man; he was able to keep a couple of hundred pounds a year for himself for his pains, as his commission. Anthony, the youngest of the four brothers, who was a solicitor and helped with the estate administration, got a bit too.

Racketty died in 1812. Margaret had remarried in 1806 to Thomas O'Meara, a solicitor from Athy, Co.Kildare where they lived for a time. The two oldest of the children, Christopher and Bartholomew, were retrieved from school in London and continued their education privately under the tutelage of a priest in Celbridge in Kildare. Bartholomew died while still in his teens. O'Meara was an active man, in sport as well as in business. We have one report of a great hunt which went from Co. Wicklow all across Carlow, and O'Meara along with the Earl of Portarlington being the only ones able to appear for breakfast back in Athy. Some time later, about 1818, O'Meara, Margaret, the two younger sons, Tom and Henry, now 20 and 18 respectively, and two more children Margaret had had with O'Meara, went to live in Glencullen House. Young Christopher would have come of age in 1814; at that time he had rooms in town or in Trinity College from which he was to graduate in 1816. He was then therefore able to do a deal with O'Meara about the occupation and use of the property. O'Meara had been Christopher's guardian from 1806 until 1814, and thereafter his agent with power of attorney.

The deal of 1816 was that O'Meara would lease the house with 84 acres for sixty-one years at a rent of £128 a year. In a further deal in 1817, O'Meara said he would invest £3,000 of his own money to build a house and plant some 95,000 trees; the area to be leased was increased to 148 acres. O'Meara wrote to Christopher then in London saying how the tenants were hard up and were having difficulty paying rent. He said that Michael and Anthony had been letting the property to miserable beggars and had not made efforts to help them or make improvements. He said that he would make such improvements as would within four or five years provide Christopher with a good income. The existing house had probably been empty for quite some time and was no doubt in a shabby state. The house that O'Meara then built was not so much a new house, but an extension, to form what is the present day front part of Glencullen House. Modifications would have been necessary to the existing building to make the whole building function as one. For instance, the kitchen, dining room, drawing room, library and main entrance hall along with some utility rooms were located in the new part. The size of the house was in effect doubled from some 3,500 square feet to some 7,000. In 1818 the house was ready for the family to move in.

The reoccupation by the family made some stir locally. Among many callers, the adjoining landlord, Lord Powerscourt, was very pleased with the arrival of a sportsman of O'Meara's high reputation, hoping that O'Meara would organize a proper hunt for the district. However there is no record of this happening; shooting grouse on the mountain was thereafter the prime sport.

By this time Michael had no further interest in the property and we only hear of him from various spas in such places as Harrogate in Yorkshire, Baden Baden in Germany, and Switzerland, where he had gone to take the waters for his health. Whether it was for his health only, or he was simply having a good time, he was still able to leave his nephews legacies when he died in 1829. Around this same time, in 1818, the third of Racketty's four sons, James Henry, was to return from military service in India; if anyone was from then on was to take on the role of paterfamilias it was he.

James Henry was born in Paris in 1765. We do not know when the family returned to Ireland, but probably not long after, in the early 1770s, so James would have been brought up, it would appear, in Glencullen, before going back to France to start his military career. In 1785 he was gazetted as a sous-lieutenant in Dillon's Regiment, one of the remaining Irish regiments in the service of the King of France. He reached the rank of captain before the Revolution cut short his French career. The Irish regiments were disbanded in 1791, the King was overthrown and James fled to Dublin. Later in the year he was back on the continent with the army of the French princes at Koblentz on the Rhine to take part in the short-lived campaign when an alliance of European monarchs unsuccessfully tried to put down the Revolution.

The men of Dillon's Regiment had largely gone over to the Revolution, but its officers had not, and many officers of a range of foreign regiments were prepared to fight alongside the Prussian forces against the French, as ordinary soldiers. One of these officers was Daniel O'Connell from Co. Kerry, whose nephew, also Daniel, was then at school in France under his uncle's eye. This Daniel junior would in time distinguish himself as the "Liberator". Daniel senior had previously commanded the Royal Swedish Regiment of the French Army and had recently been promoted by the King to be major general. He had been offered high command in the revolutionary forces but preferred to remain loyal to the King, and so was to appear with the Prussians as a private soldier in a regiment of hussars. Whatever role James Henry had on the Rhine and at the disastrous Battle of Valmy we do not know, but in November 1792 at Koblentz, he was still certified as a captain. There were twenty other officers of Dillon's Regiment there.

Following the failure of the campaign, General O'Connell made his way to London, where the British authorities detained him to discuss plans to restore the French monarchy. From his personal account book, we can trace James Henry's flight to London immediately afterwards by way of Rotterdam.

James was in London from December 1792 until April 1793, and in Dublin from then until 1 July 1794. He must have lived quite a tolerable life. Again, from his account book, we can get some picture of his lifestyle. Apart from £500 which he lent to his brother Thomas to help defray a mortgage on Thomas's Gardiner Place house, his two most significant expenses recorded were for an inordinate quantity of silk stockings which he bought frequently, quite apart from cravats and waistcoats. Drapers and shoemakers bills were not inconsiderable. On the way to Koblentz he had bought a new uniform and a brace of pistols. In Dublin and London, he frequently spent one guinea on "amusements", whatever that may mean, but more clearly we learn of bills for "tavern expenses", always several guineas a time, and many losses at cards. He would typically lose £2 or £3 at a time; only once did he record a win, it being for £6. In Dublin he kept a bay horse in a hotel livery stable. From London he managed to have a visit to Bath. In France he had a servant called Louis, in Dublin one called William and later one called Thomas O'Brien, who was paid punctiliously, if not very much. From all this one might deduce that he was something of a dandy and a gambler, albeit a moderate one, something of a man about town. Like his brothers, he had been left £2,000 by his grandfather Anthony MacDermot, another £500 from a MacDermot uncle, and should have been left some of his mother's money as well. He would have been in a much better position than most of the former officers of the French service.

While James was having what looks like a good time in Dublin, General O'Connell was hard at work trying to get Irish regiments incorporated into the British Army. On the whole this did not prove to be a long term success, but employment was in due course found for many of the officers. Between February and October 1794, James passed through the ranks of ensign to captain in three successive different English regiments all in the space of five months. He was then, in 1795, commissioned as a captain in the revived Dillon's Regiment, one of five Irish regiments formed as a result of General O'Connell's negotiations. Most of these regiments were sent to the West Indies where the death rate was appalling. James was lucky not to go with them. It was O'Connell's negotiation which ended the one hundred year ban on allowing Catholics to serve as officers in the British forces. Of course the time was ripe. It was all part of the relaxation of the Penal Laws, and the motivation was the French Revolution. It was much better to have to put up with papist gentlemen on one's own side, than to be taken over by atheistical Republicans. The allowing of Catholic officers to serve in Ireland was not extended to England until some time later. James was stationed in Waterford in 1798 (though there is no record of any fighting with the rebels in Wexford just across the river). However from then on until he left for India in 1813, all his service was in England with the 65th, the West Yorkshire Regiment. He must have kept his religion under his hat. He became a Freemason while in Waterford in 1798 and membership in that body seems to have been important to him later on; at this time it was not uncommon for Catholics to be Freemasons. Daniel the Liberator was a member at one stage.

While based in England, his main role was in recruiting for his regiment. He made several visits to Ireland; the first one in 1799, for Christmas, was to stay with his brother Thomas at Swords House, where finding a good horse for him was quoted as an incentive for him to come over. By 1807 he had been promoted to major, and with reinforcements for the 65th, sailed for Bombay in 1813 to take part in the Mahratta Wars in that part of India known as the Deccan. In his first letter after arrival he said that money could be readily made there, and described a particularly fine horse he had been able to buy for a most reasonable sum. Over the next four years there was not a great deal of campaigning beyond marching about, and only a few, and not very large at that, battles. The campaign finished with the capture of Poona in 1818. James by then was a lieutenant colonel and second in command of the field force. However an aspect of the campaign would go on for him, in London, for the rest of his life, until he died in 1832.

On returning from India, he first of all went to Paris where, the monarchy now being restored, he was given the medal of the Legion of Honour and a small pension. The pension must have been too small, or it was cut off too soon, for he was later to complain that the French had "treated me shabbily". He then took up residence in London, a lieutenant colonel on half pay. A reason for living in London was so that he could monitor the progress of the distribution of the "Deccan Booty". This was the prize money of which he felt he was due a share. The Empire at that stage of history had more functions beyond looking after the natives and teaching them democracy. He maintained that he was due at least £5,000. The case was to drag on, as he lobbied Parliament and various officials, until he died. It was discovered when he died in 1832, that he had by then received some £1,700, with another £300 still to come, which then went to his heirs. He cannot have been too badly off, but he was always complaining that he was hard up. That was the reason given why he could not go over to Dublin for his nephew Christopher's wedding to the daughter of Daniel O'Connell in 1825. His absence is particularly odd because he had seen a lot of the young Christopher while the latter was in London reading for the Bar. Indeed it was James who told Christopher not to settle for less than a dowry of £5,000, and it was James himself who successfully negotiated that sum from O'Connell. Perhaps he was still inclined to spend too much time "at play", and still needed a very large wardrobe of stockings. Nevertheless, he did keep close touch with the family in Ireland until he died.

CHAPTER FIFTEEN

Early FitzSimon history and the O'Connell connection II

The young Christopher, (known at the time as Kitt, and later as Poor Dear Fitz, a name bestowed on him by his wife, are names to use here to distinguish him from other Christophers) entered Trinity College in Dublin in 1812 as a Fellow Commoner (which meant that he paid double the fees of the ordinary Pensioner, and so could dine at the Fellows' table) and graduated in 1816. He then went to London to read for the Bar. He lived in rooms in Pimlico which he shared with another ex-Trinity Bar student called Fraser. Fraser was something of a traveller and he put up the idea of the two of them setting off in the long vacation of 1818 for France and Italy. Kitt, in his letters home, sounded most enthusiastic about the trip, did a lot of planning, and secured letters of introduction from such influential acquaintances as Sir Henry Parnell and the Earl of Portarlington. In Paris he went to see his aunt, Helen Morres, where his visit was to coincide with that of his younger brother Tom, who had been sent over to learn French. Kitt had been enjoined to buy Tom a watch, as it would be cheaper to get one there than in Dublin, and to see that Tom did not get into trouble in the seamier quarters of Paris. Kitt was glad to leave Paris; he had found that he could not get into the society of agreeable people; he then travelled down the Rhone to Marseilles from where he went by boat to Genoa and then overland to Florence. We do not hear any more of Fraser.

In Florence he enrolled in language classes with a tutor who had been recommended to him by his uncle Michael, who was at that point in Switzerland for his health. The stay in Florence was to last for several months, but cannot have been much more inspiring than the one in Paris. He said that he was bored. He would go to his Italian language class, go for a walk and then go back to the hotel. Does one conclude that visual aesthetics were not part of his orientation? He made a brief visit to Naples and Rome before returning to London.

By 1821 Kitt was back in Dublin, having been called to the Bar in the Hilary Term of that year, and the following year took up residence in Middle Gardiner Street. He did start to practise as a barrister, but there is little evidence of much work coming his way. He was very well off for a 28 year old, though he was inclined to complain that he wasn't. There was occasional bickering with O'Meara about how much he should be getting from the estates. His income in 1822 was £800, and in 1823 it was £1,000 from a net rental then of over £1,600, his mother and O'Meara keeping the balance. A nasty fight with O'Meara was in the making, to be enjoined on wider issues later.

In 1822 the long running case of East Acton was to start. East Acton was the name of a farm of 160 acres in Co. Wicklow on the townland of Ballinamona, which had been bought in 1680 and leased in 1709 for a tiny sum, £10, on a long renewable lease, with fines to be paid on renewal after deaths. In 1822, it was belatedly noticed that the last renewal fine had not been paid or any rent paid, for fifteen years. Kitt set about the procedure of having the tenant evicted. This was no case of putting out a starving cotter into the snow. The tenant was a bigger and richer landlord than any FitzSimons ever were. He was a Mr Burton of Burton Hall in Co. Carlow, himself an absentee landlord living on his estates in England, and to whom a few hundred pounds one way or the other in his expenses would not have meant much. The property was later valued as worth £200 a year. However when an attempt was made to serve a writ on Burton, he decided to fight. The case went to the High Court in Dublin and Burton won. The points he won on were that not only should he have been chased up for the rent sooner, but also, that the writ was not handed to Burton himself in his castle in England, but to his butler. Kitt did not give up and in 1826 in the House of Lords, judgement was reversed and given in Kitt's favour. This was good timing, for Kitt had just been married and was able to move into the house. There was a quite large two-storey gentleman's residence on the property.

Kitt married Ellen O'Connell at Westland Row Church in July 1825, "A great marriage in high life by the Catholic Archbishop of Dublin", it was reported. Ellen was then living in her father's house around the corner in Merrion Square. Daniel was not yet the "Liberator"; he was a successful barrister and was working for Catholic Emancipation. Most of the Penal Laws had been dismantled, but it was still not possible for Catholics to sit in Parliament.

One of O'Connell's colleagues on the Catholic Committee, the body working for emancipation, was Thomas O'Meara, and O'Connell was a frequent visitor at Glencullen House, where the plans for the campaign were drawn up around the dining-room table. They and the young Kitt also collaborated on legal business. Kitt and Ellen would have become well acquainted over quite some time. Ellen had lived most of her life in Merrion Square. She attended a school for young ladies nearby, advanced for its time, run by a friend of the prototype feminist Mary Wollstonecraft. There was a time when she, with her mother and sisters and a brother, were sent to live in France. The family would spend quite some time with the old uncle Daniel, who, after the Restoration, had returned to France, where he had a large house in Paris and a chateau on the Loire. He was a friend of the new king, Charles X, and had been made a count and lieutenant general. The idea was that the family could save money. Not so much because things were cheaper in France, but because Dan had to keep up expensive appearances like maintaining a coach and four and attending social events when the family was in Dublin. Dan was making a lot of money from his legal business, and from 1825 he owned part of the family estate of Derrynane in Co. Kerry, but he was inclined to spend lavishly, lending and giving money to a large number of friends and relatives. For the first year after she was married, Ellen spent most of her time at Derrynane, while her husband and father travelled about on legal and political business. In 1826, the house at Ballinamona had now been returned by Mr Burton, and after some alterations, became Ellen and Kitt's home for the next eight years.

In 1828, Dan O'Connell was elected to Parliament. This was the breakthrough in Catholic Emancipation, and Kitt was to act as his right-hand man. In 1834 Kitt himself was elected to Parliament for Co. Dublin and went to live at Glencullen. O'Meara had moved out some time in 1829, leaving Tom, Kitt's brother, in charge as his agent or manager. O'Meara, Margaret and the stepchildren went to live in Blackrock, Co. Dublin, which was more convenient for O'Meara's work as a solicitor. But before Kitt and Ellen moved in, there was a row with O'Meara of some significant proportion and prolonged renegotiation of the deal of 1817. The basic substance of the deal had been that O'Meara would invest £3,000 of his own in the property, take a proportion of the rent for himself, and have the use of the property during Margaret's lifetime. O'Meara was to maintain that he had invested £5,000 in the property, and he might well have done so, but it looks as if some of this was Margaret's money which was supposed to be passed on ultimately to her younger sons Tom and Henry, in accordance with her marriage contract with the late Thomas FitzSimon in 1789.

Kitt took his stepfather to court. Most of the issues seem to be somewhat trivial, and may have been more likely legal manoeuvring than a display of genuine anger and spleen, which at first sight they appear to have been. After all, it was a barrister suing a solicitor, and even though it was a personal matter, they would have been posturing for advantage after the manner of lawyers. Kitt complained that O'Meara had allowed walls to fall down, had allowed tenants to graze cattle on the new timber plantations, had cut down ornamental trees, and when he left for Blackrock, had taken the locks from the doors and the hatstand from the hall.

O'Meara made a calmer reply. He had built new walls, very few cattle had got into the plantations, the only trees cut down were old rotten ones, and the only lock he took was one padlock from the cellar. It looked as if the case would go to the High Court, but an arbitrator in the person of the Liberator himself was brought in. It must have been one conflict of interest cancelling out another, the protagonists being Dan's long time business and political colleague and his favourite son-in-law. Anyway the matters were resolved. The major issues resolved were that Kitt and Ellen were able to live in Glencullen House, which had been extended and modernized by O'Meara, within Margaret's lifetime. Tom and Henry each got £2,000 of Margaret's money to be getting on with. Kitt agreed to pay O'Meara half of the £3,000 he had invested immediately, and the remainder was to be paid later, when he had it to spare, which he was able to do from a legacy following his Uncle Anthony's death. Letters from Kitt to O'Meara were icy immediately afterwards, but soon became friendly, as they had been before the dispute.

Kitt remained in Parliament for less than three years, during which time he continued as a chief henchman for O'Connell, mainly involved in constituency work. Time was spent in London, of course and Ellen visited there occasionally. Her time was more preoccupied in having babies. Between 1826 and 1846 she had thirteen children. Five of them died in infancy and two in their teens. This was not a record among the prolific O'Connells, as Ellen's great- grandmother had twenty-two children. Kitt gave as his reason for leaving politics the wish to spend more time with his family. This was before O'Connell's campaign for the Repeal of the Union, the failure of which (in 1843) would effectively end his career. In the meantime, O'Connell was well supported by his family in Parliament, having his three sons and a nephew members at various times. Kitt secured for himself a well-paid sinecure, Clerk of the Crown and Hanaper, in the Lord Chancellor's office, where he had to go to sign documents, but not very often.

Through the 1840s, Kitt continued to be active with the estate and public affairs, involved in local government and making improvements in Glencullen. For the comfort of the family, a hot water system from a boiler in the laundry, which also provided central heating, was installed in the house. As well as the building of a police barracks and a dispensary in the village, a Victorian style gate lodge was built at the front gate. The two-storey building, later to become Foxe's pub, dates from this

O'CONNELL AND LEYNE FAMILY TREES AND THE FITZSIMON CONNECTION

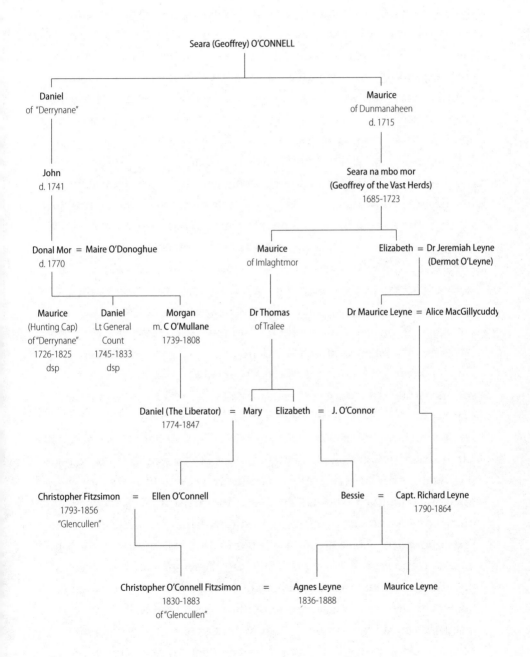

time. During the great famine of 1846/48, Kitt was active in collecting money for relief. Glencullen was not badly effected by the famine. It was one of the few places where the population kept rising right up untill the 1860s. This is probably due to the importance of quarrying and stone cutting in the local economy. The Glencullen House farm at this stage was quite large and many prizes were being won at the Royal Dublin Society including winning one for the best farm above 600 feet elevation in the country more than once. So the absolute dependence on the potato was avoided, but then again it would appear that the potato fungus never got the same hold in Glencullen as was general throughout Ireland and Scotland. The FitzSimon Wicklow property also escaped the worst of the famine because the tenanted holdings were all well above average size, commercial farms rather than subsistence holdings.

Early in 1856 Kitt and Ellen went on an extended tour of Italy, especially to see their second surviving son Thomas, who, after graduating from Trinity College, had gone there and had married an Italian lady and was working in her family building business. After attending the great Easter festivals of the Church in Rome, they had gone to Mascerata to visit Thomas's in-laws. Kitt died there suddenly, was buried there, and is commemorated by a large plaque in the cathedral. Ellen was so devastated that her practical arrangements appear to have broken down, for we find Thomas writing home to his elder brother Christopher, who had been left in charge of Glencullen, asking for money to be sent to Ellen, so that she could get her jewels out of pawn. Ellen lived on until 1888, surviving three of her children who had grown up and married. She was to spend time travelling on the continent and survived the siege of Paris in the Franco-Prussian War, where it was reported the people were reduced to starvation and were eating the dogs and cats. When my grandfather heard that she was coming to stay he burst into tears, afraid that she would eat his pet donkey. She was a very accomplished person; she could speak eight languages, including Polish, and wrote poems, several of which, even if not inspiring masterpieces, were published in her day and survive.

Kitt's brothers Tom and Henry born in 1798 and 1800 respectively, had families and careers of their own. Occasional mentions of Tom in correspondence gives the impression that he did not always measure up to expectations; I would say he was accident prone. After his time managing Glencullen for O'Meara, for which O'Meara was to blame him for the mess which made Kitt so cross, he was appointed as a senior constable in the recently reorganized Royal Irish Constabulary.

He nearly lost his position in 1840 when he was serving in Sligo. He was in a police magistrate's court on four charges, two relating to incorrect procedures, and two which were drink related. "For being intoxicated on Saturday the 12th of October last on return from Carney investigating outrages", and "For insulting a respectable female on the evening of the 8th of August in the town of Sligo whilst under the influence of liquor". He had good witnesses for his defence. He had been drinking with two priests. Father O'Callaghan, the parish priest of Carney, was asked how many tumblers of punch Tom had consumed to which the reply was "Not half as many as a certain young magistrate". Two of the constables said that they had never seen Tom drunk. Tom was able to continue his career; it was suggested that this was due to the influence of his powerful relatives; at this time Dan O'Connell was at the height of his power and influence. He later became a District Inspector in Co. Wexford. His son was known as "Austrian Tom" because he started his military career in the Austrian Army; he was later adjutant of the Inniskilling Dragoons and retired as a major. A daughter Nancy married an officer in the Indian Army and lived out her days with children and grandchildren on a farm in the Himalayas.

The youngest brother, Henry, set off in 1822 to join the Indian Army. He had letters of introduction but wrote home that when he got to Calcutta, "they didn't so much as get me a dinner". He was commissioned in the Bengal Native Infantry and later, as a major, was to serve on the Governor General's staff. He retired in 1856 as a lieutenant colonel and came back with his Anglo-Indian wife and children to live in Dun Laoghaire, where he died in 1865. In 1842 he made his one and only trip home on leave, a trip which meant several months at sea each way. His family stayed in India. He spent all his time in Ireland based at Glencullen. He had his first trip ever on a railway train, the line from Dublin to Dun Laoghaire, which was not long opened. He would from time to time go into Dublin and lunch at his brother Kitt's club, and on one occasion went to visit his cousin Sir Thomas Esmonde in Co. Wexford, where he was given "a vile dinner". He attended the confirmation of one of his nephews by Archbishop Murray in Sandyford Church, after which, at a banquet, much whiskey punch was consumed, not least, he remarked, by the Archbishop, who was well into his seventies. Whiskey punch gets quite a lot of mention in Henry's diary. When he retired, his children were still quite young, and one of his two daughters married Alderman Cotton; the other one Ellen did not marry. She lived until 1937 and was buried in Glencullen. His son Eustace "left the country for his own and the country's good" and was not heard of again.

Christopher, also known as Kitt, and latterly as Poor Dear Fitz, the name given him by Ellen, had thirteen children of whom only six survived into adulthood. Two boys had died in their teens and five babies died in infancy. Their second son Thomas, who was married in Italy, died childless not long after he was visited by his parents. Their third surviving son Henry farmed some of the Wicklow lands for many years; he rented the Ballinamona property from his brother and later his nephew, until he died in 1902 and in the meantime had bought the adjacent Ardinairy parcel of the estate. He had ten children, several of whom had children and descendants, though after his sons there were no males to carry on the name of FitzSimon or O'Connell FitzSimon as it had then become. One comes across his son, also Henry, in Joyce's *Ulysses* as "a chieftain descended from chieftains" surrounded by all sorts of vegetables - Henry junior was manager of the Corporation vegetable market. Henry junior's wife Elizabeth was the sister of the painter Charles O'Connor.

Poor Dear Fitz and Ellen had three daughters, Mary, Eily, and Catherine, all of whom were to marry and have numerous progeny. Mary was the first to marry. Indeed she eloped with a young lieutenant called Henry Redmond, who, horror of horrors, was a Protestant and to make it worse, they were married in St George's Church of Ireland Church. What would her grandfather, the poor Liberator have thought, and he only two years in his grave? Probably he would not have been too worried: after all he had himself been married into a half Protestant household and to his wife's annoyance was often giving money to Splinter, his somewhat ne'er-do-well Protestant brother-in-law. He fought for Catholic Emancipation, but there was never anything sectarian about Dan. The situation was retrieved, nevertheless, when the errant Mary and her husband were brought back to Glencullen and remarried there with Roman Catholic rites. Henry Redmond was for long a Resident Magistrate in Co. Waterford, and long after, after Mary was dead, he himself converted to Catholicism.

Eily, the second daughter, was married twice. She was first married to Charles Bianconi junior, the son and heir of the Charles Bianconi. who came from Italy and established the transport network of "Bianconi Cars" throughout the south of Ireland, providing an efficient and cheap means of travel for the general public in the years before the opening of the railways. Charles junior died young and Eily then married Charles's cousin Patrick Hayes of Dublin. Catherine the third daughter was married in Glencullen amidst great celebration, with fireworks, the village brass band, and with all the tenants attending. As well as whiskey, many barrels of stout were drunk. The groom was George Hewett, a lieutenant of the Bengal Cavalry, later a colonel. They eventually went to live in London.

Christopher O'Connell FitzSimon, my great-grandfather, the eldest surviving son, who was born in 1830, inherited the Glencullen, Wicklow and Dublin City properties which had been made over to him shortly before his father's death in 1856. He had graduated from Trinity College and been called to the Bar, but never actually practised at it. In 1862 he was High Sheriff for Co. Wicklow. Thereafter there is little evidence of much activity beyond farming the Glencullen land. He farmed most of the arable land, employing up to thirty labourers, according to the season, who were paid 1s. 6*d.* per day, the going rate at the time. There were still a number of tenant farmers, and the mountain was kept for the grouse. The Wicklow lands which made up about half of the estate were always in the hands of tenants, mostly quite large farmers.

In 1867 he married his second cousin Agnes Leyne. Ellen did not approve of the marriage, I have been told, but I have never been given the reason why. The objection would not have been on the grounds of social class. The Leynes were not large landowners like the O'Connells, but then the Derrynane estate had only become large in recent times. It had been built up by the Liberator's uncle, Maurice, known as "Hunting Cap", from the proceeds of successful legitimate trading and even more successful smuggling. The Leynes were of the professional classes with connections to the gentry. Agnes's father was Captain Richard Leyne, Resident Magistrate and former army officer. Originally a lieutenant in the Kerry Militia, Richard raised a company of Kerry men which he took to join the 73rd Highlanders, the regiment of his kinsman Charles Philip O'Connell, and so became a captain in that regiment. Charles Philip was subsequently Acting Governor of New South Wales. The 73rd Highlanders fought at Waterloo, and Richard as the senior surviving officer, led the remnants of the decimated regiment off the field. Richard married the daughter of the O'Connor Kerry, a niece of the Liberator's wife Mary. His father was Doctor Maurice Leyne of Tralee, himself the son of a Tralee doctor Jeremiah Leyne; both these doctors were trained in France. Richard's mother was a daughter of the MacGillycuddy of the Reeks.

There could have been an argument against the marriage on grounds of the degree of consanguinity. Consanguinity was not perceived to be too much of a problem to the old Kerry families. Study of their pedigrees reveals an extraordinarily complicated network of relationships, as cousins marry within a limited number of families. Ellen's parents were third cousins. Religious barriers were not an issue, as Agnes was a Catholic, but even if she had not been, it should not have caused trouble, as the old Kerry families married accross the religious divide almost as much as they married their cousins. Dr Thomas O'Connell of Tralee, Ellen's grandfather and Agnes's great-grandfather, was a Protestant, as was the MacGillycuddy. The situation was generally accommodated by the "Galway Convention", whereby sons took their father's denomination and daughters their mother's. It has to be said however that times were changing. In the eighteenth century sectarianism was about public affairs and land ownership. As the nineteenth century progressed it became more personal and intrusive; we read of Cardinal Cullen and ultramontanism and the Protestant missionaries with their soup. It caused consternation in 1849 when Mary FitzSimon eloped with the Protestant Henry Redmond.

Politics might have been an issue. Ellen thought the world of her father the Liberator, who had ended his days, though still revered, a broken man, and in a bitter dispute with the Young Irelanders. Agnes's older brother Maurice was a leader of the Young Ireland movement, and was on the run all through Tipperary in 1848 with T.F.Meagher, "Meagher of the Sword". They were captured and tried at Waterford. Maurice narrowly escaped the commuted death sentence and transportation to Van Dieman's Land with the other leaders. But then Ellen herself was tainted by the movement, having had several of her poems published in *The Nation*, the Young Ireland paper.

So if not Class, Religion, Politics or Consanguinity, what was the problem? A clue might be the case of Ellen's own parents. Dan the Liberator, who was to be heir to the great wealth of his uncle, Hunting Cap, married secretly without prospect of a dowry. Such was Hunting Cap's wrath that he cut Dan out of his will. He did eventually relent, though not entirely, for Dan was left only a third part of the old man's fortune. This was the first time in recorded history that a wife did not bring a dowry to the head of the Glencullen FitzSimons. Agnes did not have a bean. Or perhaps Ellen just did not like Agnes.

Christopher and Agnes brought up four sons and a daughter at Glencullen. The third son Dan was my grandfather. I have already referred to them in Chapter Three. Christopher, though it is reported that he kept great state while he was the High Sheriff of the Co. Wicklow, and that he was prone to lose large sums at cards, is also reported as having been an exemplary and mild-mannered man. Getting into serious debt, he sold most of the Wicklow land and all the remaining city property in 1872. He had raised a mortgage of £17,000 in 1862. Is it a little odd that the mortgagee, Magee College in Derry, a recently founded Presbyterian establishment, would choose one of the few large Catholic landlords to whom to lend money? Magee was paid out, but other debts arose. One of the creditors was the parish priest of Enniskerry, who pursued Christopher, but died before he was repaid. The priest had left his estate to four other priests, so Christopher was pursued thereafter by four priests instead of one.

Christopher died of "paralysis" in 1883; the symptoms of the condition from which he was suffering for his last six months, read very like those of motor neurone disease. He was bankrupt. The children were made Wards in Chancery, and a firm of solicitors was employed to manage the estate. Agnes lived on for only another five years and was said to have spent most of her time in prayer, when not actually attending Mass. The children amused themselves on the estate, though they all had periods at boarding schools; Carlow College, where there was a Leyne on the staff, was the most patronized. Christie the eldest, attended Trinity College but never graduated. Christie came of age the same year his mother died. He inherited the estate, what was left of it, free of debt. The Glencullen estate then had about 500 acres of arable land and about 1,200 acres of mountain and rough grazing. The Wicklow land was then only the farm at Ballinamona which Poor Dear Fitz had retrieved by way of the House of Lords, and where he had lived with Ellen when they were first married. Ballinamona was rented from Christie by his uncle Henry FitzSimon, until Henry's death in 1902.

The solicitors had done a good job. It was a time of depressed agricultural prices, and the tenants were getting a better deal than in the past, following the introduction of legislation for fair rents tribunals. This had the consequence that the total rents had reduced by about fifteen per cent in the period. The solicitors would have done well enough out of the estate themselves. Tenants (all the property, except for the top of the mountain and a few acres around the house was then in the hands of tenants) were instructed by letter, even on the most trivial of issues, with an itemised bill for writing the letter forwarded. There was one issue which was not so trivial. This was the removal of Mr Rogerson's sheep which were ruining the grouse shooting. This firm of solicitors, Maxwell Weldon, were to continue to advise the family, and well into the twentieth century were frequently brought in for all sorts of minor assistance by the erstwhile Wards in Chancery, who seem to have treated them as surrogate parents, and continued the habit until they themselves had reached middle age. This is of course no longer the "early history of the Glencullen FitzSimons".

CHAPTER SIXTEEN

Trinity College I

Trinity College Dublin could almost be considered as the FitzSimon family university. Six generations of FitzSimons have each had at least one representative attending, starting with the Christopher who matriculated in 1812 and graduated in 1816. Not everyone who went up graduated. In addition to FitzSimons, there were several Elliots and numerous MacFarlanes to attend in the nineteenth and twentieth centuries.

After several false starts throughout the Middle Ages, the university was finally founded in 1591, initially to promote English civility in Ireland, especially to promote the Protestant religion. The Vatican was to describe it as "a pernicious nest of heresy". An important, indeed predominant function, was to provide clergy for the Church of Ireland. Throughout the eighteenth century it only gave degrees to Protestant Episcopalians. Presbyterians would go to one of the four Scottish universities and Catholics would attend the numerous Irish Colleges established on the Continent. The ban on Catholics being given degrees was removed in 1792, at the same time as the foundation of the College at Maynooth. By this time Trinity was offering a wide range of subjects, and it was a university in the modern sense; it looked as if Maynooth would develop in the same way, but was soon to become a specialist school for training Catholic priests. Another Catholic to enter Trinity not long after Christopher was his future brother-in-law John O'Connell. That the Liberator himself would send his son to Trinity would be quoted by aggrieved Catholic graduates in the 1850s when the redoubtable Archbishop of Dublin, Cullen, vilified Trinity. A hundred years later, the equally redoubtable John Charles McQuaid would forbid Catholics from attending without his express permission, given only in extenuating circumstances.

In Cullen's day, the colleges of Belfast, Cork and Galway, the Queen's Colleges, were known as the "Godless Colleges", and were more strongly condemned than was Trinity. By MacQuaid's time, Cork and Galway along with the Dublin successor of Newman's Catholic University of the 1850s had been incorporated into the National University of Ireland, which was acceptable to him and the Hierarchy. Despite McQuaid's ban, in the 1950s the Trinity population was about one quarter Roman Catholic, but it had to do without a Catholic chaplain because McQuaid refused to appoint one, despite the opportunity to do so being suggested to him by the college authorities. This incentive to sectarianism was to continue until the new climate of Vatican II and talk of a government-forced merger of Trinity with University College Dublin, caused the ban to be lifted.

There were five of us from St Columba's who started the pre-med course at Trinity in 1954. "Oxo" Jackson dropped out after a term. I never entered the Medical School proper but joined the Engineering School the following year. Alex Tomkin, Donny Cheah who came from Malaya, and David Nowlan graduated in the minimum time and would become physicians, though David Nowlan flourished in later life as a medical correspondent, theatre critic and editor in *The Irish Times*. Nowlan and I worked together. By the summer, I had passed the exams and was quite enjoying the academic subjects, but it gradually dawned on me that I didn't want to be a doctor. I didn't like sick people and didn't like the sight of blood. I had thought that the medical profession was a most suitable one to join. My mother's father, brother, cousin and uncles were members of it, and I was fascinated by some aspects of biology at school. I had passed with honours the Leaving Certificate paper in Physiology, a subject which was not specifically taught at St Columba's, but I had done the exam nevertheless, so it was not a surprising move for me to enrol in pre-med.

The subject I liked best however was History, and my preferred activity was farming; however I could not see how I could earn a living at either. What I really would have liked to be was to be like Hubert Butler, to be a country gentleman with a nice farm, and scope for ongoing study and contribution to the discussion of issues, especially political ones. It is not that I was ever modelling myself on Hubert himself; it was his general lifestyle that I envied. He was much more the intellectual than I would have aspired to be, and his farming, a few acres of fruit trees and renting some fields to his brother for grazing, was far less than what I would be interested in doing in the unlikely event of having a farm or having enough money to buy one. That year, my first one in college, was when I had most to do with the Maiden Hall Butlers, though I was to keep visiting there for many years to come. I would hitch-hike up and down from Dublin. It was always easy to get a lift even though there was still little traffic on the roads, and hitch-hiking was a new idea. Nearly everyone would stop, even farmers on tractors would give one a lift for a mile or two. My best ride was all the way from Athy to Dublin with the parish priest of Athy on his way to see the Archbishop, John Charles McQuaid. He asked me my school, "St Columba's," I said, "What order runs that?" he asked. "It is a Protestant school," I said. The topic for discussion most of the way down became Henry VIII. I went down to Maiden Hall for the second of the famous Kilkenny debates. Hubert organized these debates on significant issues and brought in some of the best people in whatever field was to be discussed. The debate I went to was on peace and disarmament. He had brought the eminent military historian Liddle Hart over from England. He arrived to stay in the house in a pre-war Rolls-Royce. Also in the house was Senator Owen Sheehy Skeffington, and another speaker was Declan Costello, the Attorney General. Sheehy Skeffington was then one of the senators representing Trinity in the Senate. He taught French in the College, indeed he taught me. Everyone came back and whiskey was handed out in the drawing room, and the participants excitedly held their post-mortem. I, the most junior and humble of the audience, became disillusioned and disappointed, for these great prophets of the age, particularly Sheehy

Skeffington, did not talk about the substance or the issues of the debate. It was all "do you think I sounded good?" To the 18 year old idealist these were not prophets any more, but merely actors. When his works, articles, essays, letters to newspapers, some which had been published, and some not, were collected up in books some thirty years later, it is was clear to me that of all of them Hubert was the prophet. Many of his insights, some of which are still not general currency, I have adopted for my own illumination.

People sometimes talked of "The Maiden Hall Mafia", like-minded people of intellectual stature and people who were just friends of Hubert and Peggy. I was hardly of the Mafia, but one could call at the house in passing and find it hard to resist the invitation to stay for the night or longer. The costs of staying were immediate recruitment into some activity like picking blackcurrants or driving someone into Kilkenny to the dentist. There were usually other people staying there. The four Harrison girls, whose parents were overseas, spent their school holidays there. They had stayed with us at Annaghmakerrig, and there always seemed to be a French or German boy or two staying. Sheehy Skeffington was a quintessential Maiden Hall Mafia man. Another one was Alec Reed. It is oddly coincidental that these two were my Arts teachers in the Junior Freshman year.

It was the rule in those days that one had to have an Arts degree before one could get one in Medicine or Engineering. The authorities however made it easy by requiring only two subjects of the four needed for a pass Arts degree on its own. It was sometimes a bit tricky to find a subject which would not clash with one's professional course classes where attendance was compulsory. I chose French my first year as the least unsatisfactory subject I could get to, even though I had dropped French for my last year at school. Sheehy Skeffington was the lecturer, and he must have been quite good, because I got to enjoy reading in French, albeit simple Maupassant.

For the pre-med students, a special course in English Literature which we were all able to attend, was provided. Alec Reed was the lecturer. Alec was a plump pink-faced man so short sighted that he needed a magnifying glass as well as his spectacles to read. He could not see what the philistine would-be doctors at the back of the theatre were up to, throwing paper darts and climbing about on the pews. There were over a hundred in the class. But he had a loud enough voice to speak above the din to those of us who were not totally philistine, sat at the front and appreciated his lecture. His lectures were by far the most enjoyable I attended in my whole university career. Alec Reed was only a part-time university lecturer. I think the pre-med class was his only one; he had more strings to his bow. He taught at Drogheda Grammar School and wrote among other things, leaders for *The Irish Times*. The lectures in the professional schools were just work. In the pre-med class I had the privilege of being taught Physics by Nobel Laureate Ernie Walton, who even though he was the first man to split the atom, liked teaching Junior Freshmen: perhaps teaching first year would-be doctors was more of a challenge than splitting atoms. I got a high mark in Physics, but Nobel Laureate or not, I don't remember being inspired in any way.

It was much easier to get into Trinity than into other universities. In England one needed some subjects at GCE "A" level rather than "O" level. For the National University of Ireland, Cork, Galway or Dublin, a Leaving Certificate pass was needed, whereas for Trinity, honours at Intermediate would suffice. However, having started at Trinity, entry to the Medical or Engineering School was not so easy. In pre-med about half the class were repeats, and quite a few dropped out entirely. For the Engineering School there was a special exam called "engineering entrance", which less than half those who sat for it passed. There were about thirty in each year in the school but more than sixty tried the entrance exam. I sat it in the Summer Term and failed. It was not all that high a standard, but competitive, more a sort of intelligence and aptitude test to let through only a predetermined number for the vacancies. I passed the supplemental exam in the autumn.

Though I passed the necessary subjects in the pre-med, it was always by a small margin. It was hard work, especially with the commuting from Glencullen. We had about thirty hours a week of lectures and laboratory practicals. The chemistry lecturer proffered the view that for every hour of lecture one needed to do an hour of study; I think he was about right. I played a little rugby but slipped a disc after a few games and didn't play again for a couple of years. I had no social life that I can recall. My mother bought a little Fiat 500 for the use of Christopher and me, but our times were of course quite different, and though useful to have it, there was still quite a bit of bus travel. One night in February I spun the car around in a snow drift near the Yellow House in Rathfarnham and ran into a stone wall at right angles. It was a resilient little car and it got me home, but it cost quite a bit to repair. I found the long hours and the commuting a bit of a strain. I was beginning to find living at home more of a strain and this was the real reason, though I didn't admit it, for a request that in the second year I should take rooms in College. The expense of this was rationalized by the move to Engineering cutting two years off the duration of the course. In the meantime, with the end of the academic year, I set out for some farm work in Denmark.

David Blackwell, who had been one of the four of us who had worked on the farm in Worcester the year before, organized a trip to the farm of some family connection he had in Denmark. It was just the two of us and our intention was to see a bit of the rest of Scandinavia on the way. We passed through England and took a ship from Harwich to Gothenberg in Sweden; it took two days and we lived in a sort of dormitory with a dozen or so others. The idea was that we would hitch-hike to Oslo, but in one day we had only one lift and got less than half way so we decided next day to go east to Stockholm. It took so long getting halfway, to a place called Jönköping, that we stayed there for the week and then headed south for Denmark. We had no lifts, and walked 28 miles the first day; it was then in despair that we took the train. We were well fed on the farm with plenty of porridge, pork fat and strawberry jam. Most of the work was assisting to build a new and vast piggery, a veritable pig palace. The Danes know how to look after pigs. We were paid very little, but it was enough to cover the cost of the trip.

The second, or Senior Freshman year, in College was to be quite different from the previous one, as I was now in the Engineering School and living in rooms. The first year Engineering course was not very exciting, Pure and Applied Maths, Physics and Chemistry, Drawing and Surveying. Most of the Physics and Chemistry I had done before. Pure Maths was taught by a Mr Graham, who was normally a teacher in the Dublin High School. Rather than the usual university lecturers' performance of expanding loftily from a distance with an artistically crafted exposition, he would treat us like schoolchildren. He would keep a grip on the class calling out to unfortunates he thought were slacking "Williams! say Huygens' Rule!" or "Shanagher! What is MacLaurin's Theorem?" On the other hand, Dr Bass, who was said to be a brilliant theoretician, gave what were probably exquisite dissertations, but alas, I and many others hadn't the faintest idea what he was talking about. We would go out into the College Park to be shown how to use the surveying instruments, which would prove to be a useful skill when during the next long vacation I went to work on a construction site.

I had rooms in Botany Bay, a square of four-storey buildings, which were 150 years old. In No. 13 there were two sets on each floor, two persons per set, therefore sixteen persons had that address. I shared rooms there for most of three years with John Killen, my cousin from Monaghan. Across the landing were the rooms of Peter Williams and Jim O'Brien. Jim had been in the pre-med with me, and Peter was another first year engineer. Our combined sets of rooms in time functioned as one and remained so after Jim's replacement by his brother Nick, another engineer. I have kept continuous contact with those people ever since. The combined rooms usually also harboured Shanagher and O'Flynn from our class but who officially lived at home in Dublin. A set of rooms had two bedrooms and a living room, and a place called a skippery where there was a sink with a cold water tap and a gas ring. The skippery was the domain of the skip, whose function it was to wash up any dishes and heat the water for the young gentlemen to shave. He was supposed to sweep out the rooms as well, but I don't think our skip, a decent enough old chap, and retired from the Irish Army, did much of that. The one lavatory for the eight sets of rooms was at the bottom of the stairs. If one wanted a bath, one had to give notice to the attendant in the bath house and walk across the square to it. I bought a large solid dilapidated settee from the previous occupant for £1, and found a carpet in an outhouse at home. It had a hole in it and had had hens perching on it, but the furnishings lasted us the three years. One day Tom the skip reported that the Senior Dean had inspected the rooms and condemned the furniture. We took no notice and never heard any more. This august gentleman ranked next to the Vice Provost but I don't think I even heard his name.

The Junior Dean however, was very large in my, and many other people's lives. He was Dr MacDowell, a historian of distinction: he also was my tutor. He had become known to our family when he came to visit us at Annaghmakerrig in order to go through family papers we had which were of interest to him in his research. A remarkable man, that is one would be bound to remark on him if one was just to see him, as he trotted about, always wearing a scarf and a strange flat hat. I am sure there must have been other written attempts to do justice to him and his eccentricities. He was responsible for the students' discipline and would occasionally and erratically pursue this responsibility, sometimes with hilarious outcome. On one occasion I was causing something of a disturbance in Botany Bay: dustbins were involved. I don't remember what it was about, but when Dr MacDowell came up in something of a rage, I attempted to make an excuse which I knew was a lame one. He addressed me "O'Connell FitzSimon", (he always called me that), "That is sophistry, you are fined £10." Was the fine for me being a nuisance or for the sophistry? At any rate £10 was an enormous sum, several weeks' income. However it was never paid or the matter followed up. On another occasion I was witness to Dr MacDowell walking into the Bay, when someone emptied a bucket of water out of an upper window, getting him fully on the head. The drenched and enraged Doctor, looking for immediate retribution, dashed in through the door and up the stairs of the building, but it was the opposite building to the one from which the bucket of water was tipped. He rushed into the first set of rooms he found open where he startled a number of unaware innocents and shouted "You are all fined £10!"

Attendance at the dinner known as Commons, served in the dining hall twice in the evening, was compulsory. It was preceded by an extremely long Latin grace which referred among other things to Queen Elizabeth founding the College of the Holy and Undivided Trinity near Dublin – long before my day the growth of Dublin had engulfed the college – and was recited by a scholar who had to know if off by heart. The meal was not one for the gourmet but was substantial and very cheap. Served with it was a special college beer, and one could drink as much of it as one was capable, it was low in alcohol and though some heroes would try to get drunk on it, I never heard of anyone succeeding.

Concerning drink, though I was no stranger to it, it was during my second year in College, my first year in rooms, when I would become thoroughly inititiated into the ritual of pints of Guinness stout in public houses. The number of pints consumed, when one could afford it, and particularly on a Saturday night, might be considered to be excessive. O'Donoghues in Suffolk Street was where we started, but soon changed our custom to O'Neills. The back bar of Jammets off Grafton Street was important, as was the Lincoln at the College back gate. Further social life was limited in the main to going to a party which usually was in a flat in somewhere like Rathgar, to which one would carry a brown paper parcel of bottled stout. There might be some sort of dancing with the ladies in the front room and stout – sometimes there was even a metal barrel, an "iron lung" of it, and singing, in the back room.

Ladies at that time had to be out of the College grounds by ten o'clock, which was when the library reading room closed. Though Dublin University had been giving women degrees for fifty years, indeed it gave degrees to women before Oxford or Cambridge did, their lives were very restricted. Not only were they not allowed to be in College after ten, let alone live in rooms, they could not have meals in the dining hall, not just the ritual evening commons, but neither could they have the self-service informal lunch. About the time I was leaving, I remember Michael Knight, who was an auditor of the Hist, the main debating society, saying that he had written to some famous person to come to give the opening address of the year, always a big event. He had stressed the uniqueness of the society where Burke had honed his skills two centuries before, and that it was the only significant such institution in the British Isles besides the House of Lords which was not open to women. Despite their second class status they made up about a quarter, or perhaps more, of the undergraduate students: there was also a handful among the academic staff. Quite numerous in the Medical School, there were none whatsoever in the Engineering School.

Life for the male residents was not without restrictions. One would not be let through the gate after some hour, perhaps midnight when it was shut, without written permission from the Junior Dean. It was necessary to scale the railings after that hour, no mean feat. On one occasion a few of us were roistering down Dawson Street after hours and proceeded to climb the railings. John Killen had successfully got over and I was handing him up some advertising sign he had collected as a trophy when I was grabbed by the legs, by a Civic Guard. The Guard had been called by an irate petrol station attendant who was displeased by our behaviour. I was taken to the College Street police station and locked up for the night. The guards made a big issue of locking me in to give me a fright – they were successful at that – but let me go in the morning without reporting me to the College, which would have been embarrassing, to say the least. I shared my cell with a newspaper seller who had been accused of cheating someone with change. I recall that, on hearing his story, that I was aware of an injustice. If it had been someone higher up the social scale he would not have been locked up so arbitrarily by the police.

Commons, as I said, was compulsory, but I for one would not have missed it on any account. Indeed one paid in advance. It cost £6 a quarter, the same figure as the rent of the rooms and the pay for the skip. Chapel on Sundays was compulsory for Protestant Episcopalians – however I was to escape this as I put on my form that I was a

Presbyterian. This might appear to have been a subterfuge because, apart from that limited period of my early childhood when in the company of my Great Aunt Jane and my grandmother Killen, I had had no exposure to Presbyterianism. School exposure to religion was firmly Episcopalian, and also the denomination with which my mother mixed, so that any churchgoing at home was to the Church of Ireland. However I liked to establish my identity on my own terms, despite my ignorance of the finer points of denominationalism. I had already avoided confirmation at St Columba's, where it was an almost universal rite of passage, and got away with it. I discovered later that this was not from religious tolerance on the part of the authorities. They would, I am sure, never have forced it on me, but would have treated the issue in a gentlemanly manner. It was simply their lackadaisical failure to notice that I didn't attend the class. I was never anti-religious and was content to call myself a Presbyterian, albeit a non-practising, somewhat agnostic one and content to stand outside the whole issue. I was a good example of the Irish practice of limiting religion to the wearing of a tribal badge of identity; spirituality or theology were not matters of moment: they were a very small part of the equation. I was not as partisan as one medical student, who, over pints of stout in the Lincoln Inn pub, forcefully informed me that he would commit adultery and fornicate without compunction, as often and as much as he could, but would never, never, as a Catholic, use any artificial birth control device.

Religion, Politics or Sex are forbidden topics for discussion in an officers' mess, and only warily approached in polite society. I rather think that they were the main topics of conversation in our rooms or the pubs. Religion came up fairly quickly, and I was forced to look outside my non-practising agnosticism. This was because Jim O'Brien and Peter Williams in the adjacent rooms had recently arrived from a Jesuit school, and were perhaps curious to explore the contrariness of a heretic, and to let the heretic know where he was wrong. I don't think Jim was all that much that way inclined, but Peter certainly was, as was Nick O'Brien who was to join the rooms later. My first conversation with Nick, who had also just arrived from a Jesuit school to sit the engineering entrance, was a theological debate, albeit one strongly promoted by a large recent intake of stout. To add to debate there was John Black, who had arrived from Monaghan to join the pre-med class. He was no subtle Jesuit. He was, like me, a tribal Presbyterian, but if I was a fringe one and quiet, he was a noisy and extrovert one. I don't know that he increased anyone's knowledge of theology, but nothing whatsoever to do with theology – taught me to cheer very loudly, as they do in Co. Monaghan across the hills on St Stephen's Day when hunting a hare, indeed loud enough to wake the dead.

Though awareness of religious difference came up quickly, it didn't take long for the issue to settle down. Respective positions were recognized and were respectfully shelved. Orange sectarianism had little support. Catholics who made up a quarter of the student body, would not have been likely to attend if they came from a militant background. The ones who did enrol had to pass, or bypass, our Glencullen tenant's nephew, Archbishop MacQuaid. He would let the likes of Williams and O'Brien attend, as their school had been in England; Jesuit though it was, their innocence would already have been contaminated.

I was in an all male society to start. Rooms in College were all male, the Engineering School was all male and at meals it was all male. Most of us came from all male schools: one might have been in the army if not actually in a monastery. Women were very distant. I don't remember any of my associates consorting with them in the early days. A very few would have had what might be called girlfriends, but these souls would be seen as either eccentric or particularly adventurous. Sex was much discussed, but that was about all, apart from wishful thinking. It seems to have taken several years of monasticism before one was tempted and steeled oneself to break out of celibacy.

Politics made little impact, besides a good deal of talk about Partition and North South issues. Elections in Ireland and England were noted, but raised little response. America and the wider world evoked even less. One aspect of world affairs of which I, and some like me were aware, was the occasional fighting in little wars in a few places, especially to do with the retreat of the British from their Empire. I think this was more to do with having friends participating or undergraduates arriving from them. At this time there was still conscription in England, and a fair number arrived having done their national service. This of course did not apply to the Irish, northern or southern, but quite a few Irish joined up anyway for the adventure. Several of the leavers from my last class at St Columba's joined the British Army temporarily, and some were involved in the attempts to keep in order recalcitrant natives in Asia, Africa and Cyprus. I can remember a visit by David Plunkett, whom I had known at St Columba's. He sat in our rooms in College, having just returned after two years national service as a subaltern with the King's Dragoon Guards, telling us how when he was serving in the jungles of Malaya, the gun on his tank got too hot to work, as he had been firing it so much. Guy Eglinton, who was in the pre-med and lived above us in No. 13, had served in Korea. There was as well, a sense that if one became fed up with the unadventurous life or one failed one's exams, one would go off to the wars. It was also a time of IRA activity in the North, but that caused little particular interest. Of course the scale of activity was nothing like what it had been in the 1920s, or the much worse situation to come later from the 1970s onwards. We never went in for marches or demonstrations for any cause.

At the end of the Summer Term I set off for vacation employment. There was said to be a demand for work on hydroelectric projects in the Highlands of Scotland, so with a small knapsack of belongings I took a bus to near the airport and started to hitch-hike to Belfast. When I look at the streams of traffic on that road today, nearly fifty years later, it is hard to imagine sitting on a wall smelling the hawthorn hedge and watching a bee going about its business, while I was waiting for a car to appear. I arrived in Belfast in the afternoon and killed a couple of hours in a dockside pub waiting to go aboard the Glasgow boat. There wasn't time to seek out any of my Belfast friends or relations, having given no warning of my arrival. When one is hitch-hiking, one doesn't know when, or indeed where, one might arrive. When I set out from Glasgow next morning I had only a vague idea where I was going – north to the Highlands. That evening I was in Inverness, having had good lifts, a sharp contrast to hitch-hiking in

Scandinavia the previous year. The Labour Exchange directed me into the mountains to the Glascarnoch dam site.

There was a camp for the workers, a good one as I learned from the other inmates who had moved around the different projects: for instance we had our own beds, and we didn't have to vacate them for the night shift. Most of the workers were from Donegal, Tyrone and the Mourne mountains, with a sprinklng of Hebrideans. There were quite a few students, one of them I was surprised and pleased to see, was Ken Walsh from my own class. A distinguishing mark of the students was noted by a Donegal man, saying he would get himself a pair of pyjamas and so be taken for a student.

I was at Glascarnoch for only two weeks, during which time I painted a large part of the dam wall with bitumen. One day I was on my ladder with my brush, when the agent, the chief of the project, came up and asked me if I was an engineer. Somewhere the word among the couple of dozen students and several hundred workers, was that I was, and he asked me to move to the Vaich dam site in the adjacent valley where an engineering assistant was needed.

Vaich was part of the same hydroelectric scheme, smaller than Glascarnoch, and a more pleasant place. The workers were an almost even split between Hebrideans, mostly from the island of Harris, and out of season fishermen from the Scottish north-east coast. There were very few Irish and no students. No students as ordinary workers that is. For a time there were two civil engineering students from Southhampton University getting work experience, with tasks similar to what I was given. I had the best of both worlds, for I had what was useful and solid work to do, setting out with theodolite and level. The Southhampton students were only there for a few weeks and tended to just poke around. They were paid £7 a week whereas I had full worker's pay of two to three times that.

There was an eccentric and out of place American in the camp who I got to know well. It was the time of a presidential election campaign, and so I was to have my first really in-depth lessons in American politics. It was also the time when the Suez crisis was just starting to boil up.

The Harris men – they were all Gaelic speakers who had been in the army or navy, reckoned that I, being a young lad, would be off to the war, and as an educated one, as an officer. I didn't of course go to the war, but in September I travelled back to Glasgow, this time by train with two Tyrone men who had had enough and wanted to go home. I arrived in Dublin in the evening and went into Jammets back bar. There I saw Chris Haskins and John Campbell, two Columbans of my vintage, sitting morbidly. While I had been hitch-hiking down from Belfast, they had been at the funeral of Jeremy Taylor.

Jeremy Taylor had been my companion on the trip to Holland three years earlier: he was indeed the instigator of the trip. We had been in the same common room my last year at school, and I used to see him quite often at Trinity. He had moved into rooms in College when I did, though we were tending to move in different circles by then. He was by far the most academically gifted of all my friends or associates. He had gone up to College on the highest scholarship available in Classics and started to read both Classics and Mental and Moral Science – the Trinity term for Philosophy. These were both full-time honours courses. Getting a "double first" was something one read about in old books: it didn't happen in my time, but Jeremy would have been on the way to one. At the end of his first year he became a Scholar of the University, something normally done at the end of second year or even third. It was based on the first two years' curriculum. This was a remarkable feat. He changed, or was about to change one of his courses to Pure Science. He had told me he thought it would be useful to earn his living, like me taking up Engineering. He can't have realized that with his level of academic achievement, he would have been bombarded by the widest range of would-be employers. It was said that he had shot himself accidentally with his shotgun while climbing over a hedge. That is the official statement. It has been assumed by many that it was suicide. I didn't investigate the matter and never saw his parents, whom I had met before, again. They were devastated as one would expect, and sold up their place, Ardgillan Castle in North Dublin, a fine house in a wonderful position, long in the family. On balance I lean to the official view. He was a big and physically awkward fellow and could be quite absent-minded. As well as that, shooting was not for him a frequent sport, so he would have been very much a candidate for a shooting accident. If he was suffering from suicidal depression, it was not obvious. I have never been sure of the circumstances of his death and it has bothered me down the years when I would think of it. At last, fifty years later, I spoke to Stephen Barcroft, who had lived with Jeremy that last year, and indeed had been on holiday with him and so was more in touch with him than I had been. Stephen was definitely of the view that it was an accident, not suicide. I am perhaps lucky that no more of my contemporaries were to die before I was well into middle age.

CHAPTER SEVENTEEN

Trinity College II and Beyond

Moving on to the Sophister years was a seamless transmission compared to the move from my Junior to Senior Freshman years, the move from living at home to living in College and moving from pre-med to the Engineering School. It was at this point however, that there was a marked shift towards new acquaintances as well as my former school friends. I came back in the autumn of 1956 to be very comfortably embedded in college life.

The process of the *raison d'être* of being in the university at all, the process of getting a degree, looked up a bit in second year Engineering. In first year, the course was not much of an advance on school work, but with the widening of the curriculum, and the fact that my experience in Scotland had given me some insight into what the profession of engineering was about, there was more scope to take an interest in the work of the second year.

Engineering students at Trinity in my year and the one before were something of an anomaly, with advantage and disadvantage. The class two years ahead of mine was the last one to graduate with degrees recognized by the Institutions of Mechanical and Electrical Engineers. Technology had now become too complicated. It was deemed that there was not enough mechanical and electrical content in our course to warrant a degree in either of them. Most schools had specialist degrees for each discipline. We still had enough civil engineering to satisfy the Institution of Civil Engineers, so we were turned out as budding civil engineers, but because there was such a large content of mechanical and electrical, the civil content was less than it might have been. A good student might have benefited from the opportunity of being absorbed with mechanical and electrical issues, but most of us, certainly in my case, were not such good students, so these subjects were really rather a waste of good time. The situation was rectified for the class following our one, by making the course into two separate disciplines; civil, and industrial, and increasing the duration by, in effect, six months.

For the Arts degree, the Engineering School organized lectures in Geography and Astronomy. This seemed to be a throwback to my prep school days which was the last time I had had Geography lessons, even though this had always been a favourite subject. My other favourite subject was still History, and I determined to pursue this; however it was impossible to find history lectures at times which I had available. One had to get credit for attending lectures, but any lectures would suffice, so for my final two years I read history on my own, without attending a lecture in it, or even having a word with a tutor, and at the same time sat painfully through the astronomy lectures. When I went to the Examination Hall at the appointed time to sit the final BA exam, it was found that I was such a rare bird that there was no paper set for that occasion, so I left the examination hall for an afternoon rowing on the river. I had to come back the next day, when I was given a hastily typed set of questions. I never knew who set them or who corrected them, but I did pass. At my prep school, when about 9 years old, I used to play a game with my friend Calvert where we pretended we were space ships, and would buzz from one tree to another, each tree being designated a planet, Mars, Jupiter or the like. My astronomy has never advanced from this, despite two years of lectures, which I had to get credit for attending with no need to participate or to pass the subject. Talk of right ascensions and declinations and the application of spherical trigonometry passed over me as it bored me to distraction. It was the time the Russians put up the first sputnik with a dog in it. It was suggested by one of the class that an astronomer be put in it. This was the only time the humourless lecturer conceded a faint smile.

Another set of compulsory boring lectures was for Logic, though that was during the Senior Freshman year. Everyone in the whole university had to sit this subject in the final Freshman exam, along with some other subject which had to be different from the main ones of study. For some this exam, known as Little Go, was quite a hurdle. Tib, my Uncle Henry, had three tries at it before giving up and dropping out. For Logic we had an elderly clergyman, as humourless as the astronomy lecturer, who came in from his parish just for us. I expect he needed the money, and it was as much an ordeal for him putting up with engineering students, as it was for me having to sit through the lectures.

Social and intellectual life was opening up but not all that constructively. The role of the pub I would not decry, but there were too many visits to B grade movies in the Carlton Cinema, too much billiards in the rooms of the College Historical Society or the Philosophical Society: the debates and reading of papers in these institutions were for others. There was too much in the way of playing darts and playing poker in No. 13.

My friend from school days, Dan Brownlow, also starting his Sophister year now felt that his sybaritic existence needed a change. He was very wealthy, and whereas I and my engineering friends would have baked beans for lunch in our rooms, and scrape up small change for pints of stout in O'Neills, Dan would lunch in Bentleys and dine in the Dolphin on cordon bleu cooking and the best of wines and brandy with similarly endowed people. He put it to me that we needed some discipline and should join the boat club, and so come under its rigorous training rules. When in training, which was for the whole of the Easter and Summer Terms, it was out of bed, run around the park, down to the gym for a shower by 8 a.m., no more than two pints of beer per day, no smoking, no parties and bed at 10.00 p.m. We would be out on the river every evening no matter whatever the weather. We joined, and were put on the novice crew in January.

Competitive rowing and another section of society, the rowers, now became a large part of my life. Dan decided by the summer that he was sufficiently cured to be able to retire from the boat. I was given a place on the second eight. The summer was the time for races. We had our boat towed up to regattas at Belfast, Drogheda and Carlow. At the end of the Summer Term there was our own regatta at our club house on the Liffey at Islandbridge, which is as grand a boat club house as there is in the country, except perhaps a couple in Cork and Limerick. Following the races which marked the end of training, there was a great dance in a marquee on the riverbank.

With the end of the Summer Term, it was time to go and earn some money. Peter Williams and I set off on the mail boat for North Wales, where there was a big power station being built, and on which we thought we might get a start. We didn't know precisely where the power station was, but as it happened we found some close acquaintances on the boat, and became embroiled in a card game which continued on the train at Holyhead. The others were going on to London, and for some reason or other Peter and I decided to go on there too. We arrived in London very late, and I tried my old communist hostel for beds but it was full. One of the other chaps knew of an even more communist hostel and we were lucky to be let in and given space on the floor. There was a young Irish lad there fresh over from Cork who was pleased to see us, for he sensed that it was a communist place he was in and was afraid for his soul. It was Sunday and he didn't know where he could go to Mass. Peter was able to explain to him where he could – we were very close to Westminster Cathedral, so he went away happy.

We then somehow contacted John Black the Monaghan Presbyterian, who was working in Walls ice cream factory and he introduced Peter and me to the place where we got jobs as labourers on the night shift. We found a room in Acton with a rather unpleasant landlady. John would come to visit us at the changeover of shifts and would cheer loudly. The landlady banned him on account of his "Big yackitty laugh", as she denigrated his solid Monaghan cheering.

After a short time in a cold store 20^0 below zero, which was tough, Peter and I joined an elite squad, packing and loading boxes of all sorts of ice cream – of which we could eat as much as we liked. We had heavy padded clothes and did an hour on and an hour off, supposedly because of the cold, but it was not really cold at all. In fact it was quite an easy job. One was always aware that the job security was entirely dependent on the weather: a few hot days and the pressure to turn out the ice cream rocketed; conversely, a cold snap and there would be layoffs. First to go would be the blacks, then the Irish, and then the students. Last, if ever, would be the Jews who made up much of the supervisory staff. We were getting a bit tired of it all after a couple of months and explored the possibility of a switch to a construction site. Our classmate Ken Walsh was working nearby as a steel fixer foreman for the same company he and I had worked for in Scotland, he having kept in touch with the agent, so a start could probably have been arranged. However, we decided we had saved enough money, and seen enough of London for the time being. Not that we had seen very much of London, what with the long work hours and the urge to save money. Visits away from work tended to be to Peter's sister, whose flatmate Peter was to marry some years later. About the beginning of September therefore, Peter, John Black and I booked aboard an Aer Lingus flight to Dublin, something of a change from third class in the train and boat. It was my first plane trip. It seemed to be a bit of an extravagant adventure, but we were flush with funds.

Vacations weren't totally spent on expeditions over the sea to work. I did spend time at home in Glencullen.

Back in College for the final year, life was much as before but, there was more of it. The boat club was now my complementary pole to the Engineering School, but there was plenty of activity in between. Parties were more frequent – we didn't go into training till January. Skill at poker was being enhanced. We played for low stakes among ourselves very much for fun, and we didn't venture into the schools where there were rich Greeks and such like playing with serious money. Edwin Draper, who was in our class, joined us at cards in No. 13 from time to time, but would play in more refined circles as well. Peter Williams was the main instigator of visits to the cinema, and John Killen made great strides at billiards. John now had a small sports car; Dan Brownlow of course had his high quality car and Edwin Draper had an old wreck known simply by us all as "the car".

A wreck though "the car" may have been, it was good enough to carry a number of us to Belfast to play what was called a "coarse" rugby game against the Queen's University engineers. On this occasion, a number of us stayed with Alick Johnston and Jasper Brett (who was another Monaghan man) both of these ex-Columbans. These two were the nucleus of a flat which formed an oasis for visitors to Belfast, such as one can find in most cities for strays and hangers-on. It was on this occasion that I was injudicious enough to strike up the Republican song "Kevin Barry" in a pub. Two barmen immediately vaulted the bar and I was in the street before I had finished the first verse. My motives were almost innocent, but this was Belfast at a time not long after, the albeit mild, IRA campaign of the fifties, so that no chances were taken with any sign of coat trailing, no matter how lighthearted it was intended. There was no saying where such an incident might lead. On the way across the border, going north, the customs men didn't like the look of us and gave "the car" a very thorough going over. They were looking for weapons or explosives. Coming back we got the same treatment, but going south, however, the suspected contraband was "literature likely to corrupt faith or morals" or artificial devices for birth control.

Another important function of a car in College was to go to a "Bona Fide". This was the outworking of regulations brought in early in the century to combat excessive drinking, and especially to keep the minds of the workers on productivity during the First World War, but for decades the system had been counterproductive and downright dangerous. The idea was that the pubs would shut at 10 o'clock or thereabouts, but if one was a thirsty traveller and more than 3 miles from home one could get a drink up until midnight. In the 1950s and even later, the Dublin pubs all shut at 10.00 or 10.30, but ringing the city on its outskirts were pubs which stayed open till midnight. A Bona Fide traveller, one who in "good faith" lived 3 miles away could jump in his car when the city pub shut, and tear out to the suburbs to continue his revels. It was a system designed to promote drunken driving. It lasted a long time because it suited the publicans. In the city the publicans could go to bed and cut down on paying barmen overtime. Those publicans who elected to run

Bona Fide pubs could make a fortune. Matt Smith's of Stepaside was our most commonly patronized.

Peter Williams had been skiing with his family in Switzerland the previous winter and was continuously praising the sport. I could not see how anyone would want to slide about in snow, cold wet stuff that it was, but Peter held that you would not notice the cold, and that the snow in the Alps was not wet. There was a ski club in the College which organized a trip to the Alps for the two weeks before Christmas. John Bielenberg, whom I knew well at school and was in the engineering class ahead of me, was then the captain of the club, but it was Dan Brownlow, who had been out with the club before, who persuaded me with his enthusiastic description of après-ski social life to sign on. There might have been thirty or forty all up in our group, male and female, but we were to be vastly outnumbered by the contingents from Oxford and Cambridge, whom we joined in London to take the train, with Zurs in Austria as the destination. The idea was that with a party of 300 skiers moving into what was then a small resort, before the season, we would get cheap rates. The whole trip was very cheap, even for those days, at £35, London to London, full bed and board, ski hire, ski school and lift tickets. It was, all the same a lot of money for the likes of Peter Williams and me, but we had no problem with the finances, following our summer making Walls ice cream.

From then on skiing would be my holiday activity. I did not see a beach in summer for another dozen years, not that I had seen much of holiday beaches in the previous few years. I never became a serious skier: the combination of après-ski, with its late nights, often very late nights, and drink, often far too much of it, didn't go with proficiency at skiing. But the furious activity of sliding down, and falling down mountains for several hours a day, is a wonderful counterbalance to a sedentary and cerebral occupation, which might occupy one for most of the year, and if the holiday is to include late night carousing, it is a wonderful means of recovery from that too.

On that first trip to ski in Zurs in December 1957, I was with many people I knew. The Engineering School was very well represented.

We had a new Professor of Engineering that term: the previous one, Purser, had retired after 25 years and William Wright had just started. He was about to get the house in better order. It was necessary to have his approval to miss the final week of term, and when Brian Kidd and I went to speak to him, I sensed he was a bit surprised at the idea. I had my fingers crossed, but he said it would be all right. If all the prospective skiers had descended on him together, it might have been different, but the precedent was set, so when the train set off, its passengers from the Engineering School included, besides Brian Kidd and myself, John Bielenberg (the club captain), Peter Williams, Nick O'Brien and Hugh Delap, a boat club man of distinction. Also from the boat club was Gerry Murdoch, unless I am mixing him up with another trip. I can remember only two of the ladies in our party. I myself became greatly taken with an American girl called Sandy who was a hanger-on with the Oxford contingent and who went out of my life as quickly as she came in. With the Oxford contingent was young Winston Churchill, the grandson, and later an MP himself. Of course we mixed with the Oxford and Cambridge people despite being exclusively in our own hotel. It was however noticeable that colonials (Australians, New Zealanders, South Africans and the like from Oxford and Cambridge) tended to gravitate into the Dublin circle. It was a New Zealander who stole a small pig from a farm in the town – Zurs was still a rustic village – and brought it to the dance in our hotel, the sort of thing which appealed to the Irish.

There was little contact with Austrians, but once I was dislodged from the somewhat mindless hedonism of the sport and revelry by a couple of locals who, in the bar, told me of the last days of the war and asked me why the allies had bombed Feldkirch – a harmless mountain town – and why had they hanged Field Marshall Jodl. Of course I couldn't answer: I knew nothing of Feldkirch or Jodl, but at least I was reminded that our host country had more significance in the world than being a place to provide entertainment for undergraduates.

Back in College for the Hilary or Winter Term, it was strict training for rowing; unlike après-ski, there was no late night carousing après-rowing.

The strict limit was two pints in the widow Gilligan's at Islandbridge.

It was this term when for the first time I voluntarily, and on my own, attended divine service in a church. Perhaps I had been shamed into action. Peter Williams and Nick O'Brien would without fail on a Sunday morning go off to Mass at the Carmelite Church in Clarendon St. John Killen would put on his blue Presbyterian suit and go off to Adelaide Road on a Sunday evening. I had been there once, having registered in college as a Presbyterian and been to tea with the Presbyterian chaplain, the Revd McConnell, but was not comfortable. In fact I didn't like it at all. Over the ensuing years I had been party to plenty of informal discussions with my peers on the merits of Protestantism versus Catholicism and religion versus irreligion and was now slowly coming to rest towards the high end of Anglicanism. I was not settled or indeed interested enough to come down off the fence and attend the college chapel. However some time in the Hilary Term I went one morning to Christ Church Cathedral and several ensuing Sundays that year I went to St Patrick's Cathedral. I can date the visit to Christ Church by there having been there for an impassioned sermon on tolerance, which was in effect a protest against the Fethard-on-Sea boycott.

The Fethard-on-Sea incident involved the boycott of Protestant businesses by Catholics who had been stirred up by clerical objection to a Protestant woman defying the Pope's Ne Temere decree which said the children of a mixed marriage must be brought up Catholic. She had not followed the required pledge and had absconded with her children to Scotland. There was a lot of hurt in the local community and a good deal of heat generated nationally. The Butlers, Peggy and Hubert, would drive the 40 miles from Maiden Hall to Fethard to support the Protestant shops. It took De Valera himself intervening with the Bishop to put a stop to the boycott. I could not help feeling that the Christ Church preacher's passion was a bit lost, as there was hardly anyone in the congregation besides myself and a couple of old ladies. The congregation of St Patrick's was never much bigger, but there was a good choir, which was the attraction for me.

During the Easter vacation two boats from the boat club were taken over to England. Usually the first eight would go to London where it would take part in the Head of the River Race, where the crews row from Mortlake to Putney, about 3 miles, the reverse direction to the Oxford and Cambridge Race. In 1958, the second eight was a good one, so it went to London as well. Before going to London we went to Chester for the North of England Head of the River Race. We stayed there for a couple of days and we, the second eight, won our division, the Clinker. Racing boats were either Fine – the skin was smooth plywood, or Clinker, made of boards, heavier and more old-fashioned. In London we all stayed in a small hotel in Barnes, occupying the whole of it, and were on the river every day for a week. The race was an exciting event with 300 boats racing. The idea is that the boats start at intervals of so many seconds and race against the clock. The first one off is the one which won the year before, and so on, till the ones who were newcomers. As the second boat had not been rowing previously we started 273rd. The race is weighted in favour of the early starters, as the tide turns and from going out, it starts to come in, so it is made difficult to pick up places. As it was, we picked up to 76th. Our first boat lost places and ended up among the forties. Despite our heavier Clinker boat, we found that, during practice, we could keep up with the first boat, which I believe did not make them at all happy. They didn't practise with us again lest they should become demoralized. After the race, and the break from training, was the occasion when I drank more pints of beer in one evening – it would have been Watneys – than I had ever had before or have had since.

In the Summer Term there was plenty more rowing. Apart from our own regatta at Islandbridge there were others. Galway comes to mind. We always got on well with the College in Galway, better than the others. University College Dublin was too close geographically and there were elements of politico-religious sectarianism from earlier times, which could sometimes manifest themselves to poison the relationship. I never knew of a Protestant attending University College Dublin in those days. Queen's in Belfast was far enough away to overcome any likely antipathy.

Anyway Queen's was, like us, pretty multicultural, though sometimes a fear might surface that we might be untrustworthy Republicans or they might be bigoted Orangemen, which was of course quite unfounded either way and as politics was not of great interest to anyone, unlikely to gain much of a foothold. Galway was sufficiently far enough away and hospitable to the stranger to overcome any adverse rivalry or possible antipathy. The same would probably have applied to Cork, but we never rowed against the university there. That year we had a boat from a Cambridge college at our regatta, and though they were only there for the fun, they were patently more skilled than us. Our regatta could never be as big a one as elsewhere. The Liffey is only wide enough for two boats to race at a time. Later in the season I would row at Cork, and at Limerick on the Shannon where six boats could race abreast. An event at our regatta was the club fours, limited to non boat club members, in effect amateur races, as opposed to the club members, the professionals. I trained and coxed a crew from the Engineering School, made up of Peter Williams, Nick O'Brien, Gerry Shanagher and Mike Ancher. All of them powerfully built but quite unfit. On training outings we always had to stop at Chapelizod Bridge for Williams and Shanagher to have their cigarettes. However in the finals we won against a crew from the Divinity School, stroked by a future archdeacon.

At the end of the term we had the first half of our final exams. This was followed during the vacation by a practical project. Groups of the class would propose schemes for themselves and then go away and execute them. We would then have to do the second half of the final exams in the autumn. For the project my group consisted of the No. 13 clique of recreational poker players, Peter Williams, John Killen, Cathal O'Flynn and Gerry Shanagher. Peter had a cousin who owned a house on an island in a lake in the west of Co. Galway. The family was that of Oliver St John Gogarty, a larger than life character of the Dublin of earlier in the century. He was the Buck Mulligan of Joyce's *Ulysses*, a Senator and an author himself. We therefore occupied the house on the island, and selected a rough road along the seashore nearby to design a theoretical scheme for its improvement.

Each day we would set out with our survey instruments to chart in detail the road over a length of a couple of miles. We looked so official and professional that the adjacent farmers did not want to believe that we were only students practising. They had hopes that they would be getting sums of money from the County Council for compensation where our new road encroached on their land. When we told them the facts they assumed that we were smart politicians telling lies to minimize their chances of being in for big money. In time, maybe from enquiries elsewhere, the bitter truth that there was to be no money for them, dawned. By and large the disappointment did not show, but one unpleasant landowner became particularly shirty and threatened us with trespass, and would be on the look out in case we went onto his land.

An extraordinary coincidence was that as we progressed eastward towards Killary Harbour, we met another group of our class surveying along the same road approaching from the Leenane end. Not only had they decided to do a similar project, but of all the thousands of suitable roads in the country, they were on the same road as us. One of them had some connection with Leenane about 10 miles away from our island, which was what had determined their location. The great advantage of the house on the island was that Peter and John Killen being competent fishermen, we had an unlimited supply of trout for the whole period we stayed there.

After drawing up our highway scheme, I retired for the rest of the summer home to Glencullen. I spent a couple of months doing little but studying for the second part of the final exams. I did not want to fail any subjects. I had failed some of the June exam and therefore it would be the following January at the earliest before I would be completely finished. Our new professor, in his attempt to lift the standard of the school, failed about half the class the first time around. As well as the discipline imposed by the professor, I was a candidate for failure by my own lack of study. The boat club activity was time consuming, more even than the poker, the pictures and parties, and I was also playing tennis and swimming. Life may have been healthier, but with lack of attention to it, the academic side was bound to suffer. I had however passed all the Arts subjects for my BA degree.

I had passed the exams in October, and with no more lectures to attend, I was free to go, but only for three months, before coming back to sit the subjects failed in June. Somehow or other I found myself teamed up with Bob Coote, a graduate of the previous year, who had had a job on the building of the Cork Airport for a very meagre salary, and was now off to try his luck in England. My aim was to make enough money to go skiing again in December.

We went over by the mail boat, a very stormy crossing. Another passenger I ran into was the Revd McConnell, the Presbyterian chaplain who I hadn't spoken to for some years. We had quite a long chat, among other things, about his experience as a prison chaplain in Mountjoy Jail with its lone Presbyterian IRA prisoner. I was anxious to get to the bar where I guessed Bob would be, (I had not seen him getting onto the boat), but was too shy and respectful of the cloth to say how keen I was to proceed to the bar, or for that matter to discuss my apostasy which had left me leaning towards High Church Anglicanism in preference to Presbyterianism. In time the chaplain went his way and I found Bob in the den of vice.

In London, Bob had the idea we would save money by staying in the Salvation Army Hostel. When we looked at it, and also learned that we could not get in until eight o'clock, we recognized that it would be necessary to put in the time in a pub to take on enough drink to anesthetize us to the hostel environment. The result was that we did not save any money. The hostel was pretty basic, which was as such not too much of a problem, but the down and out inmates were herded by the officials without them showing any respect for their clients, which I thought was not in keeping with the ideals of the organization. There were obviously some tortured souls among the guests. I was woken several times during the night, by cries from disturbed sleep. The cry I most remember coming loud and anguished from the far end of the dormitory was "I don't mind Hitler, but I don't trust the bloody Japs". What history lay behind that outburst?

Next day Bob organized himself with interviews for professional employment. I had a chat with the London Education Authority, who were desperate for supply teachers, and the fact that I had passed the BA was enough for them to want to snap me up, but I was more attracted to following up on the idea of work in a sugar factory in Norfolk. Sheila Daniels, who, with her mother, had organized our Bangor house in 1944/45, had stayed with us at Glencullen a month or so before, and had said that there was always good work in the autumn in the sugar beet factory near where she was now living in Norfolk. I therefore contacted the Daniels's and they said to me to come and stay with them, so I did. I was put in touch with the sugar factory and got a job as a shift worker. It would make me more than enough for the skiing trip, and pay for my board and lodging in the meantime. The Daniels's looked after me well. They had television – this was the first time I stayed in a house with a television. I became a fan of Sergeant Bilko and somewhat differently, watched the coronation of Pope John XXIII.

I was introduced to a neighbour who had a shoot on the river. The contrast with free and open Ireland was marked. Every winter for the past few years I had gone to Monaghan for a few days to stay with the Killens and shoot duck. We would drive all over the western end of the county to different lakes and bogs looking for game – snipe and duck in the main. It was only a matter of calling in on the landowner, who we would often know, to get permission, but in many places it was not even necessary even to do that. We never got many birds, but enough to make the days sport worthwhile. The place where I was invited to shoot in Norfolk was a few square yards of the riverbank surrounded by a marsh which we went to by boat. We then waited an hour or so for the evening flight. A few duck passed over – they were on their way to a bird sanctuary nearby which seemed rather unsporting of us, but these were the only duck available, and I shot one. My host claimed he had shot it, I did not argue as he was the host – probably we had both hit it at the same time.

The only problem with the job in the sugar factory was that it was shift work, and the shift changed each week. Otherwise it was one of the best jobs I have ever had. It had enough physical activity to keep one fit and enough mental need to keep one alert and not be bored, and one was never stressed or strained. It was to do with filling up bags by machines. About seven weeks of it was however probably enough. The sugar beat harvest lasted only about three months, so I was there for half of it anyway. When I left the foreman said it was a pity I was going, because I was doing so well. He saw me as a potential lifelong bag filler. The Alps however were a more immediate magnet.

This time the universities' clubs chose Saas Fee in Switzerland, again a small and inexpensive resort. I was to discover how the Swiss approach to life was quite different from the Austrian, as it produced an unusually high proportion of humourless people, driven by formality and routine. Like in Zurs before, however, I did not go out of my way to take any interest in the local culture; again I was more oriented towards the skiing and the club's internal social life. This time, I did not have the companionship of the large number of my close friends who had been in Zurs, but there were quite a few who I had known previously, some quite well. The Dublin lot, were again all billeted in the same hotel, but it was a small one and we filled it; this led to a tendency towards insularity, and we did not seem to mix so much with the Oxbridge mob. One of this mob, a chap from Newcastle on Tyne, did become one of a our circle, for he liked to sing and he knew all the Geordie songs like the "Blaydon Races" and the "Lambton Worm". I have heard it said that the Irish, due to their eccentricity, have a tendency to sing more and more as the night wears on. It is not that the English or other races do not sing: it is a case of degree. I was also more conscious of the presence of more ladies in our group than previously, but that may have been more the lesser presence of my coarse mates with whom I would go rowling around the taverns. It was, all the same, more of a fun trip than before.

Back in College in January to sit the exams I had failed in the summer, I found rooms with Rodney Ging, whom I had known for a long time, but had got to know better on the recent ski trip. I managed to pass this time and so was ready to be given my degree in the Commencements ceremony in February. Ging featured here because his uncle owned a dress-hire business and it was necessary to wear evening dress with white tie, things I did not possess. At the last minute I found I had no black shoes, but I managed to borrow a pair from Cathal O'Flynn. Cathal was very tall with very big feet, and it was difficult going upon the stage to get my bit of paper as the shoes kept trying to get away no matter how I shuffled. Nearly a half century later, Edwin Draper remembered my stumbling on the stage, maintaining a belief that I was drunk. I was not – it was the shoes. I don't think he believed me.

In the interim before the Commencements I had a very enjoyable week's shooting in Co. Mayo. I joined Alick Johnston and John Killen who were staying with John's uncles, Sandy and Harry Pringle in the Pontoon Hotel. They had a guide who would take us to the most suitable bogs and lakes. We must have shot all the best places for snipe and duck between Crossmolina and Foxford. I was by then fairly proficient as a snipe shot, and at least did better than Sandy Pringle whose achievements included the murder of an owl. I went back with John to Monaghan for a bit more shooting. Immediately I was back in Dublin, Jim O'Brien, who was now the captain of the boat club, commandeered me to be the coach of the novice eight for the term. This fitted in well as I had committed myself to wait over for Margaret Killen's wedding before I would take off into the world. The next few weeks of coaching the eight, a six day a week affair I found as enjoyable, if not more so than rowing itself. I would ride along the riverbank on a bicycle, with a megaphone shouting at the crew. I was living then at home at Glencullen, and a mark of my growing up was my father lending me his car, then a rather stately Wolseley, to go to the river. I had not been offered the loan of his car for the previous two years having ploughed the one he had at the time into a granite wall above Stepaside, trying to corner too fast, resulting in a not inconsiderable repair bill. It was a good crew and we were practising for the Wylie cup against Queen's in Belfast. We did not win though we were expecting to and perhaps should have.

The last event in Dublin before setting off on my professional career was Margaret Killen's wedding to Peter Brittain. It was held in Adelaide

Road Church, and the reception was in Glencullen House "home of the bride's Aunt" so described in the press. It was quite a big event, perhaps the biggest held in Glencullen House in the century. Festivities continued into the small hours in the Shelbourne Hotel.

My classmate John Paul had met with London engineering consultants called Lemon and Blizard, who offered him a job he did not take up, but he put me up to it in his place and I was to be taken on. Immediately after the wedding I went over on the Liverpool boat. Also on the boat was the Revd Douglas Slator who had been a master and chaplain at St Columba's all the time while I was there. I hadn't seen him since I left school and had not had much to do with him at school, though I remembered him well enough. He was known as "Sleepy Slator" because he appeared to be so laid back. It was a misnomer, as I learned later that he was a very hard worker. He was however very relaxed: at least he appeared to be. In the chapel on Friday evenings it was the custom for the Litany to be read. The Sub-warden could do it in seven minutes, the Warden in eight, but Slator could never beat ten minutes. He was known as a keen and highly skilled yachtsman, no doubt unstoppable in any tempest. It is curious that the previous time I had crossed over to England I had met with my Trinity College chaplain.

I was travelling third class on the train and Slator was going first, but he invited me to go with him for lunch at his club in St James's, which appropriately for him was the Royal Ocean Racing Club. He told me that, like me, he too was looking for a job. Decades later I heard from one of his common room colleagues, then an octogenarian, that Slator had been forced out in some palace politics. He became a rector in a country parish where he remained until an advanced age.

My immediate destination after the club lunch was to a boarding house in Paddington run by Edwin Draper's aunt. Edwin was there as well. He was working as a deliverer of bottles for the Victoria Wine Company, and like me had graduated, but had not yet entered professional engineering, which he was to do shortly. I stayed in the boarding house for a couple of weeks until I was sought out by Gerry Murdoch with whom I had rowed in the eight, to join him in a flat. Gerry had graduated in commerce and was on a year's training course with the Ottoman Bank before a posting to the Middle East. He worked in the city, and wore a suit and a bowler hat. When I started work I too set off in a suit, but this did not last long – engineers are not noted for sartorial elegance.

The engineers' offices tended to be in Westminster, around Victoria Street. The one I went to was there. The reason they set up there was a need to be near Parliament, for in earlier days big projects needed Acts of Parliament to set them off. Big projects had tended to be public works. Lemon and Blizard were specialists in water supply and drainage. I was put in an office on my own with two telephones. The idea of having two telephones went to my head to such an extent that I had to tell everyone I met of my remarkable status. In those days, to have even one telephone was approaching the extraordinary. What my employers thought I might achieve on my own with two telephones beats me entirely. After a lifetime of supervising young engineers starting out, I well know the extent to which they have to be supervised and helped along. The firm had been in business for a hundred years, and had two rooms full of trainees and so it well knew how to look after junior engineers. I should have been put in there straightaway. In the meantime I don't know what I did; maybe I just sat and marvelled at the telephones. Like the woman in the Irish poem who had three cows and was told not to boast about it because people far greater than her had fallen from their high seats, I too learned how fickle is the possession of the trappings of status. After a few weeks I was put in with the other juniors in a room with no telephone at all.

One of my first visits in London was to Julia Butler who lived in a flat just down the road from Draper's aunt's boarding house. I was to learn from her that she had recently become engaged to an American doctor and would be married in Kilkenny shortly. After not much more than a month in exile, I was to make a flying weekend return visit to Ireland for the wedding.

I stayed at home at Glencullen for the weekend and drove down with my parents to Kilkenny for the wedding on the Saturday. It was in Ennisnag Church and afterwards at Maiden Hall. My father made the main speech which was essentially the same one with the same joke which he had made at Margaret Killen's wedding at Glencullen so soon before. He got away with it, as the guests, with a few exceptions, were from different circles.

I tried to engage Hubert in a discussion on the role of Protestants in the Republic. I thought that now that I believed myself to hold similar views to him about the need for Protestants to nail their colours to the Irish mast and participate fully in public affairs, we would have a productive conversation. It was, alas the wrong moment, as he was in too much of a fluster with all the wedding rituals and the wedding guests to give me attention on such a weighty matter. It would be many years before I would see him again and have another opportunity for a discussion.

It was a grand wedding, and a fine day, but we left about four o'clock to get back to Glencullen for dinner. We brought Tony Guthrie, who was Julia's uncle, back with us. At dinner he railed against the unedifying behaviour of the congregation in the church. Marriage was a sacrament, he said, and the chattering and reviewing of the ladies' hats should have no part in the ceremony. The famous theatrical producer was an English High Church man. I left the dinner to make my last visit to the boat club at Islandbridge. It was the evening after the regatta and there was a dance in a marquee. I did not see many of my rowing friends, as they had, like me, mostly left or were in the first eight, keeping in training for the rowing championships at Henley, though there were still plenty of faces I could put a name to. I met there one Gillian Clarke with whom I was to do more dancing than is my usual wont. This Gillian was the sister of Henry Clarke, an earlier captain of the club who was then MP at Westminster for North Antrim. Henry in time would be unseated by Ian Paisley, whose subsequent political career unfortunately was far more significant and successful than Henry's.

Henry Clarke himself showed up at Henley a week or so later. I had gone to Henley from London with other supporters of our crew, ex-oarsmen Gerry Murdoch with whom I was living and Frank Trufelli, an engineer then working with Ove Arup, but our crew had already been eliminated by the Friday, and hence had broken training. We supporters were well ready to help them break training. The one man who seemed to be a bit left out was Jim O'Brien, the captain of the club, who felt obliged to provide a bit of decorum. Perhaps he did not want our reputation to be further compromised with the English establishment. It was remembered how the Dublin crew had once shouted obscene and blasphemous remarks at King George's Royal Launch, to encourage it to get out of the way. Jim had been at school in England and would have known how badly the people there took that sort of thing. Henry Clarke MP in his rowing blazer was looking very grand amongst the elite in the members' enclosure. He too would have known how one should behave on such occasions.

This visit to Henley in July 1959 was perhaps the last occasion where I was to participate in an event particularly related to my college life in Ireland. During that year while I lived in England, I had some contact with family connections. One weekend I drove up to Norfolk to stay with the Daniels with whom I had stayed after they had introduced me to the sugar factory where I had worked the previous year, and another weekend to Buckinghamshire to stay with Sandy Pringle, who had been on the shooting party in Mayo in January. Both these connections trace back eventually to Monaghan and the Elliot side of the family.

I also went down to Hampshire to see my grandmother's cousins Tine and Odette, of the McKay connection, old ladies who had many cats. Odette lived in a caravan in the garden with one cat, and Tine had the main house with a couple of dozen cats. Not far from them was another cousin on that side of the family, Lennox MacFarlane, whom I also went to see. Lennox was Professor of Pathology at the Army Medical College, and he took me to lunch in the RAMC Headquarters where there is on the stairs a large and wonderful mural of the Zulus with spears attacking the British hospital at Rorke's Drift. He was a brigadier and had been awarded the CBE. Lennox was one of my father's few full first cousins; like me and my brother, he had passed through both St Columba's and Trinity. He had survived incarceration by the Japanese in Thailand during the war, a much more brutal experience than I was to have a half century later when incarcerated in Iraq. My grandmother,

Lennox's aunt, had a story that on release he had strangled the camp commandant with his bare hands. My cousin George MacFarlane held that Lennox might have risen to be the chief of the whole RAMC if he had had a more diplomatic temperament than a MacFarlane one. It was also said of him, and all these stories may be apocryphal, that he sent back his CBE when he heard that those low pop singers, the Beatles, had also been admitted to the Order of the British Empire. It was in Canada and Australia where I was to come across many more MacFarlanes and many as well of the Killen connection.

I decided to move on from England. When it came time to leave the firm where I worked, the partner who was in charge of me said "I suppose you are going off contracting" which was a polite way of saying "I am glad to see you are leaving the consulting field as you haven't been much use here".

I started planning a move further abroad not long into the New Year of 1960, part adventure and part a wish to make some money. I visited the Brazilian Embassy, but to go to Brazil was too complicated, especially given that I did not speak the language. I thought seriously about the USA and was considering the pros and cons of likely conscription into the American Army. One day I saw an enormous American car with bright chrome bits sticking out all over it parked outside a hotel in Bayswater, but most noticeable of all was a registration number plate with "Nebraska, The Beef State" written on it. This signalled that it might be a bit too much of a culture shock to try my hand in the States.

I settled for Canada, and so it was that I landed in Montreal in a four-engined piston-driven plane, which had stopped at Shannon Airport to collect, it being St Patrick's Day, some bags of shamrocks; "I think these are bags of turnip leaves" I heard one of the men loading them at Shannon say. As I knew that the dear little shamrock is more respected among the diaspora than in Holy Ireland, I hoped that her exiled sons would be too.

Postscript

Family History has been an interest of mine since I was quite young, perhaps since my elder brother explained to me that we were descended from the god Thor and his father Odin, the father of all the gods. The ancient Norwegian kings, forbears of our Norman ancestors had said that they were so descended. I found this idea appealing. Later I read the genealogy of some ancient Irish kings whose family tree we linked into, and it was shown how they were descended from Adam and Eve. I also found this to be of interest but not so much. I must have been older for I was suspicious of the authority of these genealogies, and any way association with a god with a winged helmet and a mighty axe was of more appeal to a small boy than two naked adults in an orchard.

On a plane of more immediate reality, when I was in my early teens, I took to asking my grandmother and my great-aunt, of the Elliot connection, about their family history. I would sit with my notebook and take down the answers to my questions. I should have written more, but the sessions tended to deteriorate into brawls as the two of them disputed facts about who was related to whom or why and when someone had moved house. They were remembering what their grandmothers had told them as best as their septuagenarian brains would allow. The best one could get from this oral history was a sense of what it was like in the nineteenth century in Monaghan, Armagh and East Tyrone. When I came to read the works of the novelist William Carleton, who wrote of this area in the early nineteenth century, I found myself in very familiar territory. There was also a MacFarlane connection with East Tyrone. My other grandmother's uncle Napier, who lived on inherited family property there, was our only known paid up besashed Orangeman. Is it mere coincidence that in the

Troubles after the 1960s, the most active brigades of the Provisional IRA were those of South Armagh and East Tyrone?

One's family history contributes, at least in my case, and I am not unique, to one's perception of one's identity; where one stands in society. With my wider ancestry with its disparate traditions, one might start with the symbols of the gods of Valhalla rather than Adam and Eve in their garden: there is plenty of scope for confusion of identity. I am not, as far as I know, schizophrenic, maybe because within and between the different branches of my ancestry I have never been conscious of racial and political type conflict. It was outside the family I came to learn of the conflicts between Left and Right, Irish and British, Protestant, Catholic and Dissenter. Within the gates, the lion lay down with the lamb, whatever they were doing outside.

In the year 1999, following some lengthy work assignments in the Middle East, I was asked, as a consulting engineer, to help with the building of a power station in Co. Offaly and lived in Co. Westmeath until late in 2000. My wife Joy joined me there from Australia, and various members of our family came to visit from Australia as well. My eldest daughter Nicola was already living in Dublin. We rented a wing of the castle of Tullynally from the Pakenhams. I had gone to look at the place because it crops up in records as an early principal seat of the FitzSimon family. I have written about this in Chapter 14. During this stay in Ireland I travelled all over the country and saw more of it than when I was growing up there. I was asked from time to time what changes I saw after half a lifetime. My immediate response was to remark on the inordinate number of magpies flying about, and how many and leafy were the trees they could fly to. I do not know where all the magpies had come from, but the regeneration of the trees was a significant change. It had been previous practice for trees to be cut down for sale as much as possible, a practice going back to the seventeenth century when the country was denuded of the great forests. Now trees were being encouraged.

This reply was hardly what was being looked for; I should have talked about the great wealth of the people of the Celtic Tiger and its manifestation in all sorts of improvements, and also the customs and practices, good and bad, which were dead or dying. A lot had happened, but it is not for me here to launch into the social and economic history of Ireland over the past half century. There are plenty of people more observant, knowledgeable and erudite than me, turning out books all the time on such topics. The one issue, apart from the magpies, which made the most indelible impression on me, was the changing attitude to religious denominationalism. In my early days, the first thing one had to learn about a person, almost as significant as determining gender (and that then was generally fairly obvious), was whether the person a Protestant or a Catholic? There were all sorts of polite ways of establishing such identity, like under some pretext unrelated to religion such as finding out where he went to school. One needed to know so as not to create embarrassment like inviting a Catholic to breakfast on Friday and offering him bacon. It was too potentially sensitive to ask outright what one was. After Vatican II, Protestants changed from being "heretics" into "separate brethren", and the Ne Temere decree was gradually dismantled and the mixed marriage became more common and less stressful. But when you cross a horse with a donkey you get something quite different, a mule or a jennet, and now I have been told the product of a mixed marriage is most likely to be neither Protestant nor Catholic but some sort of atheist or agnostic. This is the march of Western European secularism. I remember asking a young man, after a long discussion during which he said he was an atheist, whether he was a Catholic atheist or a Protestant atheist. This is a sort of old Irish joke. He said he was just an atheist and did not think the question was amusing. There I saw that the march of secularism was moving past theology and invading our tribalism. But it has a long way to go. It depends where you are. In Dublin the boundaries are more blurred; one finds, especially among the middle classes, Catholics in Protestant schools, and they make up the majority at Trinity College. How Archbishops McQuaid and Cullen must be turning in their graves. In the rural South there is much interdenominational good will, but still something of a ghetto mentality. In the border areas things have not changed, and there is fear and apprehension after a generation of near civil war. In Belfast and Derry violence and ethnic cleansing have polarized the working classes in real ghettos, while the middle classes in their suburbs try, or pretend to try , to ignore the whole issue.

I said at the outset that I wrote this book with a mindset from half a century ago; a mind formed amidst the powerful interdenominational rival perceptions with their racial undertones on the Ulster borders, but at the same time I was in a family relatively free of such rivalries: it came to terms with them or ignored them. Perhaps if I were to adopt a modern Irish mindset I would not try to tell of the reality of four old families of disparate traditions which would contribute to the palimpsest that is Ireland, as they evolved into one family. Perhaps such an idea would seem to be irrelevant or obsolete, but from where in the Ireland of my various ancestors would I get myself the best mindset today? The environs of Dublin? The stony grey soil of Monaghan ? The mountains of West Kerry? The Glens of Antrim? I think I will leave my mind set as it is.